ROUTLEDGE LIBRARY EDITIONS:
ARCHAEOLOGY

Volume 9

I0130907

NEW LIGHT ON THE MOST
ANCIENT EAST

NEW LIGHT ON THE MOST ANCIENT EAST

V. GORDON CHILDE

Routledge
Taylor & Francis Group

LONDON AND NEW YORK

First published as The Most Ancient East in 1928
First published as New Light on the Most Ancient East in 1934
Fourth Edition published in 1952

This edition first published in 2015
by Routledge
2 Park Square, Milton Park, Abingdon, Oxon, OX14 4RN

and by Routledge
711 Third Avenue, New York, NY 10017

Routledge is an imprint of the Taylor & Francis Group, an informa business

© 1928, 1934, 1952 Routledge & Kegan Paul

British Library Cataloguing in Publication Data
A catalogue record for this book is available from the British Library

ISBN: 978-1-138-79971-4 (Set)
eISBN: 978-1-315-75194-8 (Set)
ISBN: 978-1-138-81283-3 (Volume 9)
eISBN: 978-1-315-74855-9 (Volume 9)
Pb ISBN: 978-1-138-81724-1 (Volume 9)

Publisher's Note
The publisher has gone to great lengths to ensure the quality of this book but
points out that some imperfections from the original may be apparent.

Disclaimer
The publisher has made every effort to trace copyright holders and would
welcome correspondence from those they have been unable to trace.

NEW LIGHT
ON
THE MOST ANCIENT EAST

by

V. GORDON CHILDE

First published The Most Ancient East 1928
Reprinted 1929
Rewritten New Light on the Most Ancient East 1934
Reprinted with some corrections 1935
Rewritten in 1952 *and published in*
the United States of America in 1953

PRINTED IN THE UNITED STATES OF AMERICA

1 2 3 4 5 6 7 8 9 0

PREFACE TO THE FOURTH EDITION

THOUGH most of the fifteen years since the last edition appeared has been occupied by destructive war, the period has witnessed so many discoveries in the Near and Middle East as to fill new chapters and so unexpected as to render others obsolete. Perhaps the most unexpected fresh material comes from the metropolitan cemetery of Memphis at Saqqara under the First Egyptian Dynasty and from contemporary tombs, some already built of stone, on the opposite bank of the Nile near Helwan, while a sequence of 'predynastic' cultures has at last been established in Lower Egypt to compare with that familiar for fifty years from Upper Egypt. Palestine-Syria alone would have provided material for a new chapter, since there the period before 2000 B.C., almost unknown in 1935, is now illustrated by a well-documented sequence of rich cultures. But in Mesopotamia itself, the neolithic prelude, previously only a postulate, has begun to take shape since 1941. In the Indus basin Wheeler's inspired excavations have at length provided some concrete data for a reconstruction of the sociology as well as the material culture of a civilization that, while fully literate, remains for us still prehistoric. The revelation of monumented architecture in stone in First Dynasty Egypt, the recognition of superbly naturalistic portrait sculpture in Sumer in the IVth. millennium, and the rehabilitation of equally naturalistic portraiture in the Indus Valley demand new photographic illustrations as well as a revaluation of the principles of civilized art.

Perhaps the general outlines of the hazy picture, sketched in 1935, have not changed beyond recognition ; they are a little sharper in places and many rich details have been filled in. So the general form of presentation has been retained though divided somewhat differently. The reader should, however, be apprised in advance of three minor changes. Excavators of tells quite naturally number the superimposed settlements or temples in the order in which they find them—from the top downwards. Other readers may find it hard to remember that the first temple at a site was really the last to be built there, the oldest building being numbered perhaps ' 16 ' ! But settlements and temples, thus discovered, have by now

PREFACE

become so well known in archæological literature by these inverted designations that to renumber them in the historical order of their occupation or erection would hamper the interested reader's comprehension of original sources. Accordingly I have retained the established terminology but, as a concession to the layman, have inserted a minus sign wherever the levels are numbered backwards from the latest.

Secondly, I have introduced the term Early Pharaonic as a general appellation for the 'archaic' period and culture of Egypt under Dynasties I and II to balance the term 'Early Dynastic', now applied to the archaic culture and period of pre-Sargonic Mesopotamia. Finally, since the sequence of cultures, very imperfectly revealed by the French excavations at Susa, no longer provides a standard for the Near East (as it did in 1928), it has been summarized in a rather technical appendix to Chapter VII which can be passed over without impairing the intelligibility of the general narrative.

I have particularly to thank Professor Mustafa Amer, now Rector of Farouk University, Alexandria, and Dr. Rizkana of Fuad I University, Cairo, for courteously giving me access to their still unpublished discoveries at Maadi, to Y. Zaki Saad, Director of the Royal Excavations at Ezbet el-Wâlda for a like courtesy there, to Mr. F. Debono for supplementing the published accounts of his results at El Omari, and Mr. W. B. Emery for showing me fresh material at Saqqara. For Plates XIII, XIV and XXXVI we are indebted to the Director-General of Antiquities, Baghdad; for Plates XXXIII and XXXIV, to the Conservator of Oriental Antiquities in the Louvre; for Plate III *b*, to the Trustees of the British Museum; for Plate XXXVII to Professor M. E. L. Mallowan; for Plate XXIX, *a* to Professor R. E. M. Wheeler; and for Plate XXIX, *b* to the Director of the Peabody Museum, Harvard University. For information and advice beyond that acknowledged in the footnotes I am further indebted to Professor Robert Braidwood, Dr. C. S. Coon, Professor S. Piggott, and my colleagues Dr. K. Kenyon, Professor Mallowan, and Professor Wheeler. Sir Lindsay Scott and Miss Isabel Smith have kindly helped in reading the proofs.

CONTENTS

PLATES

at the end of the book

viii

LIST OF FIGURES

x

LIST OF FIGURES

LIST OF FIGURES

xiii

K E Y

△ Sites of Harappa civilization

Land over 1,000 metres

500 – 1,000 metres

Land below 500 metres

Present shore of Persian
Gulf, and courses of rivers

Scale   0   100   200   300   Miles

SYRIA

ASSYRIA

AKKAD

ELAM

SUMER

Tigris

Euphrates

Asur

Mari

Hassuna

Samarra

Kish

Erech Ur

Suez

PALESTINE

Mt. Carmel
Megiddo

Gaza

Byblos

Ugarit

Mersin

Heliopolis
Helwan
Gerzeh
Fayum

Merimde

Abydos

Hierakonpolis

NILE

RED SEA

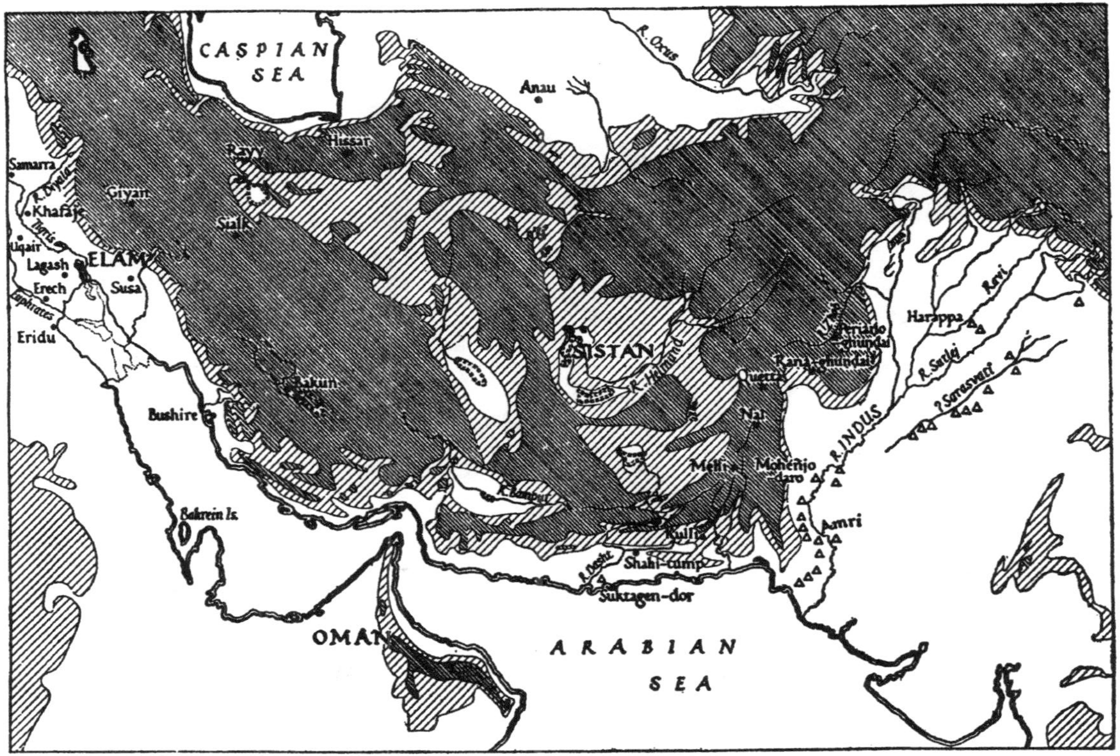
CASPIAN SEA
R. Oxus
Anau
Hissar
Rayy
Samarra
R. Diyala
Giyan
Khafaje
Tigris
Sialk
Uqair
Lagash
ELAM
Erech
Susa
Euphrates
Eridu
Bakun
Bushire
Bahrein Is.
OMAN
ARABIAN SEA
SISTAN
R. Helmand
Quetta
Nal
Mehi
Mohenjo daro
Amri
Kulli
Shahi-tump
R. Dasht
Suktagen-dor
Periano ghundai
Rana-ghundai
Harappa
Ravi
R. Sutlej
? Sarasvati
R. INDUS

CHAPTER I

FROM HISTORY TO PREHISTORY

BARELY a thousand years ago Scotland and the rest of northern Europe were still sunk in the night of illiteracy and barbarism. A thousand years earlier and history's light shines upon our dark continent merely from a few points on the shores of the Mediterranean. And in the next millennium these points flicker out one by one until only the ghostly radiance of heroic myth lights up the storied walls of Troy and Tiryns. The prehistoric archæologist can shed some light on the savage past of our ancestors and forerunners by digging up their rude tools and clumsy ornaments and arranging them in approximate temporal series or local groups. He thus wins the picture of the material life of various peoples who inhabited Britain and adjacent territories at successive epochs, and can at times even trace the wanderings of such human groups with the aid of their artifacts.

Yet the people so revealed remain almost inevitably nameless; their spiritual life is virtually a sealed book to us and their very antiquity may be a matter of doubt to many. But one thread is clearly discernible running through the dark and tangled tale of these prehistoric Europeans: the westward spread, adoption, and transformation of the inventions of the Orient. And it is from a study of objects of Oriental type found, imported, or copied, in the cultural provinces of Europe that we may hope to define in more than purely relative terms the age of the several cultural groups recognized in illiterate Europe before the middle of the first millennium B.C.

For on the Nile and in Mesopotamia the clear light of written history illumines our path for fully fifty centuries, and looking down that vista we already descry at its farther end ordered government, urban life, writing, and conscious art. There in the Ancient East, too, some episodes at least in the great drama of the conquest of civilization are enacted on the open stage. The greatest moments—that revolution whereby man ceased to be purely parasitic and, with

I

the adoption of agriculture and stock-raising, became a creator emancipated from the whims of his environment, and then the discovery of metal and the realization of its properties—have indeed been passed before the curtain rises. Yet even so, we are so much nearer the beginnings on the banks of the Nile and the Euphrates that we have better hope of understanding those most momentous advances there than from any scrutiny of kitchen-middens on the Baltic or of shell-heaps on the Scottish coasts. And frequently the data from the Orient serve as a written commentary upon European prehistory. Some of the peoples of Oriental antiquity were close kinsmen to the neolithic inhabitants of parts of Europe or descendants of the race of palæolithic hunters who had lived there before. From the Oriental kinsmen of our barbarian ancestors may we not expect to learn something even of the spiritual life of the latter? May not the practices of the Orient, glossed by literary texts, throw light on contemporary usages in silent Europe?

The prehistoric and protohistoric archæology of the Ancient East is therefore an indispensable prelude to the true appreciation of European prehistory. The latter is at first mainly the story of the imitation, or at best adaptation, of Oriental achievements. The record of the achievements themselves is enshrined in the former.

Now in no sphere of archæological or anthropological research are such startling discoveries being made as in the Ancient East. I need only instance the opening up of a quite new chapter in Egypt's remotest past at Badari, disclosing a flourishing neolithic culture older than any previously known elsewhere, or the dazzling revelation of the brilliance of Sumerian civilization at the end of the fourth millennium B.C. or again the dramatic entry of India on to the stage of Oriental history with the excavation of Harappa and Mohenjodaro. An appreciation of these revolutions from the point of view of the purely archæological story of human culture has not yet been attempted. And even the archæological context to which they belong is by no means readily accessible to the ordinary worker in the field of prehistory. That is my excuse for offering in this volume a survey, that cannot help being one-sided, incomplete, and inconclusive, of the results of the work of specialists in a field different from, though cognate to, my own.

As a preliminary it is necessary to recapitulate some conclusions of the philological historian so as to define the basis of early chronology that forms the framework for my tale and to introduce the actors who are to play the leading roles in our drama.

FROM HISTORY TO PREHISTORY

In Egypt the written records—primarily the compilation in Greek by Manetho, composed under Ptolemy Philadelphus, and then certain fragments of much older native Egyptian annals, particularly the so-called Turin Papyrus written about 1300 B.C. and the Palermo Stone inscribed some fourteen hundred years earlier—serve to date the archæological monuments from about three thousand B.C. onwards. This historical period which begins with the unification of Upper and Lower Egypt as a single kingdom by the first pharaoh, traditionally called Menes (really a composite personage), has been subdivided by Manetho into dynasties. Modern historians recognize three main periods of Egyptian greatness, termed the Old, Middle, and New Kingdoms respectively, separated by intervals of decline or even chaos; the Old Kingdom corresponds to Manetho's Dynasties III–VI, the Middle his XIth and XIIth, and the New to the XVIIIth and XIXth. Throughout the whole of this period it is possible to give the age of most monuments in terms of solar years thanks to the lists of kings and their reigns controlled by certain astronomical dates given by peculiarities in the Egyptian calendar.

The Egyptian calendar is the first recorded achievement of the application of number to accurately recorded observations. It is the parent of our own which differs from it only through small corrections, attributed respectively to Julius Cæsar and Pope Gregory. Yet its invention was a direct response to the unique conditions of farming in the Nile valley. The whole cycle of Egyptian agriculture is conditioned by the annual inundation. But this recurs with a regularity unparalleled in other river systems: fifty years recorded observations would suffice to show that the average interval between floods was 365 days to the nearest whole number.[1] Whoever knew this, could foretell when the cycle of agricultural operations ought to begin, and to peasants such successful prediction might well seem a sign of divine omniscience. But whether or no it were the basis of 'Menes' authority, he—or some unknown precursor—seems to have used the discovery as the basis for an official calendar that replaced a lunar calendar such as many barbarians and savages use still. The artificial tropic year was divided into 12 months of 30 days each and five intercalary days were superadded.

1. See Neugebauer, O., 'Die Bedeutungslösigkeit der "Sothisperiode" für die älteste ägyptische Chronologie,' *Acta Orientalia*, xvii, 1938, 169–195, and 'La Période sothiaque', *Chron. d'Egypte*, 28, 1939, 258–262.

Now remarkably accurate though this first attempt at a solar calendar was, it was in fact out by nearly six hours every year. In a century the accumulated error of a hundred quarter-days made the discrepancy between the official and the tropic year all too patent. The official names for the seasons—'Inundation,' 'Sowing', 'Harvest'—ceased to have any relation to the activities they were intended to guide, and the calendar was patently useless for just the purpose for which it had been devised. But by then it, like the Christians' Easter, must have become too sanctified by association with personal and local festivals to be safely changed; it was in fact retained till the reign of Julius Cæsar, a foreigner who could afford to ignore 'native superstitions'.

But already under the Old Kingdom the pharaohs' officials had discovered a device for directing agricultural operations. It happens that in the latitude of Memphis the heliacal rising of Sirius, the Egyptians' Sothis, coincides with the beginning of the inundation. Observations on Sothis were accordingly used by the officials for giving the signal to start the agricultural cycle. Of course once in every 1,461 years the heliacal rising of Sirius coincided with the beginning of the official year. This period is termed a Sothic cycle. One such cycle began in A.D. 139, and the Egyptians have left records showing the relation between the official and the sidereal year, defined by Sothis, under several kings of the XVIIIth dynasty and under Senusert III in the XIIth. The latter record gives us a reliable date for the Middle Kingdom which on the strength of complete dynastic lists must have begun about 2000 B.C. But there is no legitimate reason for supposing that the calendar was introduced at the beginning of a Sothic cycle. So the use of the official calendar under Dynasty IV does not prove, as Eduard Meyer contended, that the calendar was introduced a Sothic cycle earlier, i.e. in 4236 B.C. Presumably it was invented after the beginning of written records, most probably in the reign of 'Menes'. But his accession has to be dated by working back from 2000 B.C. with the aid of dynastic lists, checked by official biographies. Owing to an undoubted inflation of the record and probable exaggerations in the reported lengths of certain reigns estimates of the date in 1950 vary between 2830 and 3188 B.C.[1]

The creation of the calendar, the first approximation to a correct

1. The minimal date is defended by Stock, 'Die erste Zwischenzeit Agyptens,' *Analecta Orientalia*, 31, Rome, 1949; the higher by Sewell in Glanville, *The Legacy of Egypt*, 1941, 2-11.

estimate of the tropic year, presupposed at least fifty years of recorded observation on the Nile floods and therefore presumably a system of conventional symbols in which to keep the records, i.e. writing. Can all this be attributed to the reign of the first pharaoh, Menes? According to a tradition preserved only in late documents but generally accepted,[1] Menes was a king of Upper Egypt who united the whole Nile valley in a single Kingdom by conquering the Delta. At his death he, like all his successors, became identified with his patron deity, the Falcon Horus, and assumed a new 'Horus name'; Menes whose name has not certainly been found on any monument, became on one view, 'the Horus, Nar mer.'[2] But various native traditions point to the previous existence of independent kingdoms in Upper and in Lower Egypt,[3] each with appropriate insignia—Red and White Crowns, etc.—which were ultimately combined in the double crown and regalia worn by pharaohs after Dynasty I. At the same time there had been a seat of the Horus cult in the western Delta, and its focus at Hierakon-polis may have been a secondary centre. Sethe has accordingly argued that the unification by the Falcon chief, Menes, from the south was preceded by an earlier union effected by the Falcon clan starting from the western Delta; the struggles between Horus and Seth (of **Nubet** = ?Naqada), mentioned in Egyptian myths, would then reflect this conquest of the South. Its result according to Sethe would have been the establishment of a 'predynastic' United Kingdom with its capital at Heliopolis near Cairo. If the Helio-politan Kingdom ever existed, it might have been under it that the Egyptian conventions for writing were established; plants and animals peculiar to the Delta were notoriously prominent among the Egyptian hieroglyphic signs. But, though Breasted[4] claimed to find references to kings of a united Egypt prior to the First Dynasty on the Palermo Stone, the united Heliopolitan kingdom remains a matter of speculation not directly attested either by archæological or literary documents.

1. Doubts have been expressed as to the existence of a single 'Menes', e.g. *Annales du Service*, xli, 1942, 290.

2. So Petrie in his later years and Edwards; Reisner, Emery, and at first Petrie identified Menes with 'the Horus Aha'.

3. See Ranke, 'The Beginnings of Civilization in the Orient,' *JAOS.*, Suppl. 4, 1939, 1–15.

4. *Bull. Inst. Franc. d'Arch. orient.*, xxx, Cairo, 1932, 702, cf. *OLZ.*, 1932, 704.

On the other hand we shall find evidence for a period when the North exercised a cultural, if not a political, hegemony over the South, and the North at that time was profoundly influenced from Asia. Now philologists have detected in the Egyptian language an infusion of Semitic elements into a substantially Hamitic, African stock and have deduced from the coincidence of the words for 'left' and 'right' with the designations for 'east' and 'west' respectively that the Semitic element was introduced into Egypt from the North by Semitic tribes or conquerors who worked their way up the river; for the words in question belong to the 'Semitic' stratum in Egyptian.

Comparative ethnography at this point offers us some further clues. The social and religious institutions that face us in such maturity at the dawn of Egyptian history not only challenge us to investigate the process of their growth but also provide us with clues to facilitate the task. Behind the impressive figure of the omnipotent and deified pharaoh looms the shadow of a humbler personage—the divine king, as Frazer has depicted him, who holds his sovereignty by virtue of his magic power and as its price must lay down his life ere that power grow enfeebled with the decay of his body. The pharaoh was in fact not only accredited with many of the functions assigned to such kings among contemporary barbarians; he escaped their fate only through the performance of a magic rite that was equivalent to a ritual death. The *Sed* festival, celebrated periodically by every pharaoh from Menes, was a magical identification of the king with Osiris, the god who had died and risen again. Its meaning and function were to confer upon the monarch renewed life and vigour by a symbolic death and resurrection[1]. And so it presupposes a time when pharaoh's predecessors were actually put to death ceremonially to make room for young and potent successors lest their magic efficacy vanish with their enfeebled frames.

Similarly a contemplation of the weird animal deities of the Egyptian pantheon has suggested that the Falcon Horus, the Cow Hathor, the Serpent Neith and the rest have grown out of totems. And that implies behind the unified Egyptian State a multiplicity of totemic clans whose patron ancestral animals and plants had become local deities and then, with the unification of the land by the Shemsu-Hor, had taken their places under the Falcon totem of the victorious clan in a national pantheon.

1. So Moret, *Tribe to Empire*, 151 ff.; Seligman, *JRAI.*, 1913, 665.

Now on the Upper Nile there dwell to-day people allied to the oldest Egyptians in appearance, stature, cranial proportions, language, and dress.[1] These are ruled by rain-maker magicians or by divine kings who were until recently ritually slain, and the tribes are organized in totemic clans. The Shilluk, ruled by a centralized king with animal (i.e. totem) ancestry who was ritually slain, illustrate a stage immediately prior to the divine monarchy of Menes. A still older phase is seen among the Dinka: they are a congeries of autonomous totemic clans, often at war with one another, and each ruled by a 'rain-maker' who was ceremonially killed before old age overtook him. It really looks as if among these tribes on the Upper Nile social development had been arrested at a stage that the Egyptians had traversed before their history began. There we have a living museum whose exhibits supplement and vivify the prehistoric cases in our collections.

Legends and philology, comparative religion and ethnography thus cast some light on tribal and dynastic movements, on spiritual and social revolutions in the Nile valley long before 3000 B.C. The archæologist's spade has revealed a concrete record of man's progress from savagery to civilization in the same region. It largely substantiates the traditions and deductions just summarized and at the same time it supplements them and enlarges their scope. But further it brings the reanimated body of most ancient Egypt into living contact with Europe's own remote past, infusing for a moment the glow of life into those pale lips.

In due course we shall deal in detail with archæology's revelations that disclose no abstract evolution but the interaction of multiple concrete groups and the blending of contributions from far-sundered regions. But first we must explain one point in the framework on which that picture must be based. Our knowledge of Predynastic Egypt, as it is called, is derived almost entirely from graves that contain no written document from which a calendar date might be obtained. We can do no more than guess at the length of time represented in each of the cemeteries, but thanks to

1. Seligman, *JRAI.*, 1913, 597 ff.; Petrie, *Anc. Eg.*, 1915, 70. The attempt to connect the *Shemsu Hor* with the Land of Punt (e.g. Hall, *Anc. Hist.*, 92) must be abandoned in view of Sethe's researches. And the 'Mesniu' associated with them are not 'smiths' but rather 'harpooners' who harpooned hippopotami in the Delta marshes; cf. Moret, *Nile*, 108, and Hall in *CAH.*, i, 261. The traditions about the Land of Punt cited by Hall none the less prove conclusively an element in dynastic Egypt allied to the people of this unidentified southern region in Abyssinia or Arabia.

Sir Flinders Petrie we can arrange the graves in their relative chronological order. Petrie began by an analysis of the way in which the wavy ledges that once served as handles for certain types of jar in the course of years lost their true function as hand-holds and degenerated to mere decorative wriggles. Then he correlated the several stages of this orderly process with phases in the development of other associated articles of tomb-furniture. Eventually he worked out a numerical scale by which the position in time of any one grave relative to the rest can be defined in figures.[1] The scale consists of the so-called sequence dates (S.D.) numbered from 30 to 80, which of course give no true idea of duration but merely mark successive points in the temporal series without offering any clue as to the intervals separating them. The accession of 'Menes' was assigned to S.D. 77, but would now seem to come near S.D. 60; the 'predynastic' used to begin with the Amratian at S.D. 30 and the Badarian was then fitted in before that S.D.

Attempts have been made to give an approximate absolute value to S.D. 30 by estimating the length of the predynastic age. Sir Flinders Petrie, by a comparison of the number of prehistoric and pre-Roman dynastic graves near Diospolis, came to the conclusion that the predynastic and pharaonic periods were approximately equal in length. Hence S.D. 30 falls in the sixth millennium on the short chronology or about 9000 B.C. on Petrie's. Peake and Fleure, using a different method of computation, assign to the predynastic period about half this duration. MacIver and Mace state that the total number of graves in a cemetery in use throughout the whole period approximates to 500. Assuming that the community whose graves are discovered was similar in size to a modern fellahin village, the period represented by the cemetery would be two thousand years, the adult death-rate averaging to-day one in four years.

It may not be amiss here to recall how extremely new our knowledge of Predynastic Egypt really is. The whole volume entitled Egyptian Prehistory is just over fifty years old. Prior to 1895 the record in Egypt really began with the Pyramid age. Then Amélinau and de Morgan chanced upon the tombs of the First Dynasty while Petrie laid bare the still older series of graves that took us back to a time when only poor villagers ignorant of writing dwelt upon the banks of the Nile. The prefatory chapter of this volume entitled

1. First worked out in *Diospolis Parva*. The system is elaborated in *Prehistoric Egypt* and the new sequence dates are appended to *Prehistoric Egypt, Corpus of Pottery*.

'Badari' was only opened in 1924. Incidentally, the discoveries at that site did more than open a new chapter; they confirmed our reading of the older ones by providing the first stratigraphical confirmation for Petrie's system of sequence dating. In the settlement near Badari the ceramic types, assumed on the theory to be later, were actually found in ruined huts superposed upon those containing sherds of the supposedly older wares whose priority was thus demonstrated. And now before the Badarian preface Brunton has discovered a Tasian introduction! On the other hand this sequence is valid only for Upper Egypt. Since 1940, excavations near Cairo have revealed assemblages which cannot be paralleled further south.

In Mesopotamia surviving fragments of a chronicle composed in Greek by Berosus and incomplete clay tablets embodying parts of native annals and written in the cuneiform script purport to present a complete list of kings and dynasties reigning there since 'the Flood' together with the names of some 'antediluvian' monarchs. By adding up the regnal years, but for lacunæ in the record, we should obtain a complete chronological framework for all events since 'kingship descended from the heavens'. But the antiquity of Mesopotamian civilization too has been very drastically deflated between 1930 and 1950. In the Tigris-Euphrates valley unification came much later than on the Nile. At the beginning of continuous written history Lower Mesopotamia was still divided among a number of autonomous city-states. These were finally united in a single kingdom or empire under Hammurabi, a king of the First Dynasty of Babylon. But even his unification was not quite complete, and in the sequel his empire was temporarily divided between different and contemporary dynasties. So even the Babylonian king list gives an inflated age to the First Dynasty since its compiler, ignoring overlaps, arranges all rulers of any part of Babylonia in a continuous sequence. Fortunately about the time of Hammurabi, Assyria also became a single kingdom, and its unity was never so seriously interrupted till the fall of Nineveh before the Medes. Hence to-day by checking the Babylonian lists against the Assyrian, against Egyptian records and against purely archæological data it has been possible to fix the accession of Hammurabi about 1790 B.C.[1] or at least 1760±30.

But Hammurabi's empire was not the first. Previously the Sumerian kings of the Third Dynasty of Ur and still earlier Sargon

1. Sidney Smith, *Alalakh and Chronology*, London, 1940; but Albright, *BASOR.*, 88, 1942, 28–33, puts Hammurabi's succession sixty years later, in 1728 B.C.

and the remaining Semitic kings of Agade (Akkad) had established empires uniting the whole of Sumer and Akkad—Lower Mesopotamia—for about a century each. Under the Empire of Ur a Sumerian scribe had compiled a list of cities which from time to time had enjoyed sovereignty, together with the names and regnal years of the rulers of each imperial city. Taking the list at its face value a mere summation of the recorded reigns would yield historical dates for any king back to the Flood and for the antediluvian period as well. But the list cannot be taken at its face value. In the first place the reigns not only of the antediluvian monarchs, but also of many early rulers after the Flood are patently fabulous; the twenty-three kings of the First Dynasty of Kish, the first after the Flood, reigned together 24,519 years, 3 months and 3½ days! Then between the last ruler of 'Kish III' and her son, who initiated the 'IVth Dynasty of Kish' there is intercalated a 'Dynasty of Akshak' occupying 117 years! Thirdly till 1924 no monarch mentioned in the king list before Sargon of Agade was known from any contemporary monument; then turned up an inscription of A-anni-padda, first king of the 1st Dynasty of Ur which in the king list was succeeded by a Dynasty of Uruk with fabulous reigns. Finally contemporary documents after Sargon of Agade show that kings, separated in the list by several centuries, were actually reigning in their respectives cities at the same time.

Jacobsen[1] has satisfactorily explained what has happened. The compiler has collected lists of local 'kings' from Kish, Erech, Ur, and other cities. But, assuming that each of these kings must, like those of Ur III, have ruled over all the cities, he has broken up the lists and rearranged the sections in a serial order. He has also supplemented this probably reliable documentary material with bits of epics and mythological poems. Adjustments of the lists in the light of contemporary documents allow the accession of Sargon of Agade to be placed with some confidence about 2325±25 B.C. and A-anni-padda of Ur I perhaps as early as 2580 B.C. There may well have been earlier kings at Ur and elsewhere, but though writing was developed long before A-anni-padda, no earlier name in the king list has yet been identified on a contemporary document.

The Antediluvian section is doubtless based upon poetic, rather than historical sources. But 'flood deposits' have in fact been observed at Ur, Erech, Shuruppak and Kish, albeit at quite different archæological horizons. So we cannot identify which was 'the

1. 'The Sumerian King List,' *OIAS.*, 11, Chicago, 1939.

Flood' of the king list nor assert its historicity. Still it is significant that the oldest recognizable temple found in Mesopotamia was uncovered in 1948 at Eridu, which is named in the king list as the first antediluvian city of royalty after 'kingship had descended from the heavens.'

Linguistics may none the less throw some light upon these earliest days of human life in the Tigris-Euphrates plain. In historical times the valley had been occupied by two distinct ethnic elements speaking different languages. The southern part, including the cities of Eridu, Ur, Larsa, Lagash, Umma, Adab, Erech, and Shuruppak (Fara) was dominated down to the unification of the land under the First Dynasty of Babylon by a curious people known to us as the Sumerians (from Sumer, the Semitic name of the country)—a people distinguished by language and dress. At an early time the Sumerians had spread also over the northern part of Babylonia and even into Assyria as the archæological remains show. But there they were mixed with people speaking a Semitic dialect, akin to Hebrew, Assyrian, and Arabic. As early as the First Dynasty of Kish, the first after the Flood, we find persons with Semitic names among the rulers mentioned on the dynastic lists, and the towns of the north, Kish, Sippar, Akshak, Opis, and Agade (which latter gave its name in the form of Akkad to the whole of North Babylonia) were traditionally the homes of Semitic rulers.

Political power eventually passed to the Semites. But long after that the Sumerian language, like Latin in medieval Europe, continued to be used in ritual and in magic formulæ, while elements in later Babylonian law are traceable to Sumerian sources. The Sumerians have accordingly been generally regarded as the founders of civilization in Babylonia.

But the Sumerians themselves may have been a composite people or have had forerunners of a different nationality. Their traditions are somewhat contradictory; the legend of Oannes, a fish-man who swam up to Eridu and taught the people to build cities, points to a southern origin. The worship of deities on artificial high places suggests a mountain people. The names of some cities mentioned as seats of royalty 'before the Flood', e.g. Shuruppak and Zimbir, are not easily explained as Sumerian. The terminations resemble those proper to languages such as the Anzanite of Elam, spoken in historical times in the hill countries east of the Tigris. For this vague group Speiser[1] has proposed the name Japhetite. A people

1. Speiser, *Mesopotamian Origins*, Philadelphia, 1930; for a criticism of Meyer see Meissner in *AfO.*, v, 1–10.

neither Semites nor Sumerians, and distinguished from the latter by fairness of skin, certainly dwelt in early times in the highlands from the Zagros westward. Smith terms them Subaræans, and their language may have been Japhetic in Speiser's sense. Their kinsmen may once have occupied even Sumer.

Fortunately the archæological record provides an unusually clear sequence of cultures even if it be hazardous to attach linguistic names to any of them. The peoples of the Tigris-Euphrates valley lived continuously on the same site for many generations in villages, and eventually cities, of mud brick houses. In course of time houses collapsed, but then the component mud was just stamped flat and a new house built on the raised platform thus formed. By that time the street level had probably been raised too by the refuse dumped in it. Eventually each inhabited site became a mound or *tell*, composed of the superimposed ruins of successive habitations.[1] In the scientific excavation of such a tell each superimposed floor level with the rubbish accumulated on it illustrates the culture of a period in a chronological succession, the lowest floor being obviously older than the one above. So the dissection of a tell reveals the sequence of cultures at the site, and many excavated tells have yielded parallel sequences. Of course mortal men do not want to build their houses on slopes nor on the peak of a high mound so that settlements tended to be shifted after a time. It was different with the houses of gods. Now historical Sumerian cities had grown up round temples. Just as in the Middle Ages Christian burghers kept on enlarging and embellishing cathedrals, so pious and prosperous Sumerians repeatedly reconstructed their temples on an ever more ambitious scale. But they did not usually begin by levelling the sacred edifice to the ground. On the contrary its walls would be left standing, perhaps several feet high, but the interior was filled up with clay while outside the old walls were encased in a mud brick platform on which the new temple should stand. Superimposed temples therefore conveniently supplement the stratigraphy of domestic sites.

The consistent picture resulting from the excavation of a score of sites may conveniently be summarized here. Beneath buildings of the age of Sargon and the Dynasty of Agade come structures built in plano-convex bricks (bricks with one face flat but the other cushion-shaped). The period thus defined used to be termed simply 'Pre-Sargonic'. Christian suggested 'Plano-convex Period', but the

1. For an excellent description of the process, see Frankfort in *Town Planning Review*, xxi, Liverpool, 1950, 100.

designation 'Early Dynastic' has eventually won acceptance. Since 1936 Frankfort has divided the period into three phases. The details are not yet fully published, but even A-anni-padda is assigned to Early Dynastic III. Under the oldest plano-convex walls, are stumps of others built with flat tile-shaped bricks associated with distinctive styles in pottery, glyptic and epigraphy. These define the Jemdet Nasr phase, named after a site in Akkad where the culture was first identified in 1926. Then in 1930, below temples of the Jemdet Nasr age, the German excavators at Warka, the ancient Uruk and biblical Erech, recognized remains of a new culture which define the Uruk period. Both these cultures are found throughout the later Babylonia and are already generally associated with some kind of writing so that Delougaz would group them together as 'Protoliterate'.

Still older and purely prehistoric are villages of the Ubaid culture, so called after a site near Ur explored in 1922, and most easily recognized by its painted pottery. In Sumer Ubaid remains are found on virgin soil at Eridu, Ur, Erech, and other sites, but, save for one site, they seem to be missing in Akkad. They reappear in Northern Mesopotamia where they occur at many sites from the Kurdish foothills in Assyria, east of the Tigris, to the bend of the Euphrates near Carchemish and even further west. There in the North the Ubaid culture is preceded by one termed Halafian, first identified by Oppenheim before 1914, but fixed in the stratigraphical sequence only by Mallowan in 1933. Since 1945 two or three still earlier phases have been recognized in Assyria, first at Hassuna, excavated by Lloyd and Safar. Hassuna I represents the earliest farming culture known in 1950 in the Tigris-Euphrates valley, though Jarmo on the foothills to the east may reveal something older as well as simpler.

Having thus mapped out the world that became historical about 3000 B.C., it remains to mention one region which, though not yet historical for us, could nevertheless already boast a civilization fully equal to that of Egypt or Sumer. That region is the Indus valley, where discoveries made since 1920 have revealed a true urban civilization where writing and the other arts of civilization were already flourishing. The script is still undeciphered, and no legends can be plausibly used to interpret the new archæological data. In a later chapter we shall give some account of the remains. Here it suffices to signalize the existence at the dawn of history of a third province that ought to be historical.

CHAPTER II

THE SETTING OF THE STAGE

THE three oldest centres of true civilization named in our last chapter lie on a belt between the twenty-fifth and thirty-fifth parallel that constitutes the hottest and driest climatic zone in the world to-day. Extreme aridity and excessive summer heats are features common to the three ancient foci and to the intervening regions, though the causes are not precisely the same in each case. Geographically, too, a certain unity characterizes the whole region. Egypt, Sumer, and the Punjab lie in the valleys of great permanent rivers that traverse a more or less continuous desert plateau. The plateau is of course interrupted by marked physiographical features. The Sahara, which constitutes its western section, is by no means flat; its surface is interrupted by quite considerable ranges and depressions that sometimes fall below sea-level. The Arabian desert forms the natural continuation of the Sahara, but is separated from it by the rift of the Nile valley, and is itself broken by the great chasm of the Red Sea. East of that gap and the high gable beyond it the desert slopes away to the depression of Mesopotamia and the Persian Gulf. The farther side of the hollow is bordered by the Zagros and the parallel chains of Western Persia that frame a still more elevated desert, belonging geographically to the Anatolian-Armenian tableland, but climatically nearer to Arabia. And then at the other extremity the plateau breaks down again to the low sweltering plain of Western India. Thus from the Atlantic coasts to the monsoon region of Central India there is a continuous zone of desiccated countries, which, however much diversified, are connected without any insurmountable physiographical transverse barrier to impede intercourse. The unity of the strip between the Atlantic and the Tigris at least is of such an order as to justify the employment of a common term Afrasia to denote the whole region.

On the south the Sahara is fringed with savannah passing over into tropical forest while farther east and in Southern Arabia the monsoon rains promote the growth of a jungle border. Then the Indian Ocean forms the southern limit of our zone and beyond the Indus it is again hedged in by the monsoon forest. The northern frontier would seem to be provided by the Mediterranean but climatologically the winter-rain regions of Spain, Italy, and Greece approximate more closely to the Sahara than to the cyclonic lands north of the Pyrenean-Alpine-Balkan ridges. And physiographically the last-named chains constitute a more real dividing line than the inland sea. So in Asia, although the desert extends north of the Elburz into the Turanian Basin, it is the continuation of the same lines of folding in the Anatolian massif, the Caucasus and the Elburz and then in the Hindu-Kush and the Himalayas, that forms the true northern border of our zone. None the less, conditions in the Central Asian desert, particularly in the Tarim Basin, are not very different.

At the present time the whole region suffers from a terrible insufficiency of rain that makes it virtually uninhabitable outside the range of irrigation channels that tap the great rivers crossing it. The Atlantic cyclones that water Northern and Central Europe reach the Mediterranean only in winter and miss the Sahara altogether. The same winter storms do indeed reach Mesopotamia, the Iranian plateau and even the Indus valley, but they have been so largely drained by crossing the highlands of Palestine-Syria that the precipitation farther east is inadequate save along a narrow belt in North Syria, and even the high country of Central Persia is virtually desert. At the same time a complicated set of causes prevent the precipitation of the monsoon rains on the Indus basin, which relies on cyclonic rain from the West.[1] In such conditions the whole region, except for the river valleys that cross it, can support only a sparse and exiguous population who have little encouragement to cultural progress and have in fact remained backward.

But these conditions did not reign at the time our story opens. While Northern Europe was covered in ice as far as the Harz, and the Alps and the Pyrenees were capped with glaciers, the Arctic high pressure deflected southward the Atlantic rainstorms.[2] The cyclones that to-day traverse Central Europe then passed over the Mediterranean basin and the northern Sahara and continued, undrained by

1. On the monsoon in India see Simpson, *Q.J.Met.Soc.*, 1921, 151 ff.
2. In *Q.J.Met.Soc.*, 1921. Brooks gives maps showing the assumed paths of rainstorms in various prehistoric phases. See also his *Evolution of Climate*, London, 1924.

Lebanon, across Mesopotamia and Arabia to Persia and India. The parched Sahara enjoyed a regular rainfall, and farther east the showers were not only more bountiful than to-day but were distributed over the whole year, instead of being restricted to the winter. On the Iranian plateau the precipitation, although insufficient to feed extensive glaciers, filled the great hollows that are now salt deserts with shallow inland seas whose presence tempered the severity of the climate.

Such are the deductions of climatology, and geology confirms them. The dry wadi beds traversing the Sahara, entering the Nile on either side and draining the Arabian plateau, testify to the erosive power of the rain-waters they once carried off. In Persia and Baluchistan,[1] the high strand-lines encircling the old lakes bear witness

FIG. 1. Rock engraving in the Sahara at Kef Messiouer near Guelma, Algeria.

to the flooding of those inland seas as just forecast, and into them flowed many streams that are now lost in the desert.

We should expect in North Africa, Arabia, Persia, and the Indus valley parklands and savannahs such as flourish to-day north of the Mediterranean at a time when much of Europe was tundra or windswept steppe on which the dust was collecting as loess. While the mammoth, the woolly rhinoceros, and the reindeer were browsing in France and Southern England, North Africa should have supported a fauna such as is found to-day in Rhodesia.[2] Its former existence in areas that are now totally desert is in fact proved by pictures, engraved, pecked, or painted on rocks by men who hunted

1. Sven Hedin, *Overland to India*, ii, 214 ff.; *AJA.*, 1950.
2. Boule, *L'Anthr.*, x, 1900, 57.

there elephants, hippopotami, gazelles, wild cattle, wild asses, and other parkland ruminants and the panthers, lions, and bears that preyed on them. Such pictures are common in the Saharan Atlas,[1] in Fezzan, Tripolitania,[2] the Ouenat Oasis, the deserts on both sides of the Nile[3] and even Arabia.[4]

But most of these pictures are now believed to belong to the Recent period of geology when the glaciers and ice-sheets in Europe had already melted away.[5] Their passing did not, as was once supposed cause a sudden catastrophic reversion to desert conditions in North Africa and Hither Asia. The existing regime of absolute drought is the result of a very gradual process to which man and his stock may well have contributed. After all it was no climatic change that turned Oklahoma into a dust-bowl in half a century. In fact the rock-pictures just demonstrate the survival of the 'Rhodesian fauna' and the appropriate vegetation to a time when stock-breeders were actually using the latter as pasture.

Nevertheless, the grasslands of North Africa and Southern Asia are likely to have been as thickly populated by men in the last Ice Age as the tundras and steppes of Europe. They should have provided a more favourable environment. Now all over North Africa, in Syria, Palestine, Kurdistan, and the Iranian plateau, we do find remains of hunters equipped with stone tools—single-edged and pointed double-edged knives—similar to those used by Moustierian mammoth-hunters in Europe and Upper Asia at the beginning of the last Ice Age (Würm I). But most were made by the Levalloisean technique which demands greater foresight and intelligence than the methods usually, but not exclusively, used by European Moustierians. Moreover, while the European makers of Moustierian implements and some of their African contemporaries in Morocco,[6] East Africa, and Rhodesia,[7] belonged to aberrant (Neandertal or Nean-

1. Frobenius and Obermaier, *Hadschra Maktuba*, Munich, 1925; Flamande, *Les Pierres écrites*, Paris, 1921; Solignac, *Les Pierres écrites de la Berberie occidentale*, Tunis, 1928, etc.
2. Graziosi, *L'Arte rupestre della Libia*, Naples, 1942; Reygasse, *L'Anthr.*, xiv, 1935, 534–570.
3. Winckler, *The Rock Drawings of Southern Upper Egypt*, i, 1938; ii, 1939.
4. *Man*, xxxii, 297; *AJA.*, xxxvii, 383.
5. Vaufrey, *L'Art rupestre nord-africain,*' IPH., Mém. 20, 1939; Winckler, op. cit.; Graziosi, op. cit., 238; *L'Anthr.*, lv, 1951, 48.
6. Howe and Movius, 'A Stone Age Cave Site in Tangier,' *Peabody Museum Papers*, xxviii, Harvard, 1947.
7. *Nature*, cxxxviii, 1936, 1082–4; *JRAI.*, lxxvii, 28.

dertaloid) branches of the human family that could hardly have evolved into modern men, some at least of the Levalloiso-Moustierians of Palestine[1] represent a less specialized stock, well on the way to the modern type, *Homo sapiens* as we proudly call ourselves.

Now the first representatives of the latter type, known in Europe till 1947, appeared there equipped with a vastly superior set of stone tools made for the most part on blades—long narrow flakes prepared by a different process to those used in the manufacture of Moustierian and Levalloisean flakes. It was accordingly believed that blade tools were always and exclusively produced by *Homo*

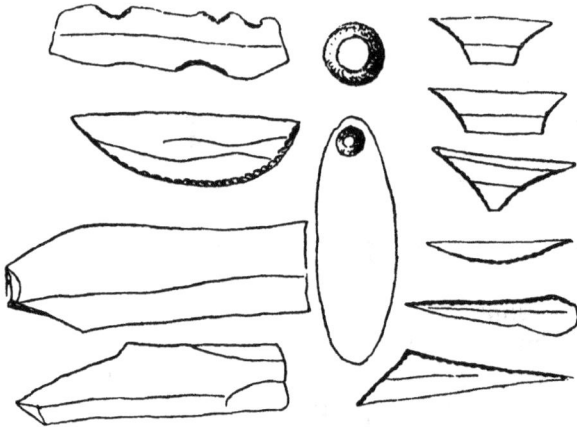

FIG. 2. Capsian flint blades and ostrich egg-shell disc bead from Aïn Mauhaâd, ¼.

sapiens, and industries based on blades were termed 'neanthropic' in contradistinction to Moustierian and Levalloisean assemblages, supposedly produced only by more primitive 'palæanthropic' species. This terminology now turns out to be misleading. In our area blade tools do not everywhere replace the older flakes as they do in Upper Palæolithic Europe.

Still in Palestine and Syria, just where Levalloiso-Moustierian men showed modern (neanthropic) characters, the latest assemblages of Levalloiso-Moustierian tools comprise a marked proportion of genuine blades. Indeed these assemblages, termed Emirian,[2] have

1. Keith and McCown, *The Stone Age of Mount Carmel*, ii, Oxford, 1939.
2. Turville-Petre, *Researches in Prehistoric Galilee*, London, 1927, 3–14; Garrod and Bate, *The Stone Age of Mount Carmel*, i, 50–53. Professor Garrod now holds that layer F at Mugharet el-Wad contains not a mechanical mixture but a transitional industry.

a better claim to illustrate the transition from the palæanthropic or Lower Palæolithic flake tradition to the neanthropic Upper Palæolithic blade tradition than any other culture recognized anywhere in the world. Then in the immediately overlying strata this transitional Emirian industry is succeeded by assemblages of true blade tools, closely allied to the Aurignacian that is found in the Crimea, the Balkans, Central Europe, France, and England.[1] At the same time in Kurdistan blade tools from the cave of Zarzi[2] are just as closely allied to the Gravettian equipment, familiar from encampments in South Russia, Moravia, and Lower Austria. Even in Africa Minor great heaps of snail shells in the desert and rock shelters yield blade industries (Figs. 2–3)—Capsian and Oranian—comparable to the Châtelperronian and Gravettian of Europe and similar tools

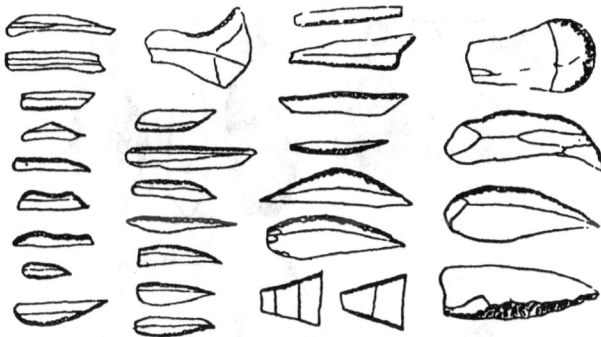

FIG. 3. Late Capsian or Getulan blades and microliths Morsotte and Ali Bacha, (Constantine), ¼.

characterize contemporary encampments in East Africa.[3] But in both areas their makers showed a predilection for composite weapons armed with minute geometric flints—microliths—such as became popular in Europe only in recent times and 'mesolithic' cultures.

On the other hand, over large tracts of Africa the place of blade industries is taken by flake industries continuing the Levalloisean tradition in Upper Palæolithic times. But most of these flake industries are distinguished from the earlier flake industries and from the contemporary blade industries by a frequent use of bifacial trimming

1. Garrod, *PPS.*, iv, 1938.
2. Garrod, American School of Prehistoric Research, *Bulletin*, vii, 1931.
3. L. S. B. Leakey, *The Stone Age Cultures of Kenya Colony*, 1931; *Stone Age Africa*, 1936.

in which the primary flake is thinned and shaped by the removal of fine secondary flakes from both sides or faces and along both edges. Other flakes have been converted into gravers, ingenious tools once regarded as peculiar to neanthropic blade industries.

Of these Upper Palæolithic flake industries, one, termed Aterian, represents groups of hunters well known all across North Africa from the Atlantic coasts to the Kharga oasis in Egypt.[1] These managed to convert their flakes into very efficient bifacial points for lances and even into tanged arrow-heads (Fig. 4); they must have possessed, if they did not themselves invent, a bow to propel the latter. And points, like the Emirian of Palestine, sometimes recur in Aterian contexts. In the Nile valley itself the Sebilian seems to represent a parallel development of the Levalloisean tradition. But

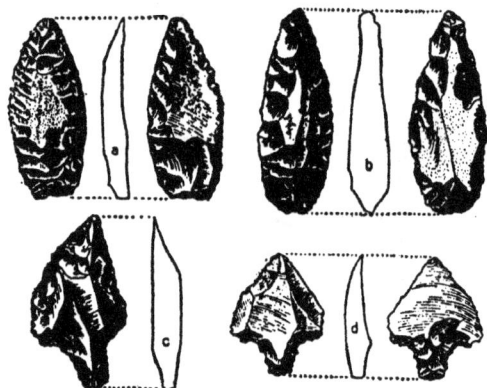

FIG. 4. Aterian bifacial points (a–b) and arrow-heads (c–d): a, c, d, ⅓; b, ¼.

here bifacial trimming was scarcely practised while a penchant for composite weapons led to a multiplication of microliths.[2] Finally in Somaliland and East Africa the so-called Still Bay industry displays bifacial points like the Aterian, but no arrow-heads. In the sequel we shall find the bifacial 'Aterian' tradition dominating later flint work in Egypt, while in Asia it is the blade tradition that shows through.

In Europe it was early recognized that tiny flints carefully trimmed to geometric shapes were especially popular in the period

1. Caton-Thompson, 'The Aterian Industry,' *JRAI.*, lxxvi, 1946.
2. Vignard in *Bull. Soc. Préhist. Franç.*, 1928, 200 ff.; Huzayyin, 'The Place of Egypt in Prehistory.' Institut d'Egypte, *Mém.*, xlix, Cairo, 1941; Caton-Thompson, *PPS.*, xii, 1946, 100–118.

extending from the end of the Pleistocene and the Old Stone Age to the beginning of the New with the advent of the first farmers. Hence the descriptive term 'microlithic' was often confused with the taxonomic term 'mesolithic'. But in reality geometric microliths were used by some groups of European hunters during the last Ice Age (Würm II- III),[1] and in North Africa and Kenya microliths may be just as truly palæolithic. On the other hand geometric microliths were still used both in Europe and Africa after farmers had already colonized the locality, that is, when the neolithic stage had dawned. So collections of pigmy flints, however beautifully made, are by themselves no guide to the relative antiquity of their makers. Indeed, Dr. Leakey has shown by practical experiments that darts armed with microliths are peculiarly deadly weapons in

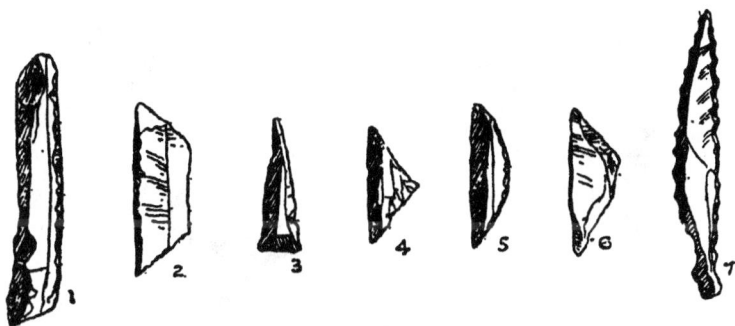

FIG. 5. Microliths from Vindhya Hills, India (nat. size) after British Museum *Stone Age Guide.*

the pursuit of certain types of game and that the microliths themselves can be made both from blades and flakes with far less trouble than armchair archæologists have supposed. It is not, therefore, very surprising that they were widely used in the Old World and deservedly enjoyed a long popularity. Though we find assemblages of very similar microliths, scattered about from John o'Groats to the Cape of Good Hope and from the Atlantic coasts to the Vindhya Hills in India (Fig. 5) and the Mongolian Desert, alone they can be used to prove neither mesolithic settlement nor folk-migrations, and their attribution to a 'pigmy race' is a gratuitous assumption, expressly contradicted by the skeletal remains of their makers.

1. e.g., Peyrony, 'Laugerie Haute,' IPH., *Mém.* 19, 1938; *L.Anthr.*, xlix, 1939–40, 702; Bouysonnie, ib., L., 1946, figs. 61, 63; Lacorre and Barral, *Rev. Etudes Ligures*, xiv, Bordighera, 1949, 19–34.

Art styles alone have proved equally unreliable for the diagnosis of age or race. Quite striking agreements have indeed been detected between paintings in shallow rock shelters in south-east Spain (Fig. 6), at In-Ezzan in the Central Sahara and even in South Africa.

FIG. 6. Scenes painted on the walls of a rock-shelter at Alpera, South-East Spain, $\frac{1}{8}$, after Breuil.

But even the first named now turn out to be not older than the very end of the Pleistocene (Würm III), and quite probably early Holocene, while some Bushmen paintings date from historical times. In general naturalistic or seminaturalistic pictures are painted, engraved or carved upon rocks for magical purposes by hunters, but hunters do not necessarily abandon the practice if they begin to supplement the products of the chase by stock-breeding or corn-growing. Petroglyphs, like microliths, attest hunting over many areas now uninhabitable, but otherwise do not demonstrate any special antiquity for the artists.

Again huge heaps of shells and bones of game animals, often covering also human burials, in Africa Minor, the Nigerian and Egyptian Sudan, and similar deposits in caves in Hither Asia illustrate the presence of communities who either resided permanently on the spot or camped there regularly every year. At present it is seldom possible to determine the age of such a settlement or camp. All that can be safely said is that its occupants had not abandoned hunting even if they had perhaps begun farming. But whether they lived as pure food-gatherers or no, the conditions of life in Afrasia must normally have imposed frequent and extensive wanderings. Huntsmen, above all in a steppe region such as the land was becoming in post-Moustierian times, have to roam long distances in pursuit of herds of game. They may have to shift their abodes altogether in the event of droughts or other causes reducing the game supply. Through such normal or abnormal movements the several groups would be brought into mutual contact—friendly or hostile—and have opportunities for an exchange of gifts and ideas or stealing alien objects and imitating the manners of their foes. Hence an environment, thus populated, provides exceptional facilities for the diffusion of inventions and discoveries.

These facilities are augmented if the invention constitute an economic revolution. Food-production—the deliberate cultivation of food-plants, especially cereals, and the taming, breeding, and selection of animals—was an economic revolution—the greatest in human history after the mastery of fire. It opened up a richer and more reliable supply of food, brought now within man's own control and capable of almost unlimited expansion by his unaided efforts. Judging by the observed effects of the Industrial Revolution in England, a rapid increase of population would be the normal corollary of such a change. Incidentally children who are liable to be a burden to the hunter can, while still quite small, be usefully employed by the food-producer weeding fields or minding cattle. But the mere numerical growth will involve soon an expansion over a wider area. The pastoralist is notoriously inclined to nomadism, but certain types of cultivator cannot be strictly sedentary.

A simple form of cultivation still practised over wide areas in Africa is generally termed hoe-culture or garden-culture. Small plots are tilled with hoes—generally by women—and the grains sown thereon until the crops begin to deteriorate. Neither manuring nor regular fallowing is observed. When a plot becomes exhausted a new strip of virgin land is cleared and tilled. Eventually, when one area is used up, the whole settlement is transferred to a new site. Hoe-culture may thus actually entail nomadism.

But if the cultivated area happens to be a terminal oasis, or a wadi bed subject to periodical flooding, migration ceases to be necessary. The inundation brings down new soil which is deposited as silt upon the fields, renewing their virtue.

If, again, the flood be sufficiently regular and come at the right season, it may take the place of rain in watering the fields. In that case permanent settlement,possible when flood-lands are cultivated, becomes almost inevitable. To reap the full benefits of irrigation, channels have to be dug to remove surplus water or supply deficiencies. And the cultivator will not willingly leave the field thus made fruitful by his labour; capital has been invested in the land. And the drainage and irrigation works generally demand the co-operation of a whole community. They form an economic bond promoting social solidarity. And the possibility of restricting access to the water supply puts a sanction in the hands of the community. It ought eventually to lead to the political unification of the whole area dependent on a single river system. Actually we shall see that the higher civilizations rested primarily on irrigation cultivation. That does not imply that irrigation cultivation is necessarily later than garden culture. Perry and Cherry maintained the very contrary.

Nor has any agreement been reached as to the relative roles of agriculture and pastoralism in creating the food-producing economy. Professor Menghin[1] represents a school which holds that domestication of animals and cultivation of plants were initiated by distinct groups. Domestication would arise among hunting peoples, agriculture among those already devoted to the collection of roots, seeds, and berries. Mixed farming would only result from the fusion of pastoralists and cultivators. Others assign the primacy to agriculture; the cultivator could induce wild animals to submit to domestication by the food his operations guaranteed. The nature of the archæological record is liable to favour the latter view unduly;

1. *Weltgeschichte der Steinzeit*, Vienna, 1931.

24

herdsmen living in tents and using bone tools and leather vessels are less likely to leave recognizable traces than cultivators who will leave about sickle-flints and querns and very likely pot-sherds.

In any case, the conditions of incipient desiccation at which we have hinted would provide a stimulus towards the adoption of a food-producing economy. Enforced concentration by the banks of streams and shrinking springs would entail a more intensive search for means of nourishment. Animals and men would be herded together in oases that were becoming increasingly isolated by desert tracts. Such enforced juxtaposition might promote that sort of symbiosis between man and beast implied in the word 'domestication'.

And in Afrasia noble grasses and animals suitable for domestication were growing wild ready for man. Indeed, only in this zone, but probably in its Asiatic rather than in its African section, were suitable species of plants and animals simultaneously at hand.

From the present distribution of wild grain[1] it has been argued that the cultivation of cereals probably began in Asia. Wild barley is as a matter of fact found in Asia Minor, Transcaucasia, Turkestan, Afghanistan, Persia, Palestine, and perhaps Arabia Petræa. But it has also been detected in Marmarica, implying an extension of the natural habitat of the ancestral plant from Palestine across the Isthmus of Suez and the Delta during the pluvial period. Moreover, Vavilov, arguing not from the discovery of stray ears of wild barley but from the number of varieties cultivated, would place another centre of domestication in Abyssinia where, however, no wild barley has yet been found. The wild ancestor of emmer wheat (*Triticum dicoccum* with twenty-eight chromosomes) is alleged to grow native in Western Persia and Mesopotamia, in Syria, and Palestine. According to Vavilov, however, the cultivation of emmer must have begun in North-East Africa, but this area was more probably only a secondary centre of dispersal, the primary centre being Syria. The uncultivated form of another group of wheats, *Triticum monococcum*, grows wild in the Balkans, Asia Minor, North Syria, and Kurdistan on the frontier of Persia. Some botanists hold that common bread wheat, *Triticum vulgare*, and allied species, with forty-two chromosomes (e.g. *Triticum compactum*), are the

1. On the cereals see *Antiquity*, vii, 1933, 73 ff.; Schiemann, *Entstehung der Kulturpflanzen* (Ergebnisse der Biologie, 19), Berlin, 1943; Helbaek, University of London, Institute of Archaeology, *Annual Report*, ix, 1952.

results of crossing between the groups just mentioned. No wild ancestor is known. On Vavilov's principles the original centre of their cultivation must be located in or near Afghanistan. There would thus be several primary foci of agriculture. If bread and club wheats (and small seed flax) come from Western Asia, emmer, barley, and large seed flax may have been cultivated first in North or East Africa.

A better argument is founded upon the animals, especially the sheep.[1] No wild sheep exists in Africa; for the so-called Barbary sheep does not really belong to the genus. On the other hand three wild sheep exist in Asia all of which have given rise to breeds of domestic sheep. The mouflon, *Ovis musimon*, lives north of the Mediterranean in Corsica and Sardinia and once had a wider distribution in continental Europe. A slightly different variety inhabits the highlands of Hither Asia from Anatolia to the Elburz and the Zagros. The Asiatic mouflon appears domesticated on a Sumerian vase dating from the IVth millennium B.C. (Plate XX*b*), but his European congener was only tamed at a relatively late date in European prehistory. The oldest domesticated sheep found in the Swiss lake-dwellings and other early deposits in Central and Western Europe, *Ovis palustris*, is the domesticated descendant of the Asiatic urial (*Ovis vignei*), a long-tailed sheep. The home of this variety is the northern slopes of the Elburz, Turkestan, Afghanistan, Baluchistan, and the Punjab. The oldest Egyptian[2] sheep, *Ovis longipes*, is said to belong to the same stock. The third variety of Old World sheep, the argal, lives to the east of the urial. If one may argue from the present distribution of the animals, it would be clear that the sheep at least was introduced into Africa and into Europe from Asia. Still it is just possible that in the pluvial period some sort of mouflon or even a urial lived in North Africa. Though Asiatic or European species are conspicuously rare in the pleistocene fauna of North Africa, it would be possible to point to rock-drawings of camels as evidence that some such types were represented there. Bones vaguely diagnosed as 'sheep or goat' are really not rare in the later palæolithic or mesolithic sites of North Africa.[3] And there are

1. J. Cossar Ewart, *Proc. Highland and Agric. Soc.*, xxv, 1913, 160 ff.; Antonius, *Grundzüge einer Stammesgeschichte der Haustiere*, Vienna, 1922; Hilzheimer, *Zeitschr. f. Säugtierkunde*, iii, Berlin, 1928.

2. Hilzheimer, *Antiquity*, x, 1936, 195 ff.; Keimer, *Annales du Service*, xxxviii, 297.

3. *L'Anthr.*, xlii, 476.

the mysterious petroglyphs depicting tame wethers obviously belonging to the species *Ovis longipes*.

The existence of various bovids is well attested; special attention should perhaps be called to the existence in North Africa of a small ox side by side with the huge beast of *Primigenius* race.[1]

The conditions for the rise of a food-producing economy were thus fulfilled in Afrasia. And in some of the 'mesolithic' cultures there are hints of its advent. Smoothed blocks of stone, shaped like saddle-querns and certainly used for grinding something, have been found on Capsian or Oranian sites in North Africa.[2]

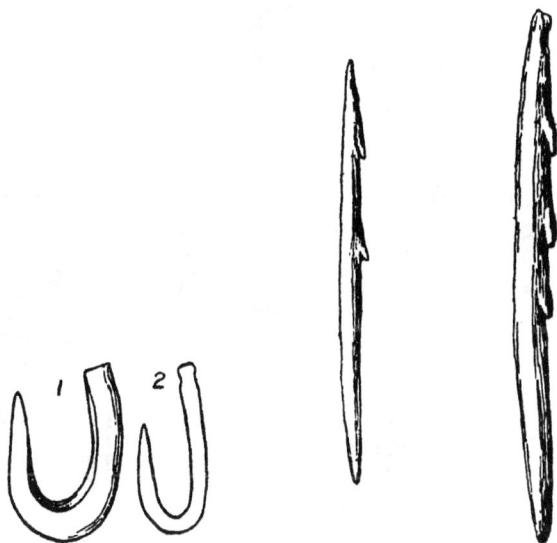

FIG. 7. Natufian fish-hooks, $\frac{2}{3}$, and harpoons, $\frac{3}{4}$.

Similarly many petroglyphs, in addition to game animals, depict sheep or cattle that are certainly tame. Such observations cannot, however, be taken as documenting the revolution itself. They patently disclose a mixed economy, not necessarily a transitional one. Till the refuse-heaps and pictures be dated more accurately, it is arguable that the farm implements or domestic animals represented therein have been introduced, perhaps only belatedly, from the cradles of agriculture and stock breeding. As far as Africa is concerned it seems very unlikely that the pictures and middens in

1. *L'Anthr.*, xlii, 476.
2. *L'Anthr.*, xlii, 429; cf. Vaufrey, *L'Art rupestre nord-africain.*

question are absolutely older than the first farming villages in the Nile valley; on the contrary they may be substantially later.

Only one culture is known to-day that can lay claim plausibly to

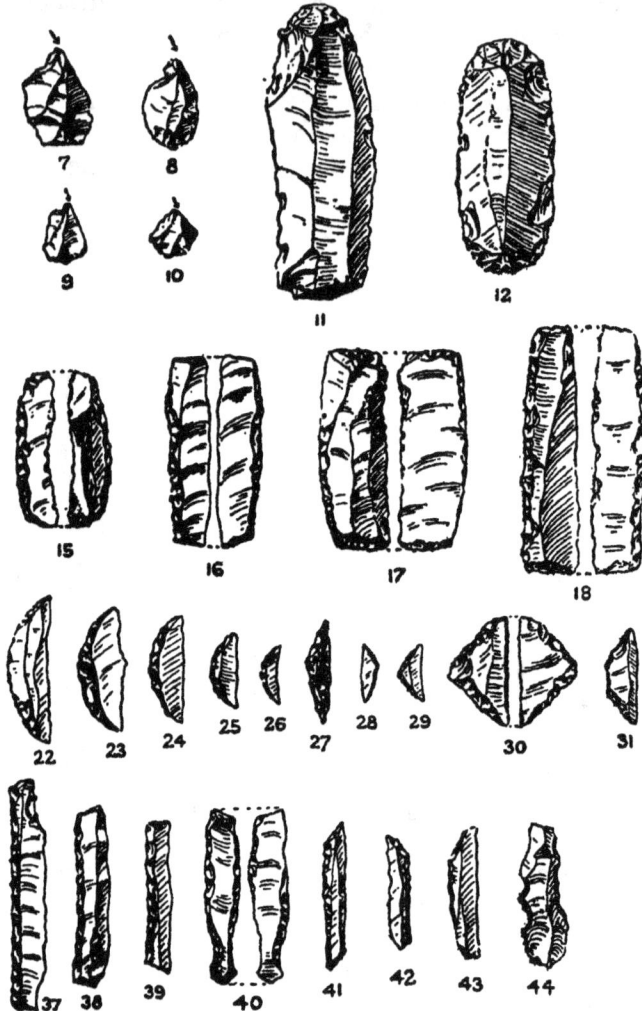

FIG. 8. Natufian microliths, ⅓, after *JRAI.* 7–10 microburins; 22–6 lunates; 27–30 triangles, 30 showing Helwan retouch; 31 trapeze.

temporal priority and transitional status. The chronological position of the Natufian[1] before the local neolithic in the Palestinian culture-

1. Garrod and Bate, *The Stone Age of Mount Carmel*, i, 1937, 9–16, 30–40, 119.

sequence has been stratigraphically established at Jericho, and, as we shall see, the neolithic there is probably comparable to the Egyptian in absolute age.

The Natufians were hunter-fishers who frequented caves, conveniently situated for game and water supplies. Physically[1] they were small folk standing only 5 feet to 5 ft. 3 in. high with long narrow heads. They practised evulsion of the incisors, like modern Bantu tribes and some early inhabitants of the Saharan fringes. They fished with hook and line—their bone hooks are probably the oldest known[2]—and with slender bone harpoons (Fig. 7). They armed their hunting implements with geometric microliths—lunates (Fig. 8, 22–6), triangles (ib., 27–30), and trapezes (ib., 31); these are sometimes trimmed from both faces (Fig. 8, 30)—a very unusual way of shaping microliths, hardly known outside Palestine save at Helwan in Egypt—but micro-burins (Fig. 8, 7–10) are a normal concomitant of all microlithic industries. But in the latest Natufian deposits appear triangular arrow-heads, notched near the base for hafting[3] (Fig. 110). Some small blades were mounted serially in handles made from ribs of deer grooved along one edge and sometimes carved at one end to a deer's head. Gloss on the blades shows that these knives were used for cutting some sort of grass, and the representation of a grazing animal on the handle may have been intended to enhance their efficiency by sympathetic magic.[4] In front of their home in the Mughâret el-Wad, Mt. Carmel, the Natufians had hammered out circular basins with raised rims that might have been used for pounding grass seeds as well as for 'ritual purposes'. Pestles of basalt, one carved to represent a deer's hoof, were certainly used for stamping something; why not the grass seeds reaped with the rib knives? No one knows what sort of grass was cut and pounded, but Palestine is a likely habitat for wild barley and emmer. These annuals may well have been reaped by the Natufians; why should they not have begun to cultivate them? They did in fact make rather heavy pointed implements of flint that could have been used for digging.

They decked themselves with chaplets, necklaces, bracelets, and girdles composed of strings of perforated shells and bone pendants

1. Keith, *New Discoveries relating to the Antiquity of Man*, 1931, 209–213; cf. IPH., *Mém.*, 9, 1932.
2. *JRAI.*, lxii, 1932, 272; *Ant.J.*, xxviii, 1948, 52–4.
3. Neuville, *RB.*, xliii, 1934, 253.
4. Curwen, *Plough and Pasture*, London, 1946, 89.

carved to represent deer's teeth; some of the latter foreshadow the so-called winged beads, popular in late neolithic Europe.[1] The dead were interred by the camping place. Some, buried in the cave itself, lay extended on their backs, ten skeletons being laid together in three layers as a single group. Others were buried on the terrace in front of the cavern, at first strictly contracted, later merely flexed, but again sometimes forming groups of five or seven skeletons.

As already remarked, there is some stratigraphical evidence that the Natufian settlements are really older than the first villages of regular farmers in Palestine. But the determination of their absolute age depends upon relations of later cultures with those of Egypt and Mesopotamia. For it is in the valleys of the Nile and the Tigris-Euphrates that the literary record and historical chronology reach back furthest, and in them the sequence of prehistoric cultures is most complete. Admittedly the record of farming life, thus documented archæologically, may not be the longest. Yet the Egyptian and Mesopotamian culture sequences must provide the standards by which those recovered in regions historically more backward must be measured. So it is only logical to describe them first before considering the subsequent fortunes of Natufians, or Capsians, or other inhabitants of regions that remained illiterate much longer.

1. Garrod and Bate, op. cit., pl. xiv, 2, xv, 1; cf. Childe, *Dawn*, index, s.v., beads, winged.

CHAPTER III

THE OLDEST EGYPTIAN FARMERS

EGYPT appears to-day above all as a corridor of fertile and habitable country drawn athwart the desert zone which divides the grasslands of the Sudan from the coastal belt of Mediterranean rains. This character is due exclusively to the Nile which is not only itself a moving road but which also fertilizes by its annual inundation a strip of the valley on either bank. Yet Egypt is no physiographical unit. The Delta, or Lower Egypt, is an open and once marshy plain continuous with the coastlands of Libya and Palestine and accessible from both quarters and from the sea. Upper Egypt, on the contrary, is a narrow rift bordered on either hand by rocky walls above which lie the now arid tablelands of the Libyan and Arabian deserts. Yet these rock walls are pierced at many points on either bank by the gorges of old streams that drained the plateaux on the east and west during the pluvial period. These dry watercourses constitute entries to the valley for the caravans coming from the Red Sea coasts or from the chain of oases that lie in a depression parallel to the Nile's course.

To-day the country south of Cairo is virtually rainless and would be utter desert save for the annual irrigation by the Nile flood. But in the pluvial period conditions[1] must have been very different. The valleys of the wadis running in from the high desert must have been clothed with spring grasses, including quite possibly wild cereals, and this herbage must have nourished herds of wild asses, Barbary sheep, urus, antelopes, gazelles and giraffes and the lions and leopards that preyed thereon. Even in the historical period hunts for such animals are depicted on the walls of Middle Kingdom tombs. In the valley itself spread extensive swamps, fringing the river, and elephants, kudu, and two kinds of wild pig roamed in the

1. On the climate, flora, and fauna of predynastic Egypt, see Newberry, 'Egypt as a Field for Anthropological Research,' Presidential Address to Section H of the British Association, 1924.

jungle besides the hippopotami, crocodiles, and wild-boars that survived till recent times. To find a floristic and faunistic environment comparable to that encountered by the most ancient Egyptians one must travel far upstream into the monsoon zone. On the White Nile the traveller will find, growing wild, plants that survived in historical Egypt only in gardens:

Hunters from the high plateaux had been visiting the valley from Lower Palæolithic times leaving their implements on the high terraces on either side. Quite recently flint industries in the Levalloisian tradition but tending to microlithic forms and Upper Palæolithic in date[1] have been recognized in the valley itself at Sébil,[1] just above Gebel Silsileh, and along the channels leading to the Fayum. It is only to be expected that, as the droughts became more frequent and acute on the surrounding deserts, the influx of nomads towards the well-watered valley would be accelerated. And such would be faced with conditions calculated to induce the change from a parasitic to a productive life. Mr. Perry[2] has stated in glowing terms Egypt's claim to be the cradle of agriculture.

Granting the existence on the edges of the valley of the nobler grasses, ancestors of wheat and barley, the idea of their deliberate cultivation would be suggested on the banks of the Nile as nowhere else. The annual flood and the rich soil it deposited would cause grains dropped on the ground to germinate without human intervention. 'The Nile valley,' writes Perry, 'would, by means of its perfect irrigation cycle, be growing wheat and barley for the Egyptians. . . . All that would be needed, would be for some genius to think of the simple expedient of making channels for the water to flow over a wider area.' Modern observers have described, among the Nilotic tribes of the Sudan, a mode of life that might well represent the stage intermediate between the food-gathering culture of Sebilian hunters and the settled agriculture of the oldest sedentary inhabitants of Egypt. The Hadendoa lived last century as nomadic herdsmen in the eastern desert. But they maintained more or less permanent villages within reach of the flooded lands to which they would repair in force in the late summer. Then they scattered millet seeds on the wet mud left by the recent inundation and awaited the harvest. Such people, fixed south of the belt of extreme desiccation, have perhaps preserved for us precisely the mode of life attributable

1. Vignard, *Bull. Inst. Franç. à Caire*, xxii; Huzayyin, *AJA.*, li, 1947, 191.
2. *The Growth of Civilization*, 30.

to the immediate ancestors of the Tasians, the oldest agriculturists certainly disclosed to our gaze by archæology in the Nile valley.

From encampments on desert spurs near Badari, projecting into the marshy valley, the Tasians[1] certainly cultivated emmer and barley, the grains of which have been found in their settlements. To grind them to flour they already used saddle querns, slabs of stone up to 50 cm. long by 27 cm. wide on which the grains were rubbed back and forth with stone rubbers that may measure 25 cm. by 11·5 cm. by 7·5 cm. How the crops were watered—by the annual inundation of the Nile, by freshets in the wadis that once flowed in from the Eastern Desert or perhaps even by rain—is still uncertain. Nor is it clear how far grain growing was combined with animal husbandry; bones of sheep or goat are, however, reported. In any case a really sedentary economy had not been attained for the graves are scattered sparsely in small groups. Hunting and fishing must still have provided staple foods. Arrow-heads indeed are

FIG. 9. Tasian fish-hook, ⅓, after Brunton.

surprisingly rare, but fish were caught with little hooks of shell or horn (Fig. 9), rather more evolved than the Natufian.

Of course the Nile valley was still swampy, and sizable trees grew along its edge and fringed the tributary wadis. So there was wood for carpentry. To work it axes were made by grinding to an edge pebbles of fine grained rock or by flaking nodules of flint collected from the ground surface. Possibly the ingenious 'tranchet' device for resharpening the latter by a blow at right angles to the long axis of the nodule was already in use, but conclusive evidence is lacking.[2]

To contain food and drink the Tasians already made pots, generally very rough. The vessels are grey to black in colour, but often blotchy owing to uneven firing, and rarely reddened on the outside by exposure to the oxidizing effects of the atmosphere. Even the last-named vessels are, however, blackened on the inside, presumably because the vases were stood bottom up during firing so

1. Brunton, *Mostagedda*, 1937, 26–33.
2. Huzayyin in Mond and Myres, *Cemeteries of Armant*, 1937, 209–211.

that the interior was protected from oxidization and exposed to smoke. They would thus be technically the prototypes of the 'black-topped' pottery that in later times will be found characteristic of Middle and Upper Egypt.

Though the shapes of the vases are simple, many have flat bases (Fig. 10). Notable forms are a shallow rectangular trough, and a

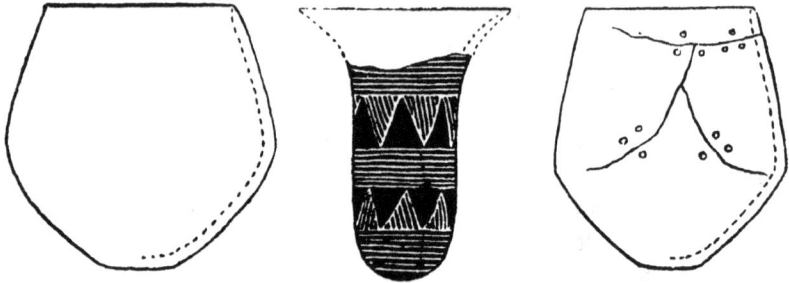

FIG. 10. Tasian pots, ⅛, after Brunton.

shallow ladle with a flat, tongue-like projection from the rim to serve as a handle. Most important of all are beaker-shaped vessels of black ware, with a rounded base and flaring trumpet-like rim. The form might ultimately have been copied from a leather receptacle. But the Tasian beakers (Fig. 10, centre) are decorated with incised lines filled with white paste to make the designs stand out. The patterns, arranged in zones, might have been suggested by basketry, and, in fact, baskets of similar shape and ornamentation are made in Africa to-day. The importance of the type lies in the appearance of similar vessels in Western Europe. With the possible basketry ancestry before our eyes, we hesitate to assume a direct connection. In fact, we shall find analogous forms, again decorated in zones, on the Tigris.

There are some faint traces of linen, but details of Tasian costume are unknown. But the face or eyes were probably already painted, since palettes are found in the graves as in later periods. The Tasian palettes are, however, generally made of alabaster, thick and rectangular in contradistinction to later forms. Ornaments were certainly worn. Perforated Red Sea shells, cylindrical beads of bone or ivory, and an ivory bangle have come down to us.

The Tasians were buried in the contracted posture wrapped in skins and enclosed in straw coffins in large pits. The people were dolichocephalic, but some of the skulls seem broader and more capacious, the face wider than among later pre-dynastic Egyptians in Middle or Upper Egypt.

The Tasians might, as noted, conceivably be compared to the Hadendoa, and treated as very primitive irrigators. But they have cultural and physical relatives in the Fayum and the Delta to whom that designation could be less easily applied.

The Fayum settlements[1] lie along the edge of an extensive lake that then filled the Fayum depression to a height of 180 feet above the surface of the present lake. The settlers indubitably cultivated emmer wheat and barley identical with that grown in Egypt to-day. Flax was also grown. The cereals were reaped with sickles formed of serrated flint flakes (Fig. 11a) set in a straight wooden shaft, were stored in silos dug in the earth and lined with straw matting, and were ground on saddle-querns. Swine, cattle, and sheep or goats

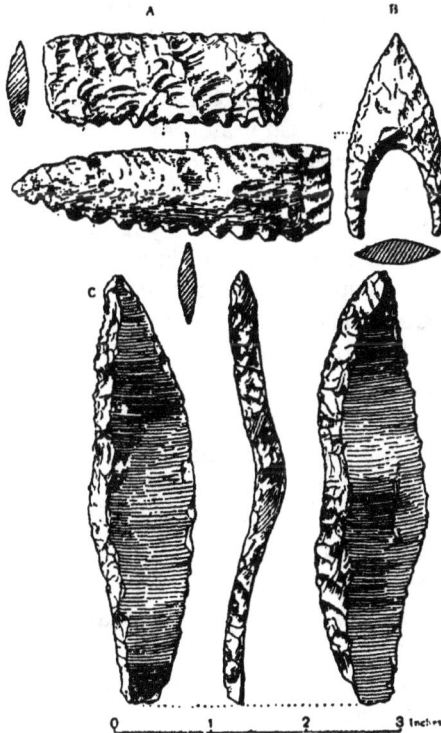

FIG. 11. Sickle-teeth (A), arrow-head (B), and side-blow flake (C) after Caton-Thompson in *Antiquity*, i. (The flake c has been detached by a blow struck near its centre as shown by the bulb visible in the middle view.)

1. Caton-Thompson, *The Desert Fayum*, London, 1934.

35

were kept. Hunting and fishing were naturally practised. The hunts-men relied principally on bow and arrows; the arrows were tipped with hollow-based flint heads, the long curving wings of which sometimes give them the shape of a mitre (Fig. 11b). Cylindrical bone points, sharpened at both ends as in the Capsian and Natufian, may also have tipped arrows or darts. Maces were loaded with thick discs of stone perforated or perhaps also with pebbles grooved to take the thong that bound them to the haft. Fish were harpooned. The bone harpoon-heads have barbs projecting from a cylindrical stem, precisely like the Natufian harpoons of Palestine.

Axe-heads with ground edges were made from pebbles as at Tasa, but also from flint. The latter material was also efficiently worked for the manufacture of many other tools, including blades polished on the face. Peculiar is the so-called side-blow flake. It was detached from the core by a blow at right-angles to its length and then retouched on both sides as shown in Fig. 11c. (The age of this type is not quite certain.)

Pottery was manufactured as at Tasa, and the forms are some-what similar, notably biconical vessels rather like Fig. 10, 1. But the beaker was absent, whereas we meet rectangular dishes rising to peaks at the corners and bowls on a sort of very low pedestal. The excellence of the basketry is shown by Plate III, and weaving is attested by remains of loosely woven linen.

Numerous scrapers suggest also the preparation of skins for use as clothing. Palettes of alabaster closely resembling the Tasian were doubtless employed as on the Nile. Disc-shaped beads made out of ostrich egg-shell, as in the North African Capsian, and perforated shells were worn as ornaments. The shells were brought both from the Mediterranean and from the Red Sea or the Indian Ocean, and amazonite was somehow carried from Tibesti in the central Sahara or the Eastern Desert. So there is proof of some sort of rudimentary trade relations with the outside world such as could so easily arise in the environment described in Chapter II. No graves have been found so that the burial rites and physical characters of the neolithic Fayumis are unknown.

A third culture allied to the foregoing, has been brought to light by Austrian excavators at Merimde[1-4] on the Western edge of

1-4. Junker, 'Vorlaufige Berichte über die Gräbung der Akademie der Wissenschaften in Wien auf der neolithischen Siedelung von Merimde-Benisalâme' in *Anzeiger d. Akad. d. Wiss. Wien, phil.-hist. Kl.*
1. 1929, 156–248.   2. 1930, 21–81.   3. 1932, 36–88.   4. 1940, 4–16.

the Delta. The site occupies a sandy spur, now 2 km. west of the Rosetta branch of the Nile, and covers an area of 600 × 400 m. Here the first settlers built flimsy shelters which were often buried in drifting sand and of which only hearths and rubbish pits remain. In time the settlement grew, and in phase II[4] more substantial shelters were erected, 5 to 6 m. across, oval or horse-shoe shaped, outlined by posts which presumably supported reed matting as among the fellahin to-day. Finally in phase III some structures of similar plan were walled round with lumps of mud, up to 1·5 m. thick, which gave better protection from the sandstorms. The huts were never closely juxtaposed; probably each hut or cluster of huts stood in its own yard. But the groups were arranged in rows as if along streets.

From the very beginning barley and emmer were cultivated and reaped with sickles like those of the Fayum. Still the grain was stored in the several compounds in silo pits, enclosed during phase II in mud-coated baskets, in phase III in large pottery jars or pithoi.

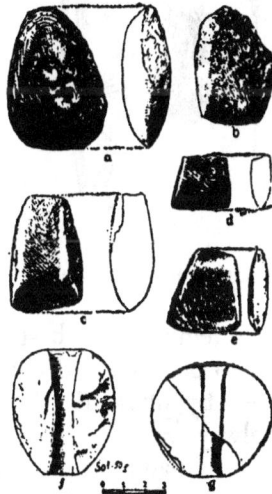

FIG. 12. Axe- and mace-heads
from Merimde, after Junker.

The same animals were kept as in the Fayum. Hippopotami still wallowed in the Delta marshes and were apparently eaten by the Merimdians as by the Fayum people. The huntsman tipped his arrows with hollow-based flint points which, however, generally

4. Ib., 1940, 4–16.

had straighter sides than in the Fayum. The mace-heads were pear-shaped (Fig. 12), as in Asia, or spheroid. Flint blades retouched along both edges, but sometimes polished on the face, may have served as knives or daggers or even been mounted at right-angles to the shaft for use as halberds.[2] The sling is also attested by round sling-stone.[2] Fish were caught with antler-hooks,[2] shaped precisely like the Tasian one of Fig. 9, or with harpoons,[1] which are flat in comparison with the Fayum type. Small grooved pebbles may have served as sinkers while flint nodules flaked to a point at one end but with the cortex intact on the butt may have served as picks. The axe-heads agree closely with those from the Fayum. Needles, bodkins, and chisel-shaped smoothing tools of bone reproduce some Natufian forms (Fig. 13).

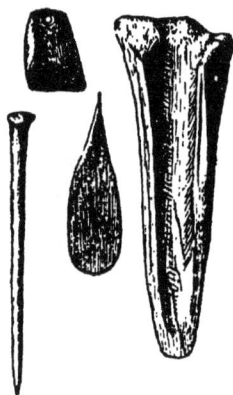

FIG. 13. Bone implements and axe-amulet from Merimde, ⅔.

Merimdian pottery was tempered with straw, but often coated with a slip, that is liable to peel off, and burnished. At first a red colour was preferred, but by phase III the best made vases are black.[4] Decoration was always rare; in phase I only, a herring-bone (a design incised on late Amratian vases too) pattern was sometimes incised on a horizontal band, left unpolished below the rim. Some forms agree with the Tasian while rough pedestalled bowls occur as in the Fayum. Some of the latter have openwork feet on a flat rectangular base. Boat-shaped troughs replace the rectangular Fayum form; the numerous ladles may have broad tongue handles as in the Tasian or thick round handles (Fig. 14, 1–2) as in western Europe. Double vases with intercommunicating compartments, are

1. Ib., 1929, 156–248.   2. Ib., 1930, 21–81.   4. Ib., 1940, 4–16.

38

FIG. 14. Ladles, ⅔, and pots, ⅓, from
Merimde, after Menghin.

represented by some fragments (Fig. 14, 5).[2] Many vessels were provided with lugs for prehension or suspension, and these might develop into genuine handles.[3] One bowl, or dish, had a pocket for the thumb inside the rim,[3] a type attested in the later Amratian culture of Middle Egypt.

A textile industry is attested by spindle whorls. Rough palettes remotely resembling the Tasian may have served for the preparation of cosmetics. Ivory bangles, bone finger-rings, boars' tusks, and disc or cylindrical beads of bone and shell were worn as ornaments.[2] Miniature celts or axes of stone, pierced for suspension, served as amulets (Fig. 13).

The dead were buried among the dwellings, flexed in the attitude of sleep and generally facing east. No vases to contain food accompanied the bodies. Junker[1] suggests that burial among the houses

1. Ib., 1929, 156ff.   2. Ib., 1930, l.c.   3. Ib., 1932, 36–88.

instead of in regular cemeteries made such offerings superfluous, since the ghost could eat with its kinsmen around the hearth. The majority of skeletons[2] belonged to females. They were appreciably taller than the later women of Upper and Middle Egypt, approximating rather to the Tasians in stature. The skulls too, though dolichocephalic, have the same sort of wide brain case as the Tasian in contrast to the narrow skulls of the Badarians, Amratians, and Natufians.

East of the Nile a very similar culture has been revealed since 1942 by Debono's[1] excavations in the extensive settlement of El Omari near Helwan. The site lies above the south bank of the Wadi Hof, just below the point where it debouches from the plateau, and is now $4\frac{1}{2}$ miles from the east bank of the Nile. Here, as at Merimde, the dead were buried among the flimsy huts and silos of the village, but the orientation is different, the corpse lying on the left side with the head to the south facing west. Again the skeletons belong to a taller, larger-headed people than the familiar predynastic folk of Upper Egypt. The villagers' diet included wheat, barley, vetch, and dates, cattle and goats, wild pig, hippopotamus, tortoise, and antelope, snails and fish. But the wheat they grew is described as *Triticum monococcum*, a distinctively northern species, not previously found south of the Taurus or Amanus. For the rest the equipment of flint sickle-teeth, saddle querns, nodule picks (like Fig. 111, 4), hollow-based arrow-heads, shell fish-hooks, grooved stone 'sinkers' and ground stone axes agrees very closely with the Merimdian. But the proportion of blade tools is higher and some knives have neatly blunted backs and a short tang. Technically the Omarian pottery resembles the Merimdian, but red seems always to have been preferred, decoration is much rarer and the forms are rather different; straight-sided flower-pots with everted rims and globular flasks were popular. In addition to earthenware, a few basalt vases, perhaps imported, were used in the village. Red Sea shells were certainly imports.

The dead, wrapped in mats or skins, were, as at Merimde, poorly furnished with gifts other than flowers. But one tomb contained a wooden baton carved at both ends and said to resemble the *ames* sceptre, borne in historic times as insignia of kingship over Lower

2. Ib., 1930, 21–81

1. *Annales du Service*, xlviii, 1948, 561–9; for the cereals see Täckholm, *Bull. Inst. d'Egypte*, xxxii, Cairo, 1950, 127.

Egypt. Perhaps then El Omari was already ruled by chiefs. Was one of them destined to make himself 'king' of Lower Egypt?

Evidently the four sites just described do not represent a single culture. Particularly significant is the contrast between burials within the settlement at Merimde and El Omari and in cemeteries outside at Tasa and presumably in the Fayum and in all later cultures of predynastic Egypt. Still the common traits are numerous, and it has been convenient to treat the four groups together as the best examples known in the Nile valley of 'neolithic culture', so familiar in Europe, without prejudice to the question of the contemporaneity[1] of all or any of them. In each case the inhabitants are food-producers living in a very favourable environment; they have used the leisure, made possible by the new economy and exceptional opportunities for applying the old hunting one, to elaborate arts or crafts not normally found among gatherers. But they have remained content with local materials save for luxury ornaments and have thus preserved their self-sufficiency; no dependence upon imports for supposed necessities has driven them to build up a commercial nexus with the outside world. (Such economic isolation, of course, goes far to explain the local divergences noted above.) Nor, it would seem, have they been obliged to organize their forces for works of public utility nor to sink much capital in the land. If some genius among them has thought of 'making channels for the water to flow in', nothing suggests that his fellows have united to carry out his idea. They remain free to shift their settlements and send out colonies.

But the conditions which made this simplicity possible were already passing. Both in the Fayum and at Merimde layers of drift sand interlarded among the refuse of occupation illustrate the menace of the encroaching desert. Eventually the settlements had to be abandoned. Round the shrinking Fayum Lake, indeed, survivors of the old population can be watched for a while. But their culture is degenerating; the flint axes are no longer polished, and old specimens are resharpened by flaking, the implements diminish in size, though the little arrow-heads may be provided with a tang. At last they too disappear, as the wadis dry up and the desert advances. Even the large village of El Omari was abandoned though, perhaps

1. Baumgärtel, *Cultures of Prehistoric Egypt*, Oxford, 1947, 15–17, argues that the Fayum settlements are contemporary only with the Amratian of Upper Egypt, Merimde with the Gerzean, stressing the similarity between incised domestic pottery of late Amratian sites and the Merimdian, 95.

after an interval of uncertain duration, another settlement, this time with a distinct cemetery, was established about half a mile further up the wadi. One result is that the culture sequence in Lower Egypt is still incomplete and even the relative age of the sites just described is somewhat uncertain. In Middle and Upper Egypt on the contrary the archæological record is uninterrupted and presents a continuous sequence from Tasian onwards.

The Tasians stand at the head of a long series of cultures in the Nile valley. The Badarian culture[1] can be regarded as just an elaboration of the Tasian and was first found, like the latter, in cemeteries and settlements near Badari in Middle Egypt. But, though found no further north, the same culture is known in Upper Egypt at least as far south as Armant[2] and in 1950 was recognized also in the Wadi Hammamat basin.[3] The wadis flowing in from both sides of the Nile still carried occasional freshets while there was still enough herbage in the desert to support wild cattle, asses, giraffes, and even elephants; for perhaps it was Badarians on hunting trips or on seasonal migrations with their herds who carved pictures of these beasts on rocks in the Eastern Desert and just west of the Nile.[4] For the Badarians were not much more firmly rooted to one spot than the Tasians. But anthropologically they exhibit rather different physical characters; standing only 5 to $5\frac{1}{4}$ feet high, they were small, slender, and delicately built with just a hint of negroid or South Indian traits.[5]

The Badarians still camped on desert spurs. For habitations they were content with matting wind-screens, like the Merimdians. But they made mud-lined storage bins for their grain. Barley and emmer wheat was certainly now cultivated as in the Fayum and the Delta, but sickle-flints are very rare. Cattle and sheep were kept and sometimes given ceremonial burial, but pig bones, so common at Merimde, have not been reported. Hunting and fishing were still important. Arrows were tipped with hollow-based flint heads as in the Fayum, but also with leaf-shaped types. Wooden throwing sticks or boomerangs (Fig. 15) were also employed. Fish-hooks like Fig. 9 were still used.

1. For points not otherwise documented, see Brunton and Caton-Thompson, *The Badarian Civilization*, London, 1928; *Mostagedda*, 43–59.
2. Mond and Myres, *Cemeteries of Armant*, 8.
3. *Annales du Service*, li,, 1951, 74.
4. Winckler, *Rock Drawings*, i, 20.
5. *Biometrika*, xix, 1927, 110 ff.

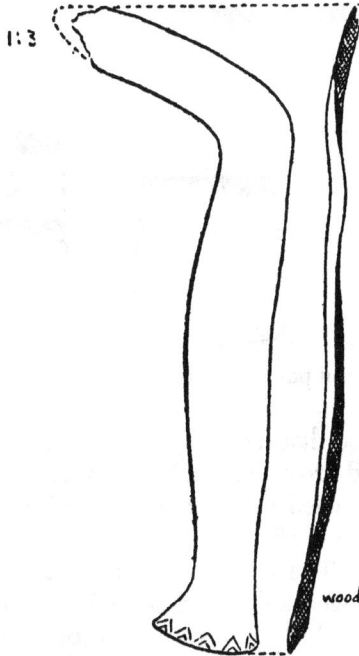

FIG. 15. Wooden boomerang, Badari, ⅓, after Brunton.

A new economic factor was introduced by an incipient depend-ence on imported materials involving some sort of more or less established trade. Malachite in any case was regularly employed for painting the eyes, and must have been brought from Sinai or Nubia. Shells imported from the Red Sea are also quite common, and pieces of cedar and juniper wood and resin,[1] suggestive of Syrian connec-tions, have been found as have rare beads of turquoise, carnelian, and glazed steatite. At the same time metallic copper becomes known; its malleability was already appreciated, but not the truly metallic property of fusibility. And pottery models of boats illustrate attempts at navigation that had already got beyond the simple log raft.

The pottery vessels, especially those designed for funerary use, exhibit a perfection of technique never excelled in the Nile Valley. The finer ware is extremely thin, and is decorated all over by burnish-ing before firing, perhaps with a blunt-toothed comb, to produce an exquisite rippled effect that must be seen to be appreciated (Pl. III, b). The vases, sometimes coated with a ferruginous wash, were

1. Brunton, Matmar, 1948, 11.

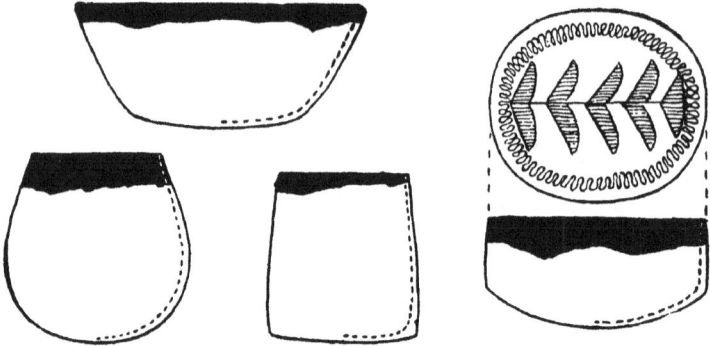

FIG. 16. Badarian pottery, $\frac{1}{6}$, after Brunton in *Antiquity*, iii.

often fired inverted so that the lower part was exposed to the free air and became coloured brown or red by oxidization, while the rim and the inside were blackened by impregnation with carbon and smoke and by its deoxidizing effect, the ferric oxide in this case being reduced to ferrous. The chief shapes manufactured in this fabric were bowls, often steep sided and sometimes carinated (Fig. 16). A globular flask of pinkish buff ware with four handles on the belly is quite exceptional and may be of later date.

Vases, of almost cylindrical form with overhanging rim, were ground out of basalt. Flasks, small cylindrical vases, and ladles

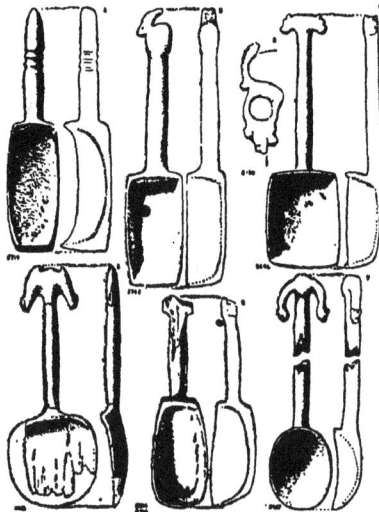

FIG. 17. Carved ivory ladles, Badari, $\frac{1}{6}$.

were made of ivory; the handles of the ladles generally end in carved ibex or other animal forms (Fig. 17).

The Badarians wore clothing of skins, but some vegetable fibre similar to flax was also woven into rather coarse cloth. The eyes were painted with malachite. It was ground on narrow rectangular slate palettes, generally with concave or notched ends, but sometimes simply rectangular. Ivory combs ornamented with carved birds were stuck in the hair, and pins (or needles) of the same material, sometimes with grooved heads or an eyelet in the neck, perhaps fastened the clothing. Copper tubes, beads of glazed quartz or felspar, discs cut from ostrich egg-shell, segmented bone beads (Fig. 18), and Red Sea shells were strung together as necklaces or

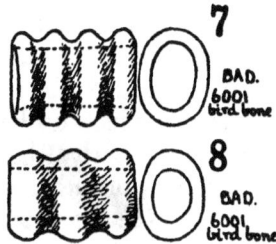

FIG. 18. Badarian segmented beads of bone, Matmar (after Brunton), ⅓.

girdles. Bracelets and rings of ivory were worn on the arms or fingers. Stone plugs were inserted in the nose as ornaments, and the lips may have been embellished with pottery plugs.

Female figurines, carved in ivory or moulded in clay, have been found in some graves. Such may be images of a mother goddess or substitutes for wives. The ivory figurine (Pl. IVa) does not conform to the physical type suggested by the Badarian skeletons, but might perhaps be a Tasian. Amulets are represented only by small carvings of an antelope and a hippopotamus. The Badarians were buried, flexed, or crouched, wrapped in skins or encased in hampers of sticks, in trench graves, sometimes lined with matting and grouped to form small cemeteries. The corpse was generally facing west, but the rules for orientation were far from strict.

It is now possible to examine concretely the question of the origin of Egyptian farming. Did the neolithic cultures of the Nile Valley arise where we find them through the initiative of African food-gatherers in exploiting the opportunities so glowingly described by Perry and Cherry? The existence in North Africa of possible wild ancestors for wheat and barley is admittedly un-proven; the presence of wild sheep is positively unlikely. The neolithic flint industries with their bifacial technique certainly can-not be derived from the North African Capsian or Oranian blade tradition, nor from the rather microlithic Sebilian of the Nile valley. They could, however, go back to the North African Aterian or the East African Still Bay. On the other hand Caton-Thompson[1] remarked in 1928 that even the Badarians failed to utilize the excellent tabular flint that lay ready to hand in the Eocene cliffs anywhere north of 25° N., but, like the Omarians, relied on surface nodules. Hence she concluded that their ancestors had lived 'south of the region where tabular flint was available. Brunton,[2] Junker,[3] Scharff,[4] and Baumgärtel have likewise insisted on the Nubian affinities of the Badarian and even the Merimdian cultures.

Since 1945, Arkell's discoveries in the Sudan allow this hypothesis to be tested against archæological facts; for near Khartoum he has brought to light archaic cultures which do have traits in common with the Egyptian neolithic. The Early Khartoum or 'Khartoum Mesolithic' culture[5] is the product of rather negroid hunter-fishers who camped seasonally near the Nile at a time when the rainfall was higher than it is to-day. They armed darts and arrows with micro-lithic lunates of quartz or larger lunates of rhyolite and speared fish with stout bone harpoons, barbed unilaterally and rather like those shown in Fig. 22.) They grew no grain nor did they breed stock. But they made excellent well-fired pottery and decorated the vases with wavy lines and other patterns executed with a cat-fish spine. Arkell suggests that the Badarian rippled ware might have developed out of this. The dead were apparently buried in the camping place itself, not in cemeteries. Evulsion of the upper incisors was certainly practised.

This 'mesolithic' culture developed into the 'Khartoum Neolithic' or Gouge Culture,[6] distinguished primarily by the breeding of very small goats. Its authors still grew no grain, but hunted, using disc-shaped mace-heads[7] as well as darts armed with lunates, and fished

1. Brunton, *Badarian Civilization*, 75.
2. *Man*, xxv, 1925, 103.
3. *Schmidt-Festschrift*, Vienna, 1928, 867.
4. *Die Altertümer der Vor- und Frühzeit Ägyptens*, 1931, 24.
5. Arkell, *Early Khartoum*, 1949, 40–84.
6. *PPS.*, xv, 1949, 42–9; in *Early Khartoum* the term 'Gouge culture' had been used.
7. Arkell, A. J., *Shaheinab*, 1953.

with shell fish-hooks (notched like the Natufian) as well as with bone harpoons. They also made 'celts' of bone with polished edges, perhaps for chopping hippopotamus and elephant flesh, but for wood-working manufactured axe-heads and gouges of rhyolite, again sharpening the edges by grinding. The designs on their pottery can be derived from those of wavy-line ware, but the pots themselves were often slipped and sometimes covered with a ferruginous wash and then so fired that parts are red and parts black; indeed techniques and shapes alike approximate to the Badarian. Finally these goat-herders wore beads of ostrich-egg shell and exceptionally of amazonite which they presumably obtained, like the neolithic Fayumis, from Tibesti in the Sahara or the Eastern Desert.

It is no doubt tempting to identify these savage or very barbarous negroid tribes of the Upper Nile with the hypothetical southern ancestors of Badarian, Tasian, or Merimdian farmers. But, of course, there is no stratigraphical nor other evidence to establish the chronological relation of these Sudanese cultures to the Egyptian. They might belong to backward contemporaries of the Amratians or Gerzeans, just as even in Nubia barbarism still reigned long after the historical pharaonic civilization had been established below the First Cataract. Even if temporal priority be conceded to the Sudanese and if they be supposed to have worked their way down stream to emerge at Tasa and even at Merimde, they would still have had to begin cultivating wheat and barley and breeding sheep at some point in their long trek. But as we have seen, it is very doubtful if there were any wild ancestors of those cereals for them to cultivate in the tracts they would traverse. Adametz[1] has contended that the early Egyptian sheep were brought into Africa from Asia across the Strait of Bab el-Mandeb. And, despite agreements in fishing tackle and mace-heads, the bifacial flint work so distinctive of the Egyptian neolithic is unrepresented at Khartoum. For that one might look further west to the Aterian province.

Now comb-decorated and impressed pottery, more or less akin to that from Early Khartoum, has in fact been reported from widely separated sites right across the Sahara.[2] In the Nigerian Sahara[3] it is actually associated with bone harpoons and fish-hooks and stone axes, as in Khartoum Neolithic, but even with hollow-based arrow-

---

1. *Antiquity*, x, 195.
2. Vaufrey, *L'Art rupestre nord-africain*, 78, 97, 101.
3. Arkell, *Early Khartoum*, 117 ff.; *PPS.*, xv, 46; *L'Anthr.*, l, 325.

heads too. The age of these assemblages is admittedly extremely vague. Vaufrey indeed would derive the pottery and other distinctively neolithic aspects of the Saharan cultures from Egypt. But theoretically the process could be reversed, provided wild cereals and sheep be admitted for instance on the Central Saharan highlands (Tibesti and Tassili). Assuming there cultivators or herdsmen, heirs of a neo-Aterian tradition, some of them might gradually be squeezed by drought into the Nile valley, both into Egypt and into the Sudan. But then Khartoum Mesolithic and Neolithic would be parallel, rather than ancestral, to Upper and Lower Egyptian neolithic.

Either thesis, the Sudanese or the Saharan, makes heavy demands on ignorance, and both might be said merely to push a stage further back the origin of Egyptian farming. The discussion has indeed shown that distinctive traits of the first Egyptian neolithic cultures were widely scattered about North Africa from the White Nile to Lake Chad in quite early times. To that extent it has disclosed a fundamentally African character in the Tasian-Badarian and also in the Merimde-Omarian traditions. In linguistic terms this should correspond to the Hamitic element in historical Egypt, and ethnographically it might account for the striking parallels between early pharaonic institutions or equipment and those of modern Nilotes or Saharan tribes.[1] But what makes the Egyptian cultures neolithic is left unaccounted for.

Now there are northern or Asiatic elements in the neolithic cultures at least of Lower Egypt. The most explicit of course is the *Triticum monococcum* grown at El Omari, but it does not stand alone. The blade industry there and at Merimde is neither Aterian nor Sebilian, but might be Asiatic. The Fayum harpoons and the Merimdian fish-hooks recur in the Natufian of Palestine, and outposts of Natufian culture itself have been recognized in Sinai and even at Helwan by distinctive microliths (p. 29). It has long been seen that the plain dark-faced pottery of Merimde with its ladles and leathery vessels has striking parallels in the Western Neolithic of Europe[2] from the Iberian Peninsula to the British Isles. It is now known that the earliest pottery from the site with its herring-bone patterns incised in reserved bands is significantly like some neolithic

1. Cf., e.g., Seligman, *JRAI.*, xliii, 1923, 597–680; Huntingford, *Ancient Egypt*, ii, 1927, 36; Forde, *Ancient Mariners*, London, 1927.
2. Childe, *Dawn of European Civilization*, 280.

wares from Palestine.[1] So it is not impossible that cereals and domestic animals and some other neolithic arts were introduced into Egypt from that quarter. Even so this Asiatic tradition would have blended even in Lower Egypt with the African-Aterian traditions already admitted. It might, however, follow that the idea of farming spread up the Nile first to Tasa and still later to Khartoum. But to decide whether that were chronologically possible, it is necessary to examine the subsequent culture sequence. That is clear and complete only in Upper Egypt where Petrie's system was elaborated. Nothing comparable has yet been established for Lower Egypt where till 1940 there was nothing to fill the typological gap between the neolithic village of Merimde and the pharaonic city of Memphis! We shall accordingly begin our survey with Upper Egypt.

1. E.g., in the Middle and Upper Neolithic of Jericho, *LAAA.*, xxii, 169, and pl. xliv, 1; xxiii, 77, 87, 89. Cf. p. 227 below.

CHAPTER IV

AFRICANS AND ASIATICS ON THE NILE

I N Upper Egypt the *Amratian* (or Naqada I)[1] culture succeeds, and may well be directly descended from, the Badarian and initiates the long familiar culture sequence documented from numerous cemeteries.

Its bearers, the Amratians,[2] had lost those faintly negroid traits, observed on some Badarian skeletons. They stood about $5\frac{1}{4}$ feet high and were slender and lightly built, with a long small skull, delicate features, and straight hair. A type almost identical in every feature may be seen among the Beja of the Eastern Sudan to-day. Figurines of clay or ivory supplement the information yielded by the well-preserved corpses. The early statuettes, Pls. V*a* and VII*a*, depict men clean-shaven or wearing long pointed beards with a prominent aquiline nose and a high domed forehead. The women on the other hand often shaved their heads and wore wigs that are separately modelled on the clay figurines. Besides a slender type, corresponding to the skeletal remains and the male statuettes, there is a group characterized by marked steatopygy (Pls. IV*b*, VII*b*). Petrie thought these represented survivors of a conquered race, to be equated with the assumed substratum of Eurafrican proto-negroids to whom such fat was a mark of beauty.

The Amratians must have initiated the systematic cultivation of the naturally irrigated flood plain of the Nile; for the desert wadis can hardly have any longer provided reliable water supplies. Yet at least one village site has been reported in the Eastern Desert but three settlements along the Wadi Hammamat trade route and a

1. On the predynastic cultures of Upper Egypt, Petrie, *Prehistoric Egypt,* London, 1917, remains the standard source; cf. also Scharff, 'Grundzüge der äg· Vorgeschichte,' *Morgenland*, 12, Leipzig, 1927; the terms Naqada I (Amratian) and II (Gerzean) were suggested by Baumgärtel (*CPE*).

2. *Biometrika*, xix, 1917, 110 ff.; Elliot Smith, *The Ancient Egyptians*, 49; Seligman, *JRAI.*, xliii, 605; Petrie, ibid., xxxi, 250.

FIG. 19. Designs scratched on Amratian pots.

factory site for the production of shell bracelets are probably of later date.[1] In any case cultivation was now better balanced with animal husbandry and cattle were bred for milk as well as meat. But the economy was still 'mixed'—a mixture, that is, of the new

1. *Annales du Service*, li, 75.

techniques of 'food-production' with the older pursuits of hunting, fishing, and collecting. The distribution of rock-drawings,[1] including pictures of the sickle-shaped Amratian papyrus boat must reflect expeditions in pursuit of game or in quest of grazing; for in style the pictures resemble those scratched on Amratian pots (Fig. 19).

The exploitation in both directions of the Nilotic environment permitted and provoked a great expansion of population. The number of settlements multiplied enormously and many must have grown to sizable villages. Their size has to be deduced from the cemeteries, and few of these have been exhaustively excavated. All, belonging to permanent villages, were used over many generations and have yielded remains of several archæological periods. That at Naqada[2] comprised over 2,000 graves of two or three periods. Some villages may have been fortified; a model from Diospolis Parva seems to represent a walled town,[3] and Petrie found remains of a wall at the southern settlement of Naqada, probably the site of Nubet, the town of Seth. Of dwellings, the only trace is afforded by round hollows, excavated in the ground and surrounded with walls of mud, identified at Hammamiya near Badari,[4] and perhaps comparable to those assigned to phase III at Merimde.

Many authorities[5] think that the Amratian villages were occupied each by a totemic clan like Dinka villages on the Upper Nile. The representation on vases of crocodiles, scorpions, and other noisome creatures would be intelligible if they were totems, and some Amratian symbols reappear in historic times as emblems of nomes. The representations perhaps include a cow-headed female and the Seth animal. The former is later the guise of the mother-goddess Hathor,[6] but it might be rash to infer that either Hathor or Seth were worshipped as deities in Amratian times. The graves as yet give no direct evidence for kings or chiefs. But a palette of the period though found in Upper Egypt,[7] is carved with the Red Crown, later worn by the pharaohs as symbol of kingship over Lower Egypt!

1. Winckler, *Rock Drawings*, i, 1938, 24–5.
2. Baumgärtel, *CPE.*, 26.
3. *Diospolis Parva*, pl. 6, B.83.
4. Brunton and Caton-Thompson, *The Badarian Civilization*, 82–8.
5. E.g. Capart, *Primitive Art in Egypt*, 1905.
6. Baumgärtel, *CPE.*, 31, adduces many arguments for the cult of the mother goddess in predynastic Egypt, a view also set out by Hornblower, *JEA.*, xv, 1929, 30 ff.
7. *JEA.*, ix, 1923, 27.

Slavery may have been recognized. Figurines of water-carriers, generally female, and of captives with the hands bound behind them have been thus interpreted. The recognition of private, as opposed to communal clan, property may be inferred from proprietary marks, often scratched on vases; all the vases in one·grave normally bear the same mark.

In addition to the industries practised by the Badarians, the Amratians had begun quarrying or mining for flint, since they used the tabular blocks, extracted from the limestone, in preference to

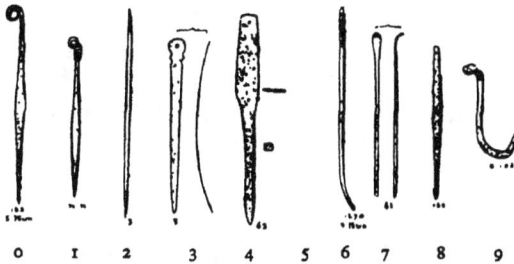

FIG. 20. Small copper implements from Naqada: o, Pin, Amratian; 1–3, Pins and Needle, Gerzean; 9, Fish-hook, Proto-dynastic, after Petrie, ⅓.

surface nodules, which are of course much harder to work. They were certainly cultivating flax which they wove perhaps on vertical, as well as on the well-documented horizontal, looms. Copper was now used for small tools such as harpoons, which were cut out of metal hammered into sheets, and pins with rolled head like Fig. 20, o. But the metal was never cast and was presumably collected in the native state, not smelted from ores. Intelligent metallurgy was still unknown.

The use of mined flint, the collection of malachite, copper, and gold, the manufacture of basalt and alabaster vases imply some degree of intercommunal specialization and accordingly trade. The villages along the Wadi Hammamat, if really Amratian, would be stations on a caravan route to the Red Sea and were certainly engaged in the manufacture of schist bracelets for export and in the distribution of malachite from the Eastern Desert deposits. The development of long distance commerce, attested already in Tasian and Badarian times by sea shells and malachite, is now illustrated by occasional imports of obsidian[1] from the Aegean, Hither Asia, or

1. Lucas, *Annales du Service*, xlviii, 1947, 123, corrects Wainwright, *Anc. Eg.*, 1927, 85.

most probably Abyssinia, of juniper berries and coniferous wood from Palestine-Syria and of emery, possibly from Naxos.

Perhaps the ass[1] had already been domesticated and was used to carry burdens in this commerce. In any case the Egyptians had by now evolved a very serviceable boat made out of bundles of papyrus lashed together (Plate VI*b*). It gave support for two square cabins amidships and was propelled by seven or eight pairs of oars, the steersman standing sheltered by a bough at the stern. Petrie believed that such boats must have been equipped with sails, as rowing would be ineffectual against the Nile current. But it is more likely that they were towed up stream; for boats of this type are never depicted with sails spread while the later 'foreign' barques are thus represented. With the same 'trade' might be connected the elaboration and widespread diffusion of those alphabetiform signs that appear scratched on our vases, signs whose origin is ultimately to be sought in palæolithic marks.

The progress in religious belief is shown by the elaboration of the funerary ritual. The marvellous preservation of the bodies in the hot sand of the desert would suggest to the Nile dwellers a peculiarly vivid idea of the continuation of life after death. The barbarous practice, till recently observed by some Nilotic tribes farther south, of slaying wives and menials and burying them with their lord to attend him in the future life (*satī*) was unknown; for sympathetic magic offered a more economical alternative. The statuettes of women and of servants bearing water-pots on their heads, are probably substitutes for living wives and attendants as were demonstrably the *ushabti* figures of historic times.

Man's dumb servant, the dog was, however, often forced to accompany his master in death and buried with him in the tomb. Other possessions such as cattle were replaced by clay models (Plate X*a*).

In dynastic Egypt paintings on the tomb walls depict the bringing of offerings to the dead, the labours of his serfs and his own pleasures at the banquet and the chase. Such scenes were not executed merely to delight the eye of the soul but, as the accompanying texts show, to secure to the defunct by their inherent magic virtue the actual enjoyment of such services and delights. In the prehistoric grave there was no room for paintings on the walls of the simple pit, but

---

1. It is apparently represented on an Amratian pot (*ÄZ.*, lxi, 1926, 17, and Baumgärtel, *CPE.*, 30) as well as on probably contemporary rock drawings described by Winckler.

funerary vases and slate palettes were decorated with comparable scenes that are linked by a continuous chain of later monuments to the earliest painted tombs, as will appear in the sequel.

To enable us to disentangle the several constituents of this culture and justify our initial assertion, let us now examine some of its archæological traits more closely.

No ground stone axes or adzes are certainly known from the Amratian period, but flint ones, some resharpened with a tranchet

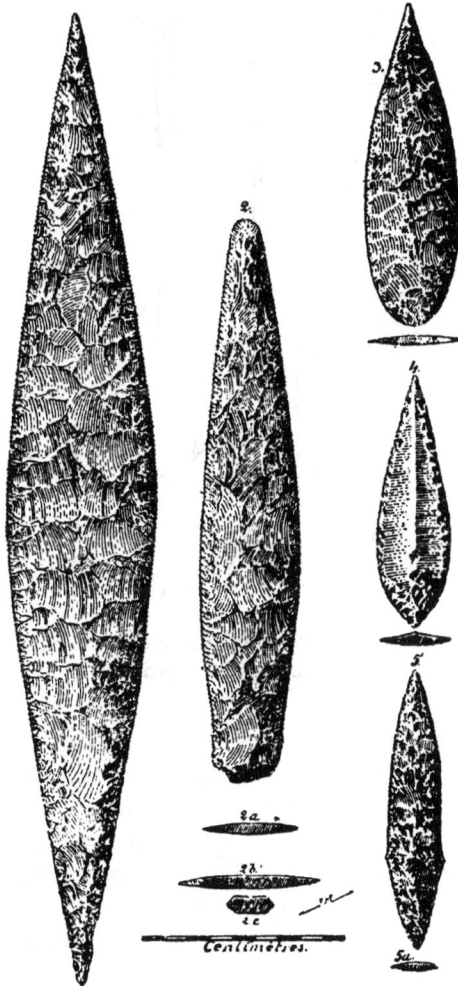

FIG. 21. Amratian flint work: 1 and 2, rhomboid daggers; 3 and 4, arrowheads (5 is perhaps Protodynastic), after de Morgan.

blow (p. 33) are common enough, other flint tools include sickle-teeth, disc- and end-scrapers, the latter probably used as razors, and a beautiful comma-shaped knife (Fig. 32, 2) that is really just a Capsian point worked all over one face by pressure-flaking.[1] The arrow was tipped with concave-based or tanged points as before,

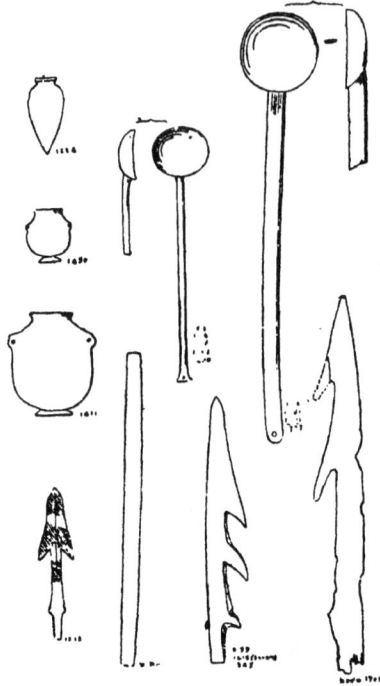

FIG. 22. Ivory vases and harpoons of Amratian and spoons of Gerzean cultures, ⅛, after Petrie.

but, at least in Nubia, transverse arrow-heads of lunate or trapezoidal form now occur.[2] Notable types are the fish-tailed blade (Plate VIIIa), hafted by its point into a wood or ivory hilt and allegedly used for hamstringing game, and the great rhomboid 'lance' or dagger blade (Fig. 21). The mace now used was weighted with a sharp-edged stone disc or more rarely with a pointed head of stone (Plate VIIb, bottom). Fish were speared with harpoons, rarely

1. Petrie's original account of the flint work in *Diospolis Parva* should be supplemented by Huzayyin in Mond and Myers, *Cemeteries of Armant*.
2. At least in Nubia, *Arch. Survey of Nubia, Report*, 1907–8, pl. 62.

of copper, more often of bone and always flatter than those from the Fayum (Fig. 22), but closely resembling the Khartoum types.

Several classes of pottery, all inferior to the best Badarian, were now in use. The commonest fabric, termed Black-topped Ware, resembles the finer Badarian in the manner of its decoration by partial oxidization of the ferruginous wash but lacks the tasteful ripple burnish and the fineness of the latter fabric (Pl. V*b*). Among the shapes the flasks, carinated bowls, goblets on a low pedestal and twin vases are noticeable, but the lank tumblers are the most distinctive. Secondly, a polished red ware, fired wholly in an oxidizing atmosphere, was current as was a black ware produced by reduction and imitating basalt. Yet more characteristic is White Cross-lined

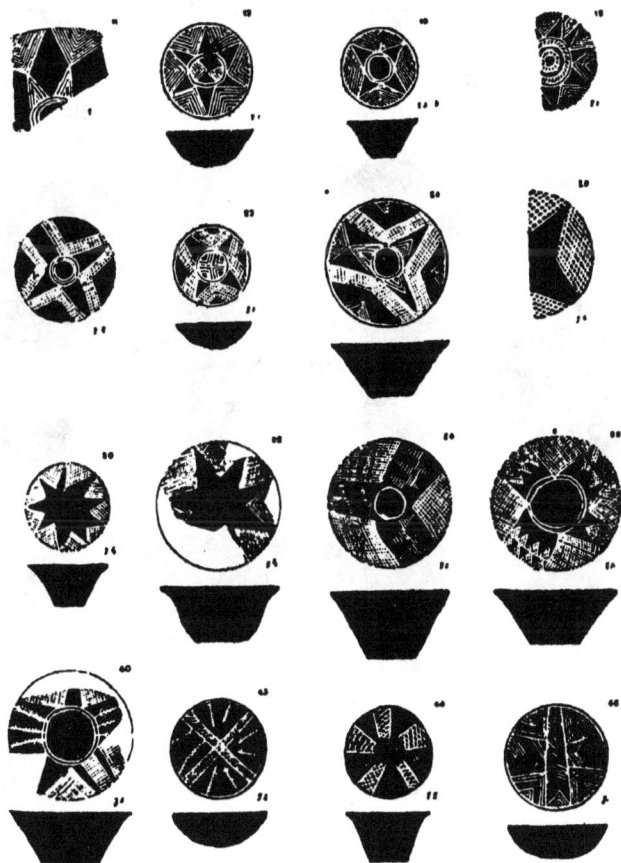

FIG. 23. White Cross-lined bowls showing basketry patterns, after Capart, $\frac{1}{12}$.

pottery that was only manufactured between S.D. 31 and 35. It is essentially a red ware ornamented with patterns in dull white paint. The designs belong to two series. First there are vases adorned with simple rectilinear motives evidently copied, like the vases they adorn, from basketry originals (Fig. 23). Others are ornamented with the representations of men and animals, already referred to as of magic purport and evidently intended to be lifelike, but the result was not always very successful (Pl. VI*b*). These painted scenes have ruder precursors scratched on Red-polished or Black-topped vases. In some cases plastically modelled animals—generally elephants or hippopotami—walk round the vase's rim. These figures and the painted giraffes, Barbary sheep, and scorpions give us a lively picture of the prehistoric fauna of the Nile valley and its immediate borders. A pendant to the White Cross-lined is the rare Black Incised ware, a fabric principally found in Nubia. It corresponds in technique to the Tasian beakers and like them is inspired by basketry models with the exception of some Nubian vases that imitate a

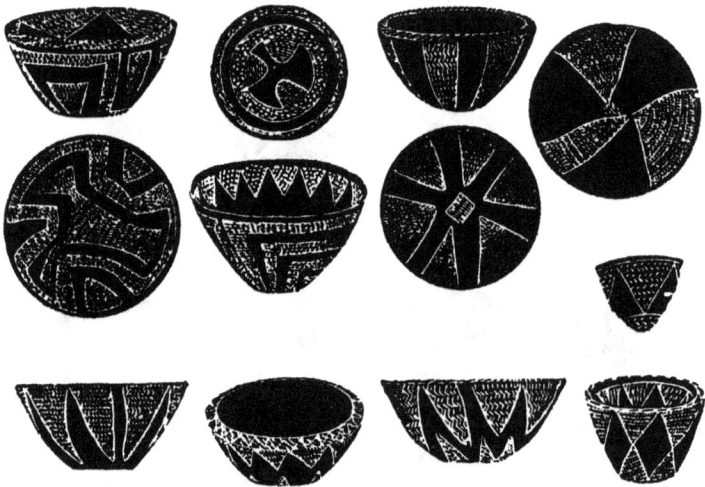

FIG. 24. Black Incised ware, ⅙.

gourd in a straw sling (Fig. 24). Finally rather coarse vases decorated with incised herring bone patterns, rather like the early Merimdian, were used on domestic sites like Armant and Hammamiya (Badari).

Stone was also used for vessels, though not very often. The only Amratian types are tall ovoid beakers on a pedestal with two lug handles just under the rim and cylindrical jars with slightly convex sides and bevelled rims (Pl. VI*a*). The material used for the early predynastic stone vessels was exclusive y fine-grained rocks, principally basalt and alabaster. Other vases were made out of ostrich egg-shell or ivory.

Turning to toilet articles we find that the eyes were still painted with malachite. It was ground on slate palettes that are now either rhomboidal (Pl. VII*b*, bottom right) or carved to represent animals (Fig. 25). The material was carried in little bags decorated with tags

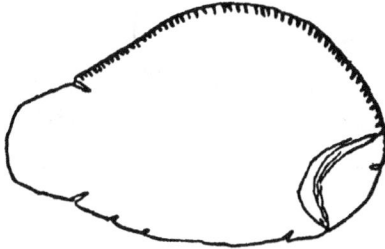

FIG. 25. Slate palette in form of a fish, Naqada, ⅜.

(Plate VIII) that may be either real tusks, or flat ivory slips of a similar shape or well-carved stone models. The body was tattooed with various patterns. Long-toothed ivory combs, like the Badarian, were stuck in the hair or wig, and ivory pins may have been similarly worn. Necklaces of ostrich-shell discs, carnelian, steatite, felspar, or green glazed beads and marine shells or coral were hung round the neck. To them were attached slate pendants representing animals, birds, or fishes that may have been totemic emblems or magic amulets. The arms were decked with bracelets of shell, ivory, or tortoise-shell. Men, to judge by the figurines, went stark-naked save for the 'Libyan sheath' or penistasche (Pl. VII*a*, centre) and plumes stuck in their hair, but were shod with sandals of grass. Women wore a linen apron, and, sometimes at least, wigs.

The graves were shallow oval pits in which the corpse was interred doubled up. Sometimes more than one body lies in a single grave, and in other cases the bones are found in disorder as if interment had taken place only after the skin had decayed from them.

The deceased was liberally provided with weapons, ornaments, and food for the future life as well as the magical apparatus already described. The figurines belong to several classes. In the first place we have the ivory tusks showing only the head (Pl. V*a*). Next comes

FIG. 26. Ivory combs, about ½.

a series of complete statuettes also in ivory. The earlier examples are fine and realistically carved. The clay or mud figures are generally much rougher. Erect and squatting types occur and the arms may be upraised or curved round below the breasts (Plates VII and VIII).

In the complex defined by the foregoing traits the sedentary life, the grains and domestic animals which made that possible, the fine flintwork, the black-topped pottery, the slate palettes, ivory combs and pins, shell bracelets and glazed beads, are all just improvements on the discoveries of the Badarians or are derived more or less directly from them. On the other hand, the scenes painted on White Cross-lined pots or incised on Black-topped vases or slate palettes betray in style and mentality the closest kinship to the rock paintings and engravings described in chapter II. They show the same liveliness and impressionism, but the Egyptian artist, experimenting

AFRICANS AND ASIATICS ON THE NILE

in a new medium, fell short of the best achievements of his North African or Spanish confreres. Indeed a detailed comparison with the East Spanish rock-shelter paintings led E. S. Thomas[1] to conclude that the painters of the latter were inspired by the same ideals and developed along the same lines as the Amratian artists.

Then there are many agreements in costume between the figures depicted on Amratian pots and those drawn on the rocks of North Africa and Eastern Spain. The feathered headdress worn by men on White Cross-lined vases reappears in Saharan rock drawings as does the penis sheath of the Amratian figurines; one of the latter wore anklets comparable to those depicted at In-Ezzan in the Sahara and at Cogul in Spain. The Amratian dog looks rather like that represented at Alpera (Fig. 6). From these and similar considerations some have deduced a fresh infiltration of Libyans to mix with the Amratians' Badarian ancestors. The facts could, however, be explained just as well by a diffusion of Egyptian fashions across that continuum of mobile tribes postulated on p. 23 or by assuming that some of those tribes were aboriginally related to the predynastic Egyptians, whether both had come from further south or had been cradled in the Sahara itself.

The Gerzean period witnessed a transformation of the rural economy of Upper Egypt, the invention or diffusion of new industrial techniques and an expansion in volume and range of 'foreign trade' that prepared the way for a second economic revolution. At the same time it is defined by a new archæological culture due to the superposition on the Amratian equipment of Middle and Upper Egypt of expressions of foreign traditions, some at least explicitly Asiatic, and that should denote the infiltration of new ethnic elements.

The Amratian culture had been based on a mixed economy of farming and food-gathering. In Gerzean[2] times farming became the mainstay of the peasant masses and was perhaps now based on some measure of artificial irrigation. Hunting weapons are comparatively rare and were seldom deposited in the graves. Dogs were no longer buried with their masters.

In flint work blades, struck from true prismatic cores, came into more general use without superseding bifacially trimmed flakes and cores, but the pressure flaking reached a new summit of excellence.

1. *JRAI.*, lvi, 385 ff.　　　2. Baumgärtel, *CPE.*, 46.

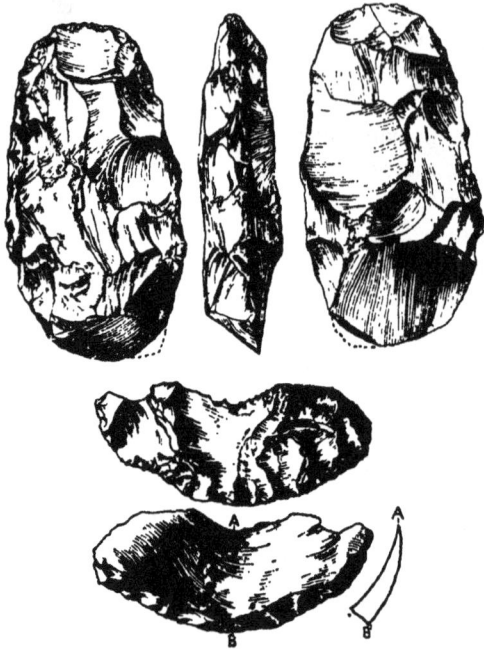

FIG. 27. Tranchet axe and resharpening flake, Armant, $\frac{2}{5}$.

Axes were regularly sharpened by the tranchet blow (Fig. 27a). More significantly the principles of intelligent metallurgy were understood and applied. Though rare, cast metal tools and weapons were

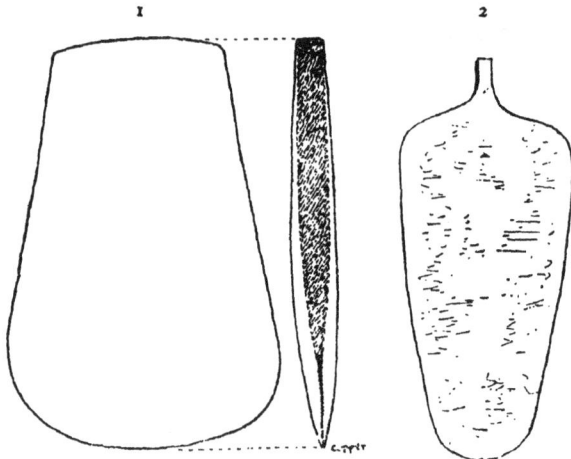

FIG. 28. Copper axe-head, Matmar, $\frac{1}{3}$, flaying knife, $\frac{1}{3}$.

in use; flat axes with expanding blades (Fig. 28, 1), rhomboid daggers and specialized knives (Fig. 28, 2) were now being cast by copper-smiths. The daggers were mounted in a hilt of wood or bone with a crescentic base (Fig. 29); the horns encircle the butt of the copper

FIG. 29. Gerzean copper dagger with ivory handle (restored), El Amrah, ¼.

blade as they had the Amratian fish-tailed flints, a method of mount-ing that helps to distinguish Egyptian from Mesopotamian tradi-tions in metallurgy. By the middle of the period at least the blade was strengthened with a stout midrib and by its close elongated as in Fig. 30. The knot headed pin (Fig. 20, 1) that in Central Europe stands at the head of the whole Bronze Age series was probably in use by this period.[1] These products must have been fashioned by full-time specialists though these perhaps still worked as perambulating merchant-smiths rather than residing permanently in the several villages.

New artificial substances were also manufactured—gesso and fayence. The latter—a sand-core held together by a glaze—is an improvement on glazed stone, used already in Badarian times, as it could be moulded into beads and pendants, but could be produced easily in Egypt where deposits of the requisite alkali are available in the Western Desert (Wadi Natron). The production of stone

1. Brunton and Caton-Thompson, *Badarian Civilization*, pl. liv, 9, from grave 16, 4; cf. Childe, *Dawn*, 117, and p. 159 below.

vases likewise increased, and now even the hardest rocks, like porphyry, were efficiently worked. These too must be the products of full-time specialists, supported by the surplus food Gerzean farmers could so easily produce.

Substantial rectangular houses of mud replaced the older wind-screens and round huts. The model from El Amrah (Plate X) represents a dwelling, estimated to have measured 25 ft. × 18 ft., and entered through a wood-framed doorway on one long side. Some villages may now have attained the dimensions of a small township. Besides Naqada, which still flourished, we may assign to this period the Falcon-town, Hierakonpolis, the debris from which extends over three-quarters of a mile.[1]

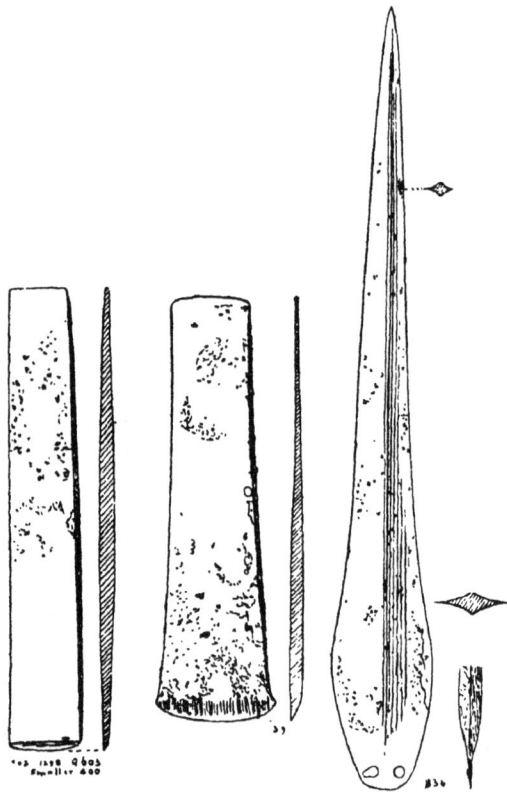

FIG. 30. Late Gerzean–Early Pharaonic adze and dagger blades from Naqada, ⅙, after Petrie.

1. Brunton in *Studies presented to F. Ll. Griffith*, London, 1932, 272–5.

AFRICANS AND ASIATICS ON THE NILE

The regular use of copper of course involved continuous contact with regions outside the Nile valley proper, whether the ore was mined exclusively in the Eastern Desert or already also in Sinai. Traffic along the Wadi Hammamat and other cross-desert routes was certainly maintained, and the distribution of mined flint, stone vases, and other local products along the river was regularized. Now long distance trade began to bring to North Africa products of Asia. From this quarter came silver, lead, and lapis lazuli. Assuming that lapis came then from Badakshan in northern Afghanistan, the only well-attested large deposit, the stone must have come through Mesopotamia. Hence it would not be surprising if manufactures from that region reached the Nile. In fact, a couple of cylinder seals found in the Nile valley do seem to be Mesopotamian products of about this age, while one local copy comes from a Gerzean grave attributed to S.D. 46.[1]

The commerce attested by these imported materials and commodities doubtless depended on the use of asses for transport; bones of that beast were in fact found in settlements of the period near Armant. Whether the camel was also utilized is more doubtful. A small model from Abusir el-Meleq[2] seems to represent a camel. But even if it do, it does not prove domestication. Nor was the beast necessarily Asiatic since camel bones occur in North Africa in pleistocene times.

These technical and economic advances increased the wealth of Gerzean Egypt. But perhaps this wealth was less evenly distributed than heretofore. Variations in the size and furniture of graves suggest a division at least into richer and poorer clansmen. Most Gerzean graves are larger and more nearly rectangular than the normal Amratian. After S.D. 40 some were further enlarged to accommodate richer offerings—particularly jars of food and drink. In some cases a ledge was left in one side of the shaft to contain such furniture; in others the shaft itself might be filled with funerary gifts, while a recess was cut in the hard desert soil to receive the corpse, forming a sort of pit-cave tomb. Or again the pit might be divided into two compartments by a wattle partition supported by upright stakes planted in the pit floor.[3] Despite such variations, the disparities in furniture are not yet such as to prove the division of

1. Frankfort, *Cylinder Seals*, 293; cf. p. 127 below.
2. Mond and Myers, *Cemeteries of Armant*, 255; Scharff, *Abusir el-Meleq*, 40, pl. 24.
3. *El Amrah*, 7.

Gerzean villages into chiefs and commoners. They may, for all we know, have still been occupied by democratic totemic clans.

Indeed to this period belong Decorated vases, painted with pictures of boats bearing standards (Fig. 34). Most of the latter correspond to the emblems of Egyptian nomes in historic times; where two or more boats are depicted on the same vase, their several ensigns are always those appropriate to contiguous nomes.[1]

The distinctive features of the Gerzean period, just summarized, could be regarded as reflecting merely a regular technological and economic evolution. But certain innovations in equipment, armament, fashions in dress or ornaments, burial rites and artistic taste

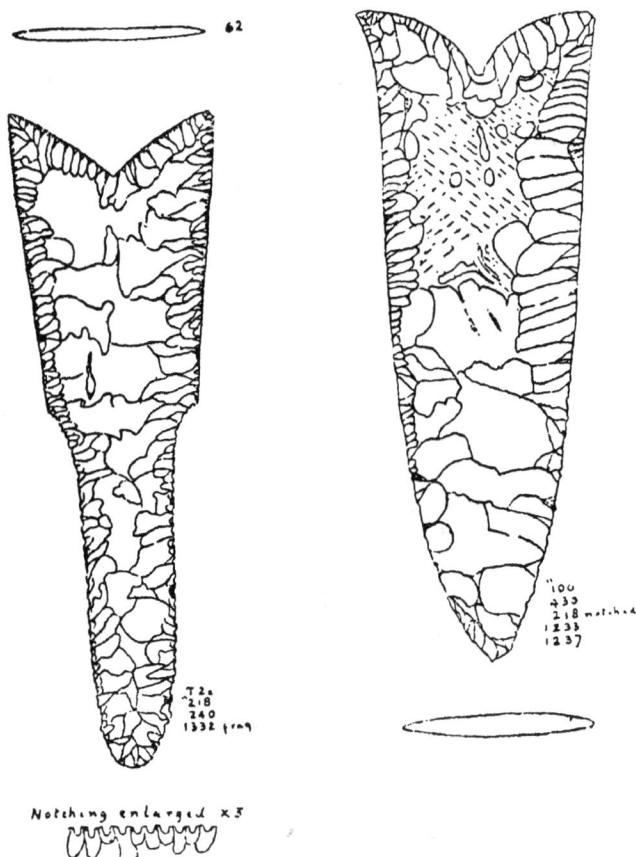

Notching enlarged x 3

FIG. 31. Flint blades with V base, Naqada, after Petrie, $\frac{1}{2}$.

1. Newberry, *LAAA.*, i, 18; v, 134.

can hardly be thus explained. They seem rather to denote an infusion of foreign traditions, an infiltration of new ethnic elements, and perhaps even a political conquest. The break with the past is most explicitly indicated in the following traits. A pear-shaped mace replaces (S.D. 42) the disc type that only survives later as a cult object; the fish-tailed blades (with U base) give place (S.D. 38) to swallow-tailed shapes with a V base (Fig. 31); scimitar-shaped

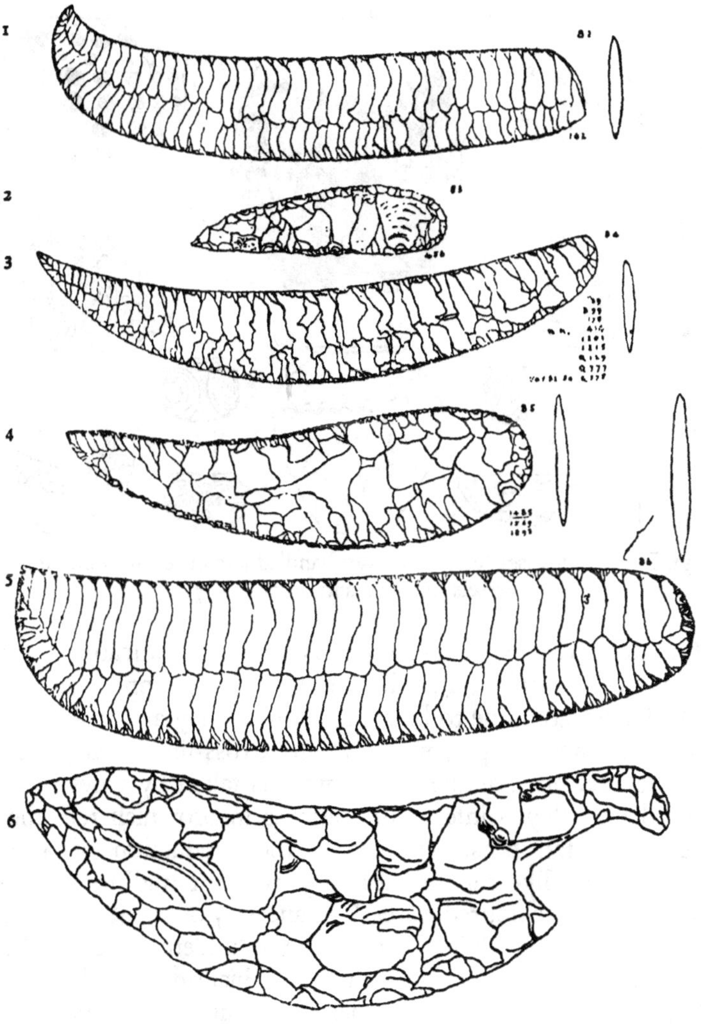

FIG. 32. Flint knives: 2 and 4, Amratian, 3, Early Gerzean, 1 and 5, late Gerzean, 6, Early Pharaonic, ⅓.

knives (Fig. 32, 3) at S.D. 45 oust the comma type; flint daggers come in and arrow-heads with concave bases go out; but the chisel-bladed arrow occurs occasionally even in Middle Egypt; figurines are no longer modelled in clay after S.D. 43 nor carved in ivory after S.D. 45; but clay and stone vases are made in the form of animals and the ivory-carver turns his attention to the manufacture of amulets and spoons strange to the Amratian culture.

FIG. 33. Decorated vases (and two wavy-handled jars in centre) imitating stone vessels in shape and ornament, $\frac{1}{4}$.

Household vessels, always the most sensitive indicator of ethnic change, are radically altered. Though Black-topped and Red-polished ware continue to be manufactured, they are no longer the vehicles for new shapes, while White Cross-lined has gone out altogether. Its place as the typical ware is taken by vases of light-coloured buff clay painted with patterns in brownish red, the so-called Decorated pots. Technically the production of a light-coloured fabric like this implies very different traditions to those embodied in self-coloured wares. The ancestry of the decorated pots, as disclosed by their shapes, especially the 'undercut' rims and long tubular handles, is to be sought in stone instead of in leather and basketry. The patterns on the earlier vases imitate either the mottling of coarse-grained stones or the protective straw jackets in which such vessels, like Chianti flasks or ginger-jars to-day, were carried.

FIG. 34. Decorated pot figuring boat.

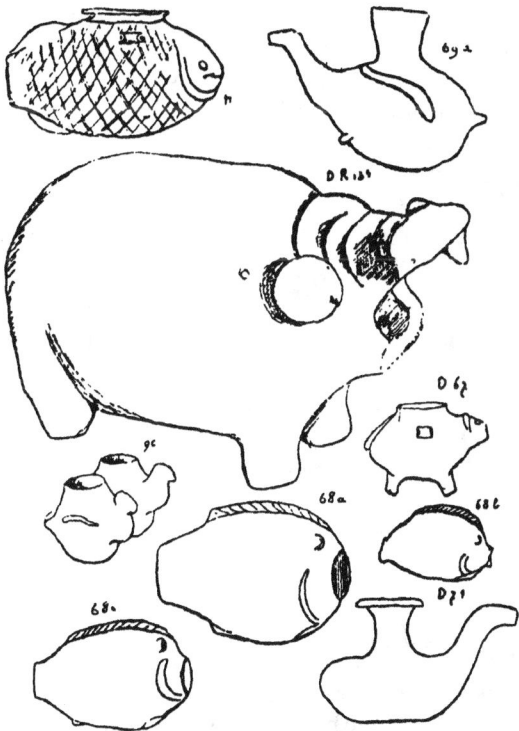

FIG. 35. Theriomorphic and spouted vases, ¼, after Capart.

And actually many graves contain stone vases agreeing precisely in form with their clay copies and distinguished from those of the previous period both by their shapes and by the preference for variegated and coarse-grained rocks (Plate IX*a*).

In addition we have the famous Wavy-handled jars whose progressive degeneration provided Petrie with the first basis for his sequence dating (Plate IX*b*), and then a multitude of 'Rough' pots, tempered with chaff, generally reddish in colour and often provided with a pointed base. There are further a few spouted jars, some stray amphoriskoi, and vessels in the shape of animals. Such 'theriomorphs' have been regarded as signs of foreign influence but the animals represented include definitely Nilotic species such as hippopotami, and some theriomorphs are made of just those variegated stones and with just those peculiarities that are exclusively characteristic of the Middle Predynastic stone-ware (Fig. 35).

After S.D. 45 subjects taken from nature, plants, animals, and ships are also depicted upon the Decorated vases and the treatment of the themes is now abstract and stylized as contrasted with the naturalism and youth of the older White Cross-lined painting.

No less radical alterations are observable in dress and toilet articles. The long-toothed comb disappears entirely after S.D. 42;

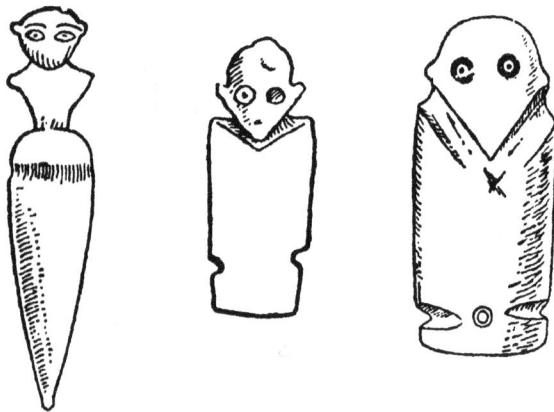

FIG. 36. Block figures, Naqada, ⅓.

its place is taken by short-toothed scratching combs or combinations of such with hair-pins. The rhombic slate palette goes out of fashion at S.D. 40 and with it the various tags and tusks that had decorated the malachite bags. Yet the eyes were still painted with

70

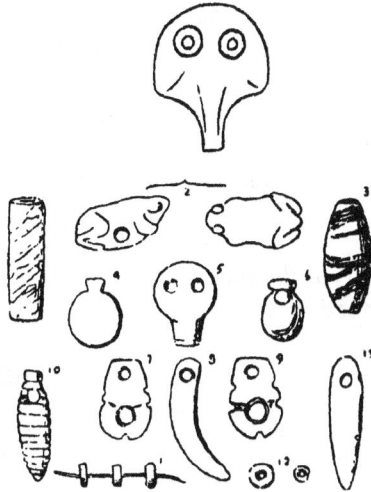

FIG. 37. Amulets: 1, Bull's head; 2, toad; 8, claw, etc., S.D. 65. $\frac{3}{4}$, after Petrie.

malachite, and theriomorphic palettes were still used for grinding it on.

In the domain of cult and ritual the naturalistic ivory figurines were conventionalized into 'block-figures' (Fig. 36), a type which was eventually adopted in Minoan Crete. The magical potency of beads was enhanced by carving them into amulets in the shape of bulls' heads (first dated example S.D. 46), flies (S.D. 48), falcons and

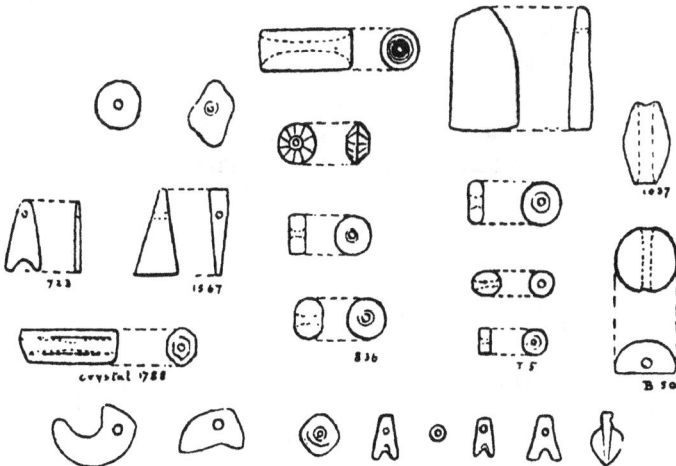

FIG. 38. Predynastic stone beads; in bottom row claw and fly amulets.

71

other creatures (Figs. 37–8). Burial rites were drastically modified. No regular orientation is now observed; multiple interments have ceased, dogs are no longer buried with their masters; weapons are rarer in the tombs. The ornaments, vases, and utensils have often been deliberately broken—ritually killed—at the time of deposition. The grave itself assumed a new shape and was steadily elaborated as already remarked.

Of course there is no complete break between Amratian and Gerzean; in Upper Egypt the innovations just enumerated gradually trickle in. Black-topped ware, for instance, continued to be made, though no new forms were developed in it after S.D. 50. To that extent it is correct to speak of foreign influences slowly dominating Upper Egypt, but not of an alien culture replacing the Amratian. For the immediate source of the innovations most authorities look to the North. The Gerzean culture never penetrated into Nubia where Amratian traditions persisted. On the other hand it is represented, without recognizable Amratian admixture, at Gerzeh and Abusir el-Meleq, about 130 miles north of the nearest Amratian village. Then there are notorious Levantine parallels to many of the Gerzean innovations. The Wavy-handled jars have strikingly close analogies in Palestine, though it now appears that these are later than the Egyptian though certainly derived from a common 'ledge-handled' prototype. Spouted jars remarkably like the Gerzean recur in Palestine,[1] but are far commoner in Mesopotamia where the type has a long history. Midrib daggers like Fig. 30, 3, can be matched at Byblos and elsewhere in Asia, but the hafting seems peculiarly Egyptian, and the type is dated only to S.D. 60 on the Nile. The piriform mace is admittedly an Asiatic type.

It would, of course, be tempting to see in the Asiatic elements in Gerzean culture archæological counterparts of the Semitic element in the Egyptian language. Now some arguments for deriving this Semitic element immediately from Lower Egypt have been mentioned on p. 6. They must be read in conjunction with the fact that the hieroglyphic signs for mace and arrow were the Gerzean piriform mace and chisel-ended arrow respectively. Moreover, the environment of the marshy Delta, like that of Sumer in Mesopotamia,

---

1. Albright, *AASOR.*, xiii, 1931–2, 31; *BASOR.*, 63, 1936, 13; cf. p. 230 below. The Egyptian spouted vases are Petrie's 'Fancy forms', especially F.58 and R.43 in *Prehistoric Pottery Corpus*, pls. xviii and xxxviii; cf. also, Brunton, *Badarian Civilization*, pl. xxxviii, and Scharff, *Abusir el-Meleq*, 1926, pl. 23, 207. They copy metal ewers like Fig. 51, 2.

was calculated to provoke that concentration of social resources essential to the effective development of metallurgy and other technical advances.

The only concrete archæological evidence for influences on the Gerzean culture explicitly emanating from Lower Egypt is provided by the boats depicted on Gerzean vases. Newberry has claimed that of 288 boats figured on Decorated pots, 166 fly the ensign of the Harpoon nome, historically situated on the Canopic mouth of the Nile, while 80 others bear emblems of adjacent West Delta nomes. Even if Newberry's identification of the emblems[1] be accepted, the vases in question reached Upper Egypt relatively late in the Gerzean period; none need be earlier than S.D. 45.[2] The argument is therefore no more relevant to the origin of the Gerzean culture than the Levantine parallels to the Late Gerzean midrib daggers.

Nor can it any longer be plausibly argued that the spread of Gerzean culture documents the conquest of Upper Egypt by Followers of Horus from the Delta and its incorporation in a 'Heliopolitan kingdom'. Even if the Red Crown on an Amratian palette and the sceptre from El Omari betoken an early kingdom in Lower Egypt, there the Gerzean culture is unknown. It is indeed found much further north than the Amratian, at Gerzeh and Abusir el-Meleq, but in Lower Egypt proper it is still missing. Of course, in the Delta itself any settlements—Gerzean or other—lie buried deep in Nile silt. But on the Delta's edge at Heliopolis[3] and then at Turah[4] and Maadi,[5] just south of Cairo, graves and settlements are known which, while certainly predynastic, are later than Merimde or El Omari. Yet there is nothing explicitly Gerzean in them.

The settlement at Maadi covered no less than 45 acres of a desert ridge, with a cemetery outside it on the slope to the flood plain. Besides the usual flimsy shelters, oval or horse-shoe-shaped and all sorts of silos and pits, spacious chambers of subrectangular or

1. The identification of most of the 'harpoon' signs has been plausibly challenged by Baumgärtel, *CPE.*, 11–12.
2. Cantor, in *JNES.*, iii, 1944, 119.
3. Debono, *Chronique d'Egypte*, 1950, 233–6.
4. Junker, 'Turah,' *Denkschr. d. k. Akad. in Wien, phil.-hist. Kl.*, lvi, 1912, 2 ff.; cf. *Schmidt-Festschrift*, 873–9.
5. Mustafa Amer and Menghin, 'The Excavations of the Egyptian University at Maadi,' Egyptian University Faculty of Arts, *Publication*, 19, 1932. The following account is based largely on the paper read to the 3rd Inter. Congr. of Pre- and Proto-historic Sciences at Zurich, 1950, and a visit to the site in 1951, by the courtesy of Professor Amer and Dr. Rizkana.

elongated plan were cut to a depth of two or three metres in the hard subsoil. Their vertical walls were hung with mats or in one case were lined with alternating courses of stone and mud brick. Stout posts along one side presumably supported a sloping roof, but one chamber was prolonged by a low annex, tunnelled in the subsoil.

The industrial equipment is strikingly different from that of El Omari and from the Gerzean. Stone axes are absent; their place must have been taken by copper celts since the wooden posts have been efficiently hewn to a point. Of actual metal tools only one stout axe or adze and a few awls survive. But an unfinished casting proves that copper was worked in the village. Among thousands of flints there are only two stray arrow-heads and these are the only bifacial tools. Sickle teeth were regularly made on blades, but the most characteristic tools are fan-shaped scrapers, made from mined tabular flint, and fine awls. The only weapons recognized are disc maces. Just like the Gerzeans of Upper Egypt, the Maadians must have relied mainly on cultivation and the breeding of food-animals, among which pigs were conspicuous.

Most of the pottery is made of chaff-tempered ware, slipped and sometimes polished, as at El Omari, but the favourite colour was now black. Besides storage jars of imposing size, the commonest forms are globular or ovoid pots with everted rims. The bases are often rounded or almost pointed, but a splayed ring foot is the most distinctive. A comparatively small group of vases with straight necks and one or two handles have obvious connexions with Palestine or Syria, as have a few sherds with incised herring-bone ornament. One or two ledge-handled jars might illustrate the model from which the Gerzean and Palestinian wavy-handled jars were both descended. Finally a couple of painted sherds are as like Early Palestinian wares as Gerzean Decorated vases.

Vessels were also made, probably locally, of calcite and more often of basalt that must have been imported from the Fayum or the Eastern Desert. The commonest basalt vase closely resembles the Amratian form illustrated in Plate VIa; squat chalices or 'egg-cups' in the same material are also represented in a few Amratian graves, but can be exactly matched in a temple deposit of the Late Uruk-Jemdet Nasr phase at Erech in Sumer; finally, conical vases with a flat broad rim, resemble some from the Libyan coast.[1] Combs

1. Mersa Matruh, *Harvard African Studies*, viii, 1927, 138–140, and pl. 27, 8; for the 'egg cups' see Baumgärtel, *CPE.*, 107.

and beads were also manufactured on the spot. The raw materials for stone vases, if not the vases themselves, copper and other raw materials were certainly imported, as were sea shells.

The dead were buried in a cemetery outside the settlement, but very poorly furnished at Maadi. At Heliopolis, where the cemetery alone is so far known, the funerary gifts are slightly richer and the orientation more regular—head to the south facing east. The bodies were wrapped in skins or papyrus mats. Gazelles and dogs were also ceremonially buried in the cemetery. In both cases the skeletons belong to taller and stouter folk than the predynastic inhabitants of Upper Egypt. But the Heliopolis skulls display a distinct prognathism which is generally reckoned a negroid feature, while even those from Maadi are pentagonoid like other predynastic crania. Neither site, therefore, shows the Giza type that is prominent in Early Pharaonic and Old Kingdom graves.

At Heliopolis three layers of graves can be distinguished, dug into as many superimposed gravels laid down by torrential freshets from the Jebel Ahmer. Maadi too was more than once flooded by torrents. Both sites therefore cover a substantial period of time. But it is impossible to fit them into the system of sequence dates worked out for the south. Some of the vases indeed might be precursors of the Rough types recovered from Early Pharaonic cemeteries at Turah and elsewhere. But actual Early Pharaonic types of pottery, flints, stone vases, palettes, or ornaments are totally absent. Considering the proximity of the great cemeteries near Turah and Helwan, that must mean that Maadi was deserted before the foundation of Memphis. Gerzean types are equally missing. On the other hand the basalt vases and disc mace-heads are in the Amratian tradition and would argue an early date. Still despite a few reminiscences in the pottery, Maadi can hardly be the immediate successor of El Omari. It must then, after all, be partly contemporary with the Gerzean of Upper Egypt.

Does the Maadian then represent the culture of the hypothetical predynastic United Kingdom? Are the Heliopolitan graves part of the necropolis of its postulated capital? There are no signs of Horus among the surviving relics. On the other hand Asiatic elements are obvious both in the flint-work and the pottery and these are different from, and look earlier than, those detected in the Gerzean. But in the Cairo region such, after all, merely denote a reappearance of older connexions. In mesolithic times Helwan had been a Natufian outpost, and the *Triticum monococcum* from El Omari must rank as a northern element in the local neolithic. If then there be an archæological counterpart to the union, allegedly imposed upon the South by Lower Egypt, it cannot be found in the Gerzean culture; but it may lurk in the neglected Rough and Late Pots which even in Upper Egypt may continue a Maadian tradition. But these have never been adequately studied.

As for the Gerzean it may perhaps have arisen in northern Middle Egypt through impulses from Asia across the Eastern Desert. After all Petrie[1] long ago contended that the Gerzean stone vases were products of pig-tailed people who inhabited that region in the earliest historical period, and Baumgärtel[2] more recently suggested that the Gerzeans arrived down the Wadi Hammamat with the 'foreign boat' described on p. 78. In any case it seems to have been Gerzean barbarism that was replaced by pharaonic civilization. But, if only because of the greater completeness of the archæological record, it is in Upper Egypt that the rise of pharaonic monarchy can alone be traced.

1. *JRAI.*, xxxi, 1911, 250.   2. *CPE.*, 44.

CHAPTER V

THE RISE OF THE PHARAOHS

As exploited by Gerzean farmers the soil of the Nile valley must readily have yielded a surplus above the peasant's domestic needs. It was no doubt used in part to contribute to the support of specialist craftsmen and merchants. Indeed the Gerzean period, as illustrated by the cemeteries of Upper Egypt, witnessed both an absolute increase in wealth, reflected in the multiplication of grave goods and the enlargement of the graves, and also a growing inequality in its distribution, suggested by disparities in size and wealth between contemporary graves. But this must not be pictured

Fig. 39. Ivory handle for a knife like Fig. 32, 5.

77

as a peaceful process of internal expansion. There are some definite hints in the archæological record of warfare for the acquisition of cattle, booty, or land. Towns and villages were certainly fortified. Scenes carved on the ivory handles for some serially-flaked, Late Gerzean flint knives, like Fig. 32, 5, point in the same direction (Fig. 39).

A whole series of ivories[1] depicts rows of animals, always represented in the same order with the elephant, historically the emblem of the first nome of Upper Egypt (Elephantine), at their head. So the animals are the totems of clans, such as have been inferred even from Amratian documents. Bénedite[1] suggests that they are pictorial records of struggles between neighbouring clans, comparable to the armed conflicts which throughout Egyptian history broke out between adjacent villages whenever the central authority was weak. It is still the clan totems that contend together, so perhaps the totem has not yet been monopolized by any chief. The Falcon, Horus, is not represented; hence Bénedite infers that the ivories date from a time before the Falcon-clan had obtained predominance in Upper Egypt.

But the series culminates (typologically; there is no independent evidence for the relative ages) in a knife-handle on which actual men are engaged in fighting; indeed, a regular 'naval battle' is depicted. This document[2] was found at Gebel el-Arak, significantly just where the route from the Red Sea down the Wadi Hammamat debouches on the Nile valley. One side depicts scenes of conflict on land and water. On the reverse is a hero wearing a long flowing robe and a turban dompting two lions on a rocky peak while two dogs gaze up at him. While the execution of the carving is purely Egyptian, its themes are reputedly Asiatic. In the naval battle the old Nilotic papyrus boat is engaged with others with high prow and stern. The latter type, while depicted often on rock-pictures in the Eastern Desert,[3] looks foreign on the Nile (Fig. 40), but resembles vessels depicted on Mesopotamian seals from the Uruk period.[4]

---

1. Bénedite, *JEA.*, v, 225 ff.; for the dating (S.D. 50–60) see Kantor, *JNES.*, iii, 1944, 125.

2. Figured, for instance, in Frankfort, *Studies*, i, and in Petrie, *The Making of Egypt*, 1939.

3. Winckler, *Rock Drawings*, i, 26 ff.; ii, 18; west of the Nile, found only at Hos, that is, still in the valley.

4. Frankfort, *Cylinder Seals*, pl. iii, d.; cf. Emery in *Annales du Service*, xlv, 1947, 147; cf. Plate XXc here.

FIG. 40. 'Foreign' ship painted on a late Decorated pot.

The dogs on the reverse again are unlike the older Egyptian grey-hound type and resemble rather Mesopotamian hounds.[1] The antithetical group above them is a motive, never popular on the Nile,[2] but thoroughly at home in the Tigris-Euphrates valley. The hero too with his full beard, turban, and flowing robe looks Asiatic rather than Egyptian. A like personage in similar attire is carved, shooting a lion with chisel-ended arrows, on a basalt stele found at Erech in Sumer in a deposit of the Jemdet Nasr phase (Plate XIII).

Scharff indeed inferred that the Egyptian ivory carvers were copying in miniature the products of a Sumerian school of monumental sculpture. The Erech stele in any case confirms the contact between Egypt and the nascent civilization of the Tigris-Euphrates delta, deduced from the other motives on the knife-handle and from other aspects of Gerzean culture.[3] But this contact need not have been direct. The hero of the Gebel el-Arak knife-handle and the Erech stele need not be a Sumerian; he is more like a Semite of the desert, as Dussaud suggested.[4] Impact on both river valleys of Bedouin tribes, living in an intermediate region, might suffice to explain the observed phenomena. But in any case some sort of contact was now established between two nascent civilizations.

1. This and other points were first noted by Frankfort, *Studies*, i, 117–135.
2. After Dynasty I it survived only in the emblem of Cusae in Upper Egypt, cf. Scharff, 'Die Frühkulturen Ägyptens und Mesopotamiens,' *Der Alte Orient*, xli, 1941, 26.
3. A cylinder, allegedly a Mesopotamian product of the Jemdet Nasr phase, is reported from a Gerzean grave of S.D. 46–50!
4. *Syria*, xvi, 1935, 322.

The sequel is best deduced from a series of documents from Falcon-town (Hierakonpolis),[1] the Upper Egyptian seat of the Horus cult and presumably once the capital of the Falcon clan. There Quibell found a tomb[2] that can be regarded as representing the culmination of the development sketched on p. 65. The shaft walls are lined with mud brick and the wattle-work partition of El Amrah has been replaced by a mud-brick wall. Its very architecture suggests the elevation of an influential clansman to the rank of chief at least. Moreover the mud walls were coated with plaster and painted in the style of the Decorated vases with a scene that reproduces on a large scale the several themes of the Gebel el-Arak knife-handle (Fig. 41). A reproduction of the 'naval battle' with the same

FIG. 41. Scene painted on the wall of a tomb at Hierakonpolis.

two types of boat presumably attests the historical importance of the event. The antithetical group of the hero dompting lions reappears together with scenes of dance, the chase, and combat.

Then a series of monumental palettes—glorified versions of the Gerzean toilet article—and huge piriform mace-heads, from the sanctuary of Horus, record the achievements of the Horus clan. The first, typologically, is the Lion Hunt palette (Plate XII). The scene is as purely 'mythological' as those on the ivories. But here the hunters are depicted as men, and the Falcon, Horus, is perched

1. All first published in Quibell, *Hierakonpolis*, and often thereafter, e.g. Capart, *Primitive Art in Egypt*.

2. The tomb, dated to Dynasty O by Reisner, is assigned to S.D. 50–60 on the strength of the contained pottery by Kantor (*JNES*., iii, 111), who, however, unnecessarily doubts its sepulchral character.

on a standard borne before them. Led by the totem standard, the clansmen, armed with chisel-ended arrows, throwing sticks (? like the Badarian specimens of Fig. 15) and grooved stone maces, sally forth to hunt lions. The scene is apparently laid in the Western Desert and is generally interpreted as symbolizing a victory over Libyans. The double-headed beast in the top right corner is a popular Mesopotamian motive, rarely used in historical Egyptian art. On this palette Horus has not yet found any single human incarnation; no chief is depicted.

On what is regarded as the next document in the series, a mace-head, the incarnation has been affected; a king is portrayed in super-human proportions, wearing the White Crown of Upper Egypt. Beside him appears a picture of a scorpion, enclosed in a conventional palace door, surmounted by a falcon, emblem of Horus. Later pharaohs' names are always thus written, so the enclosed picture must be regarded as a true pictogram, the first attempt to write the name of a king whom we can only transcribe as 'King Scorpion'. This is his 'Horus name'; for the Falcon perched above it symbolizes his identification with the deity; he has monopolized the clan totem. The mace pictorially commemorates the victory of a group of Upper Egyptian nomes, symbolized by their clan badges, over foreign and Lower Egyptian clans (represented respectively by bows and lapwings) and also the initiation of some productive, peaceful enterprise by King Scorpion; he wields a hoe, ceremonially cutting the first sod of an irrigation canal or opening the agricultural cycle. King Scorpion, with another monarch, Ka, is assigned to a Dynasty O, as an immediate predecessor of Menes.

The next document from Hierakonpolis in stylistic order should then illustrate the unification of Egypt by 'Menes'. It is another huge palette, this time carved on both faces. On one face the king, like Scorpion, wears the White Crown, but on the other the Red, signifying kingship over Lower Egypt (Udimu, fifth king of Dynasty I, is the first to be portrayed wearing the Red and White Crowns simultaneously). His identification with Horus is symbolized by the picture of a Nar-fish inscribed with another symbol in the palace gate under the Falcon. We read the symbols 'The Horus Narmer' that was the 'Horus name' of Menes or of his first successor.[1] The knife-handles and palettes have been pre-

1. Emery (*Hor-Aha*, 5) like Reisner (*Development of Egyptian Tomb*, 9–13) adopted Petrie's original identification of Aha with Menes. Edwards follows Petrie's later view in equating Menes with Narmer.

sented as a pictorial record of the emergence of kingship in Upper
Egypt, the unification of the Two Lands and the transition from
Gerzean barbarism to Early Pharaonic civilization. The sepulchral
record justifies this interpretation and supplements deductions drawn
from the figured documents.

The royal tombs[1] of the first pharaohs have been discovered at

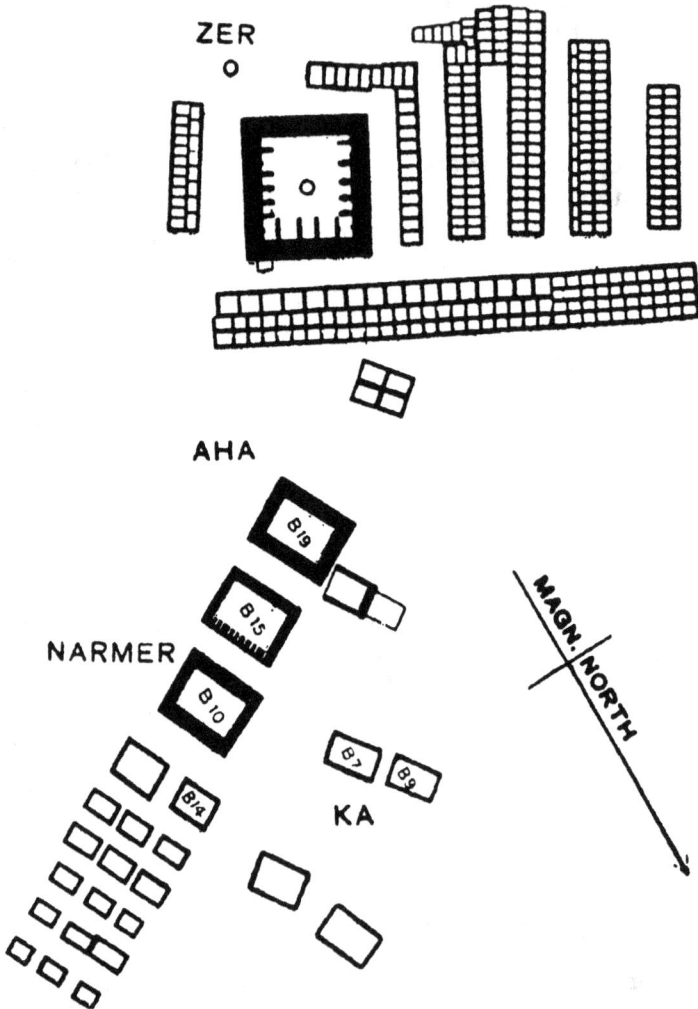

FIG. 42. Part of the Royal Cemetery at Abydos, after Petrie.

1. Petrie, *Royal Tombs*, ii, 1902. No two authorities agree in the spelling
of the early pharaohs' names.

82

Abydos, the ancient This, capital of Upper Egypt under Dynasties I and II. The tombs had indeed been plundered already under the Old Kingdom, but can still be arranged in an historical order and with their surviving furniture illustrate the rapid development of the oldest civilization on the Nile. Inscribed stelæ, jar-sealings or wooden labels enable us to identify the tombs of (1) Narmer (B.10), (2) Aha (B.19), (3) Zer (O), (4) Zet, (5) Udimu, (6) Anezib, (7) Smerkhet, and (8) Qaya with names recorded in later lists of First Dynasty pharaohs. The cemetery also comprised the tombs of the IInd Dynasty kings, those of a 1st Dynasty queen, Merneith, and a king of Dynasty O—Ka (Fig. 42).

The royal tombs can be regarded as a natural development of the Gerzean series, described on p. 65, but from the first are distinguished from the sepulchres of ordinary clansmen by their size and construction. The tomb of Narmer (B.10) was already a great shaft, lined with brick and 10 ft. 6 in. deep, with an area of 26 feet by 16 feet; at the bottom probably stood a timber chamber—a veritable mortuary house. In the course of the next seven reigns the grave shaft was enlarged and deepened; the chamber was divided by partition walls into mortuary hall and store-rooms by the reign of Zer, till under Udimu and later a stairway was needed to give access to the mortuary house.[1]

The accessories of a royal burial were no less distinctive. Of course the furniture, buried with kings, was enormously richer tnan that of any private grave. But human victims too—concubines, officials, servants, craftsmen—accompanied their royal master. At Narmer's funeral only 33 such persons are known to have been buried. But round Zer's tomb (Fig. 42, o) the accessory graves accommodated 275 harem ladies and 43 other members of the royal household, while a mile away 269 further familiars or courtiers were buried round a square that must have contained some monument to the same pharaoh.[2]

No superstructure survives to mark the sites of the tombs in the Abydos cemetery. But Aha, Zer, and Queen Merneith and probably

1. For details of the development, see Reisner, *Development*, 9 ff., and Emery, *Great Tombs of the 1st Dynasty*, 1949, 1–12.

2. Petrie, *Tombs of the Courtiers*, 1925, 1–3; similar squares of 'sati' burials surround vanished monuments of Zet and Merneith at this site. Reisner (*Development*, 109–125) suggests that these squares of sati burials surrounded a sort of 'dummy mastaba' serving as a 'valley temple' comparable to the later ones at Saqqara and Giza.

the remaining Thinite pharaohs, each had a second tomb at Saqqara,[1] the necropolis of Memphis, the northern capital founded by Menes on the border line between Upper and Lower Egypt. Each of these was surmounted by a monumental superstructure, termed a mastaba, as were the tombs of high officers of state and of some provincial magnates or princes. On the edge of the desert cliffs, overlooking Memphis from the west, rose a line of stately mastabas which, viewed from the valley, must have stood out against the skyline as does a long barrow on the brow of an English down.

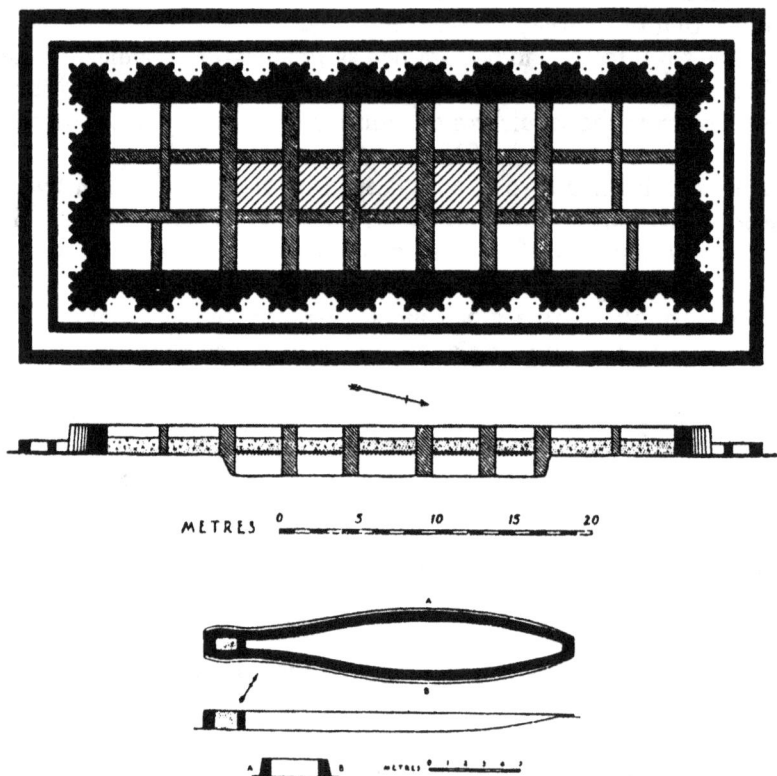

FIG. 43. Mastaba of Hor-Aha and adjacent boat grave at Saqqara, after Emery. (The grave shaft is shaded.)

1. Emery, *Hor-Aha* (Excavations at Saqqara, 1937–8), Cairo, 1939. Both tombs in each case were equally luxuriously furnished, but only one can have contained the royal corpse; there is no conclusive evidence, and no agreement, as to which was the cenotaph.

A mastaba is a huge rectangular structure of mud brick, perhaps a model in more durable material of a wooden palace (Fig. 43). The exterior is decorated by an elaborate alternation of buttresses and recesses—crenellations—that seems to imitate the wooden columns with mats hung between them[1] forming the façade of contemporary palaces. However, similar but less elaborate crenellation is found on the mud brick walls surrounding 'forts' or sacred enclosures, built at Abydos under Dynasty II[2] and is suggested on the town walls, figured on the Hierakonpolis palettes. In the mastaba no real opening pierced the continuous brick wall, though one recess might be treated as a 'false door' before which offerings would be laid. Nor was the 'palace façade' intended to impress mortal eyes. For the whole structure was surrounded with one or two stout brick walls, the innermost separated from the mastaba façade merely by a corridor, sometimes as little as ·75 m. wide. Behind the façade the mastaba was divided by cross walls into a number of chambers that when intact have been found crammed with offerings—jars of grain, wine and oil, stone vases, boxes of metal tools and ornaments, pieces of furniture, and other treasures.

The burial chamber itself lay beneath these rooms in a shaft sunk in the subsoil; it developed at Saqqara as it did in Abydos. In Aha's tomb the mud-brick lined shaft was already divided by cross walls into five compartments and was roofed with great wooden beams. Then from the reign of Udimu the stairway, down which the body was carried, passed under the mastaba wall by a sort of tunnel, but was sealed by one or two portcullis stones, slid into place after the funeral. Then, even before the end of the dynasty, the shaft was made still deeper and the funerary chamber hollowed out in the soft rock underground.

The body of a divine king or a prince was perhaps borne to its final resting place in a funerary barque. In any case such boats have been found ritually interred in the vicinity of several mastabas[3]; Aha's boat grave was built 35 m. north of his mastaba and was 19·3 m. long and 3·2 m. wide at the middle (Fig. 43b).

Burial in mastabas was not confined to pharaohs; the privilege was conceded to high ministers of state and to county governors or princes. In some provincial cemeteries the tombs can be arranged in typological series to illustrate an evolution from the Gerzean

1. Quibell, *Tomb of Hesy* (Excavations at Saqqara, 1911–12), 1913.
2. Ayrton and Currelly, *Abydos*, iii, 1904, c. ii.
3. Emery, *Hor-Aha*, 18.

trench grave to the stairway tomb of the time of Udimu,[1] or from a mud-brick chapel of offerings built above poor trench graves (Fig. 44) to the palace façade mastaba.[2] It seems, however, most

FIG. 44. Small mastaba, Tarkhan.

likely that the developments thus illustrated were inspired by the demands of the royal funerary cult and were only 'later copied by provincials; typologically 'early' tombs, like Fig. 44, are not demonstrably prior in time to the palace façade mastabas.

Still the provincial cemeteries sometimes illustrate developments not yet observed in the royal tombs. In particular, the necropolis of Ezbet el-Wâlda near Helwan, now being excavated for H.M. King Farouk by Zaki Saad,[3] has disclosed early sepulchral architecture in stone. One shaft tomb had been lined with stone slabs set on edge instead of wooden planks. In two stairway tombs, dated by sealings to the reigns of Udimu and Anezib, thick limestone slabs on end not only line the brick-walled shaft, but also replace the brick partitions enclosing the store-rooms (Fig. 45 and Plate XV). The result is something really comparable to the megalithic tombs of western

1. Cf. MacIver, *El Amrah*, 1902, 7; Garstang, *The Third Egyptian Dynasty*; Reisner, *Naga ed-Der*, ii, 14; iii, 6.

2. Petrie, et al., *Tarkhan*, ii, 1913; Reisner (*Development*, 240) dates these small 'mastabas' to Dynasty I.

3. Zaki Saad, *Cahier 3, Supplément aux Annales du Service*, 1947. I have to thank the excavator for permitting me to visit the site, examine the collections, and for unpublished information.

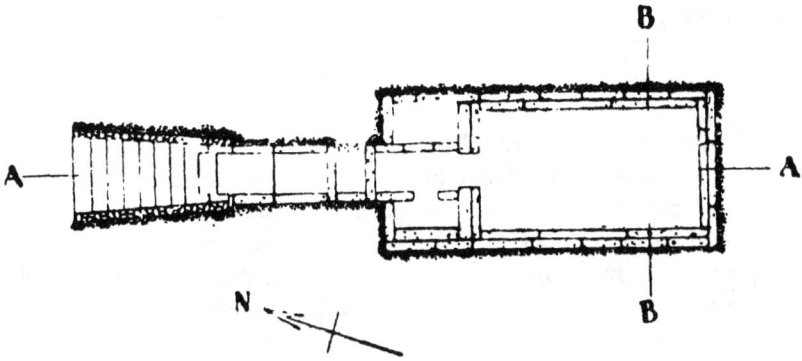

SECTION A A LOOKING EAST

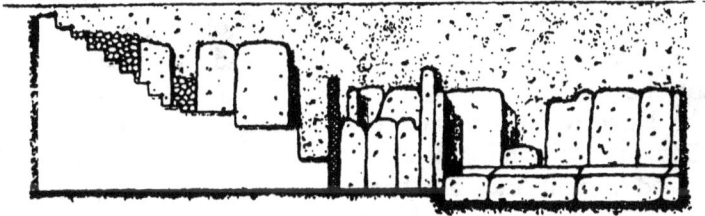

SECTION B.B. LOOKING SOUTH

FIG. 45. Stone lined stairway tomb at Ezbet el-Wâlda near Helawank, after Zi Saad.

and northern Europe, just as the boat graves in the same cemetery and at Saqqara might reveal the inspiration of boat burials of the Bronze Age in Britain and Scandinavia. Even provincial magnates were accompanied in death by a few human servants, buried beside their mastabas, and by animal servants too—asses[1] and, in one case, at Helwan, what appears to be part of a camel also.

The development of royal sepulchral architecture under Dynasties II and III can be well dated by inscribed documents.[2] On the one hand the superstructure was filled up so that the mastaba became a solid mass of brick work. Then under Dynasty III this was translated into stone for pharaohs' tombs, and finally the earliest pyramid, that of Zoser at Saqqara, can be considered six such mastabas piled one on the top of the other. On the other hand the subterranean house was enlarged by the multiplication of separate chambers to resemble more and more the dwelling of the living. Under Dynasty II the earlier wooden roof was replaced by a corbelled vault of brick, that might well have developed naturally. Under Dynasty III even this roofing became superfluous as the chambers were entirely hewn out of the hard rock. This well-dated series corresponds to a logical sequence both of technical advances and of stages in securing greater permanence for the mortuary house and greater security from tomb robbers.

The latter result was not attained. The plunderers tunnelled through the rock and split stone slabs as effectually as they had burrowed in mud brick and burst down wooden planks. But they could not of course ignite the masonry and repeat the fierce conflagrations that have damaged so seriously the contents of the earlier tombs, lined and roofed with timber. Their activity doubtless contributed substantially to the survival of the pharaonic economy, but has compelled the modern archæologists to rely very largely on the furniture of provincial tombs, poorer and therefore less thoroughly ransacked, for details of Early Pharaonic civilization.

The social and economic consequences of the Union of the Two Lands were indeed revolutionary. Zer's household alone at Abydos occupied more than half the number of graves excavated in a whole cemetery during the Gerzean and Amratian phases! A single royal tomb contained more stone vases than a whole predynastic cemetery: 10,000 were recovered intact from Zoser's magazines! Now Engelbach[3] has pointed out that, given internal peace, a single farming family could extract from the fertile soil of Egypt, if rationally ex-

1. Cf. also *Tarkhan*, ii, 6, for the burial of an ass.
2. Edwards, *The Pyramids of Egypt*, 1947, 37–50.
3. 'The Dynastic Race,' *Annales du Service*, xlii, 1943, 211–12; he argues that an aristocracy of conquerors compelled the predynastic peasantry to produce the surplus.

ploited, three times as much food as was needed for domestic consumption. By the unification of Egypt the pharaohs put an end to internecine conflicts (p. 78). With their princes they made the peasants produce the potential surplus. But, however lavish their banquets and extravagant the reserves buried in their tombs, they could not consume it all. Quite a lot was redistributed to support a whole new population of non-farmers, from labourers to clerks, and some was used directly or indirectly to pay for imported raw materials. Thus arose a new urban economy in which industry and trade were added to primary production.

Trade was certainly expanded and regularized. In addition to the

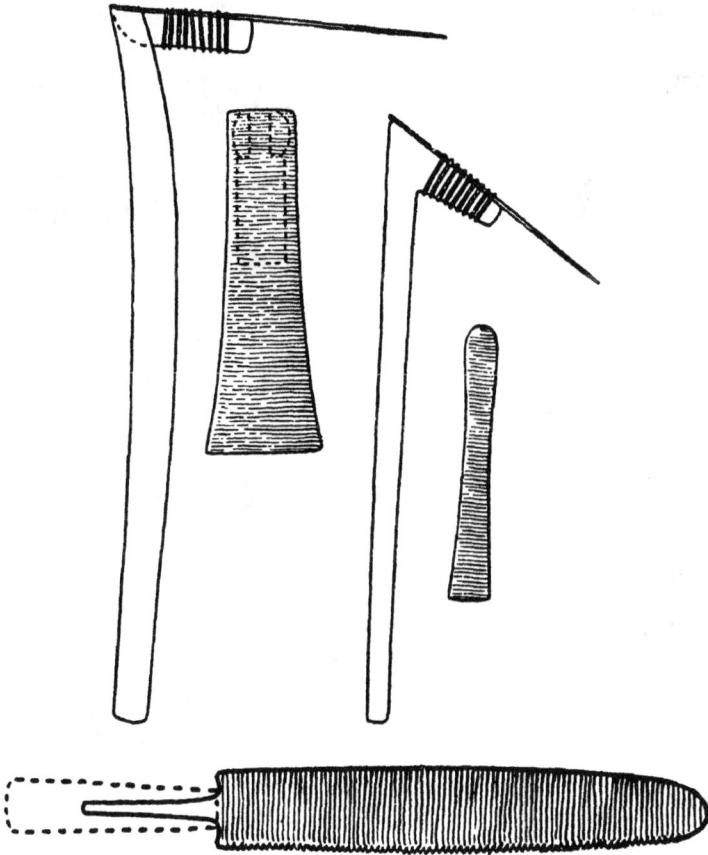

FIG. 46. Copper adzes with wooden handles and saw, Tomb of Hemaka, after Emery, ⅛.

luxury substances imported in predynastic times—such as silver, lapis lazuli and semi-precious stones which continued to arrive in even larger quantities—supplies of timber and metal were effectively organized. The beams needed for palaces and mortuary houses were obtained from Lebanon by sea through Byblos. There a sort of Egyptian colony was established in protodynastic times. The pharaohs themselves sent periodical expeditions to mine copper and turquoise in Sinai, and had their inscriptions carved on the rocks. So there was now plenty of metal to provide tools for craftsmen, weapons for the royal army, vessels for gods and nobles and even trinkets for prosperous peasants.

Specialist coppersmiths standardized a series of distinctive, Egyptian types:[1] (1) as chisels, narrow flat celts with rounded butts (Fig. 46, 2);[2] (2) flat wide axe and adze blades without any splay at the cutting edge (Fig. 46, 1);[2] (3) saws with a tang projecting from the middle of the butt[3] (only from Dynasty V does the tang continue the line of the back) (Fig. 46, 3); (4) flat double-edged knives, narrower than Fig. 28); (5) stout single-barbed 'harpoons' (Fig. 47, 1–2); (6) wiry fish-hooks, generally barbless; (7) midrib daggers with rivet holes (like Fig. 30, 3); (8) spear-heads with

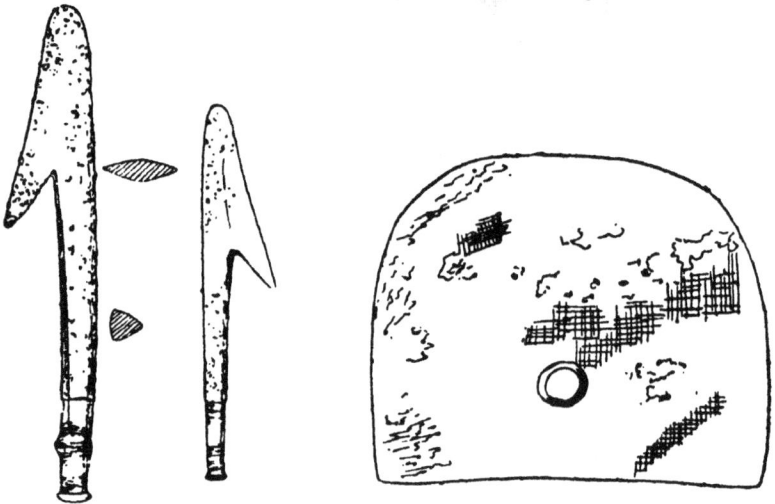

FIG. 47. Early Pharaonic copper harpoons and battle axes.

1. Petrie, *Tools and Weapons*, 1917, for points not otherwise documented.
2. Emery, *Great Tombs*, 1949, 21–33.
3. A single specimen survives, from Tarkhan, but the principle of the folded socket is illustrated by a 'sceptre head' from the Royal Tombs of Abydos.

FIG. 48. Copper chisel with 'flanged' blade from the tomb of Hetep-heres, the mother of Cheops.

a socket[1] formed by folding a broad flat tang;[2] (8) flat battle axes with a convex blade that developed into the distinctive lugged axe (Fig. 47, 3). A crescentic axe with scalloped back (cf. Fig. 91) is depicted on a protodynastic stone vase, but is apparently carried by a foreigner wearing the 'Libyan sheath';[2] (9) tweezers made from a single strip of copper ribbon bent double.

Egyptian metallurgists do not seem to have used tin-bronze;[3] to that extent early pharaonic civilization was still in the Copper Age. Axe-heads were never provided with shaft-holes, like ours. But spear-heads and sceptre-tops were fitted with a socket formed by folding a flat tang, while by Dynasty III chisels were strengthened by hammering up flanges along the sides (Fig. 48),[4] like European flanged celts.

Metal, however, had by no means ousted stone as an industrial material, and flint in particular was superbly worked. The peasants probably had no metal tools at all, but were content with wooden hoes, just possibly equipped with stone blades and wooden sickles, armed with flint teeth; these were of the efficient

FIG. 49. Chisel ended flint pike heads, tomb of King Zer, ⅓.

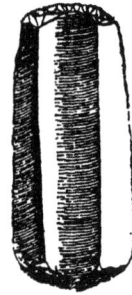

FIG. 50. Flint razor, ½

1. See n. 3, p. 90.
2. Capart, *Primitive Art in Egypt*, fig. 70; Scharff, *Altertümer der Vor- und Frühzeit Ägyptens*, ii, 1929, 79, pl. 22, 108.
3. Forbes, *Metallurgy in Antiquity*, Leiden, 1950, 325–342; cf. Lucas, *JEA.*, xiv, 1928, 97.
4. Boston Museum of Fine Art, *Bulletin*, xxv, Supplement, 1927.

type termed the 'balanced sickle'.[1] Craftsmen, too, used many stone tools—crescentic flint borers for hollowing out stone vases, many awls and perhaps even flint adzes. The royal army was equipped with chisel-ended or tanged arrow-heads, pikes tipped with blades like Fig. 49, piriform maces and throwing sticks. The weapon depicted on the Lion Hunt palette is not a double axe, but a grooved stone attached by a thong round it—perhaps descended from the 'sinkers' of El Omari. Even in royal tombs and in temples we find splendidly fashioned chopping knives, shaped with their tangs from a single tablet of flint (Fig. 32, 6) and flint razors—short blades with neatly rounded (Fig. 50) or squared edges. In the tombs of Hetep-heres, mother of Cheops,[2] such flints were found together with more gaudy but less serviceable copies in gold.

Vessels were also hammered out of copper or precious metal. The ewer with bent spout riveted on (Fig. 51) has already met us in clay

FIG. 51. Copper vases from First Dynasty tomb at Saqqara, ¼, after Emery.

in Gerzean graves and carried by the squire on the Narmer palette; a type with open spout brazed on seems to begin rather later, but is familiar by Dynasty III.[2] The stability of bowls was sometimes

1. Emery, *Tomb of Hemaka* (Excavations at Saqqara), 1938; cf. *Aspects of Archaeology; Essays presented to O. G. S. Crawford*, London, 1951, 41.
2. Boston Museum of Fine Arts, *Bull.*, xxv, Suppl., 1927, 26.

increased by hammering up a small omphalos from the outside so that the base is slightly concave.

Stone vases were now manufactured en masse, but generally in alabaster or basalt, as in the Amratian and Maadian cultures, rather than in the variegated stones preferred by Gerzeans. Even rock crystal, obsidian, and lapis lazuli were used for royal vessels. Practically all the shapes manufactured in metal or pottery were skilfully reproduced in stone, even spouted ewers. Rare, and apparently confined to the beginning of the protodynastic age, are block vases[1]—consisting of two or three cups hollowed out of a single parallelopiped of alabaster and perforated along the upper edge for the attachment of the lid (Fig. 52). The type was popular

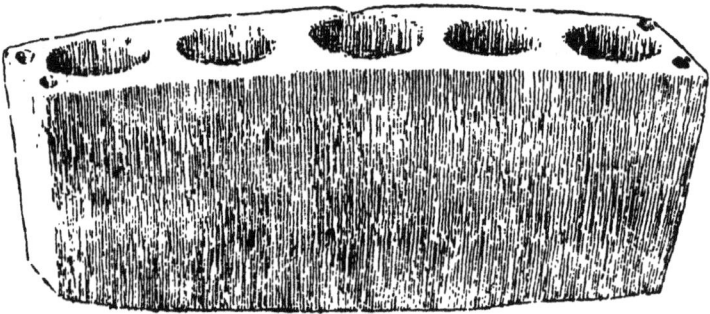

FIG. 52. Stone block vase, Hierakonpolis, ⅓.

in Sumer, Elam, and Crete, and the Egyptian specimen from Abusir el-Meleq is said to be an import from the Aegean.

Fayence, too, was now used for the manufacture of vessels and for models of boats and other objects as well as for beads and amulets.

Pots were now mass produced, too, but without the aid of the true, fast wheel. Most vessels are coarse, straw-tempered and red or pale drab in colour. Many of these Rough forms are foreshadowed in Maadian types. But a rough bowl with bevelled rim[2] like Fig. 62, 1, has Mesopotamian analogies. Of course, the well-to-do now used vessels of metal or stone. But even in royal tombs we find vases of

1. Quibell, *Hierakonpolis*, i, pl. xxxi, 3–4; Scharff, *Abusir el-Meleq*, 41.
2. Petrie, *Corpus of Prehistoric Pottery*, type R 24; the date, S.D. 63–4, may be too high, as the type lasts perhaps as late as Dynasty VI (Brunton, *Qau and Badari*, ii, pl. lxxvi, 6 E. Cf. Emery, *Hemaka*, pl. 27, 17.

fine red ware, including pedestalled bowls and (under Dynasty III) a round-bottomed carinated pot with a narrow mouth surrounded with a moulding or very short neck[1] that recalls vases from megalithic tombs in Spain and the British Isles.

Early Pharaonic earthenware was hardly ever decorated, but a few vases of First Dynasty age were coated with a genuine glaze while others were still painted in the style of Gerzean Decorated vases.[2] Then there is a small group of handled jugs adorned with designs in shiny paint.[3] Though some were certainly made in Egypt, most must be either imported from Syria–Palestine or made by Syrian potters in Egypt since the shape and technique can be matched there in 'Early Bronze II'. Spindle-shaped flasks[4] of hard red 'metallic' ware (Fig. 53)

FIG. 53. Imported (?) 'Syrian' jugs from 1st Dynasty tomb (Udimu) at Abydos, ¼.

also found in First Dynasty tombs likewise seem to have been imported from Syria or Palestine, doubtless as containers for olive oil. So were vases of combed ware found in fragments in the Abydos cemetery. Finally, a few vessels of pinkish clay, partially covered with a red wash and then adorned with lattice patterns, executed with the burnishing tool,[5] seem to have been manufactured in Palestine or

1. From the tomb of Hetepheres, not yet published.
2. *Annales du Service*, xxxix, 1939, 770 (Abydos); glazed vases from reign of Udimu (Petrie, *Royal Tombs*, ii, 36).
3. Emery, *Great Tombs*, 121; Bonnet, *Ein frühgeschichtliche Gräberfeld bei Abusir*, 1928; Petrie, *Royal Tombs*, ii, 9—tomb of Zer.
4. Petrie recognized the foreign character of the ware, but called it 'Aegean'. Its true source was identified by Frankfort, *Studies*, i, 107–8.
5. Petrie, *Tarkhan*, i, 1913, 17, pl. xvi, 4.

Phœnicia where the same 'lattice burnished ware' was very popular in Early Bronze II.

Among the products of the carpenters, now equipped with copper tools, it suffices to mention couches standing on well-carved bulls' legs,[1] a device appearing as early as S.D. 66 or under Dynasty O.

Among a fantastic wealth of toilet articles, jewelry, and charms, space permits mention of only a fraction.

Slate palettes in animal form, but generally highly conventionalized, survive till the beginning of the Dynastic age, and indeed in a magnified version serve as a vehicle for the records of the Falcon

Fig. 54. Figures of apes in stone and fayence, about $\frac{1}{4}$.

clan and of its princes, but the normal type after S.D. 70 is rectangular. Among the ornaments spiral beads of stone burnished with gold occur between S.D. 65 and 72[2] and iron beads[3] are dated to 72 likewise. Under the First Dynasty fayence is quite common and a spirally gadrooned long barrel bead (Plate XI*b*) is very characteristic. The original form is given by coiled gold wire which was copied by engraving on lapis. A large number of new animals, notably apes and lions (Figs. 54, 55), appear as pendants, amulets

1. Petrie, *Prehistoric Egypt*, 10.
2. Dated specimens in University College, London.
3. Petrie, etc., *The Labyrinth, Gerzeh*, 1911, 15.

or playing pieces.[1] Finally, engraved cylinders of stone, ivory or fayence that had occurred sporadically even in Gerzean times became common under the first pharaohs. But now they are rolled on the clay sealing jars, just as in Mesopotamia, to mark ownership

FIG. 55. Gaming piece from Royal Cemetery, Abydos.

of the vessel's contents; for they are inscribed with the owner's name.

Indeed, not the least important of the full-time specialists supported by the newly concentrated social surplus were the clerks. A scribe's palette with compartments for red and black ink was actually found in a domestic's tomb, attached to a First Dynasty mastaba,[2] and products of their craft are abundant. To the clerks of the united State must have fallen the task not only of keeping records or perpetuating in writing magic spells, but also of establishing a common convention for the transmission of ideas. The vehicle was, of course, pictographic. Indeed, the earliest Egyptian hieroglyphs are less simplified and more easily recognizable pictures than the comparable pictograms of Sumer and Elam. Still, even in documents of Dynasty O they are already stylized in form and invested with conventional meanings as ideograms.

For the formal style of the signs the clerks could draw on conventions of glyptic and graphic art already elaborated by ivory-carvers and vase-decorators. For the symbolic use of pictures, the emblems of nomes, conventionally standing for a county and its inhabitants, provided a model. On the oldest surviving documents the script is indeed highly pictorial. The king's 'name'—a scorpion, a nar-fish, a fighter, drawn in a palace gate under the wing of a falcon—is a pictogram as much as an ideogram. The falcon (Horus) may, in fact, wear the Double Crown or wield a mattock! The

1. Petrie, *Prehistoric Egypt*, 10.
2. Petrie, *Gizeh and Rifeh*, 5, and pl. iii, A.

97

scorpion or the nar-fish might indeed be the personal guardian spirit of the king rather than a mere designation. The invention of the hieroglyphic script would then be the equation of such a picture with a sound of the spoken language.[1] That is surely exemplified in the addition to the nar-fish picture of a sign that can have had no ideographic meaning as describing the personality of Menes (Narmer), but presumably served to represent the spoken syllable m.r in his name.

In the sequel the Egyptian clerks, instead of inventing more purely conventional symbols to stand for names or concepts—like vizier, exalted—that cannot be denoted by self-explanatory symbols, used the pictures phonetically to stand for the sound (or initial sound) of the object's spoken name and thus spelled out the appropriate spoken word. This stage seems to have been reached under Narmer, but is not attested earlier.[2] Very gradually under Dynasties I and II the orthography was standardized, and then for practical business the pictograms were simplified in a conventional cursive script, the hieratic. But for ritual and funerary inscriptions detailed and realistic pictographic characters were retained, and in both scripts ideograms continued to be used side by side with spelled words.

It may well be that the standardization of pictographic conventions was largely carried out in Lower and Middle Egypt since more mastaba tombs, belonging to kings and high dignitaries, occur at Saqqara, Giza, Tarkhan and other northern cemeteries than at Abydos or elsewhere in the south. It may even turn out that writing developed faster in the north than in the south. But the oldest specimens of writing from Lower Egypt are vases from Tura and Helwan respectively bearing the names of Scorpion and Ka, kings of Upper Egypt![3] There is no excuse for the assumption that the hieroglyphic script was introduced into Egypt from without. The same should apply to the remaining elements of pharaonic material culture.

It is possible to present the rise of Egyptian civilization as a self-contained process as we have just done. But de Morgan, when he

1. Gardiner in *JEA.*, ii, 1915, 61–75.
2. A sign, used as a character in the later script, occurs on a late Gerzean palette, dated S.D. 60–63 (MacIver, *El Amrah*, 38, pl. viii, 2), but might be still just the emblem of a clan or deity.
3. Junker, *Turah*, 1912, 7; Zaki Saad, *Cahier*, 3, 111 (tomb 1627).

first described the predynastic and early pharaonic cultures, alleged that the latter was introduced into Egypt by Asiatic invaders, masters of Sumerian arts like metallurgy and writing. Petrie likewise postulated a 'dynastic race' and interpolated a Semainian period to contain the conquest and a Semainian culture to result from it. The archæological record, however, leaves no room for a period between the Gerzean and Dynasty O, between the Painted Tomb of Hierakonpolis and that of Ka, or between the cemeteries of Maadi and Turah, as Miss Kantor has shown in detail.[1] Nor does it disclose a culture which is no longer Gerzean nor Maadian, but yet not pharaonic.

Nor can we point to any culture outside Egypt that was technically and economically on a par with Gerzean or Maadian and pregnant with the potentialies realized under the First Dynasty. On the other hand, on the anthropological side Dr. Derry[2] has recognized first in Third Dynasty tombs and now also in the earlier tombs near Helwan, a new racial type, the Giza type, distinguished from the familiar predynastic people by taller stature and a capacious, oval, instead of a narrow, pentagonoid, skull. But the taller stature, and possibly even the oval skull, have now been recognized in neolithic Merimde and El Omari. So Derry now prefers to contrast a 'northern' with a 'southern race' rather than a 'dynastic' with a 'predynastic' one.

New ethnic elements from outside the valley may well have filtered in during and after Gerzean times. Such may have contributed to the unification of Egypt, but they certainly did not introduce ready made a culture superior to the native predynastic. On the other hand, the archæological record clearly reflects relations with foreign parts that might well result in stimuli from exotic ideas and inventions. Owing to the natural deficiencies of the Nile valley Egypt had to import timber and metals as well as luxury substances. Cycladic marble, olive oil, and perhaps exotic wines in foreign pots,

---

1. 'Gerzean or Semainian,' *JNES*., iii, 1944, 110–136.
2. *Cahier* 3, *Supplément aux Annales du Service*, 1947, 250 ff. At Tura the skulls from graves assigned to Dynasties O to II belonged to the 'predynastic race', as did those of menials from Abydos, but according to Junker ('Rassen u. Reichen in der Urzeit Ägyptens,' *Anzeiger Akad. d. Wissen, Wien, phil.-hist. Kl.*, 1949, 485–490) the Giza type is represented already under Dynasty I, at Helwan, Saqqara and Abydos and also in the 'neolithic' graves of El Omari. But the Maadi skulls look to me pentagonoid and those from Heliopolis are called 'negroid'.

silver, lapis lazuli, obsidian and so on were demonstrably imported. In return stone vases carved in Egypt under the early pharaohs were offered in the temples at Byblos and Ai, Early Pharaonic stone vases found their way to Crete, too, and the Fish-standard, borne by boats on Decorated vases, reappears on Cycladic ships.

With imported substances and manufactures could come devices prompted by a different environment and ideas evoked by other historical conjunctures. Now lapis lazuli at least presumably reached Egypt through Mesopotamia, and there Sumerian society was, just at this time, emerging from barbarism to civilization. A fertilizing interchange of ideas between two nascent civilizations was perfectly feasible and is actually likely. Already during Gerzean times we recognized the Mesopotamian affinities of (1) certain spouted vases and (2) cylinder seals. To these were added in the Final Gerzean and Proto-dynastic, (3) the 'foreign' boats, (4) the dress of a 'hero', (5) a new breed of dog, (6) the use of mace-heads as vehicles for commemorative and votive carvings, (7) several artistic motives, notably the antithetical group, the double-headed beast and monsters with intertwined necks. Under Dynasty I the series of analogies is completed by (8) crenellated brick architecture, (9) several ceramic forms, such as bevel-rimmed bowls and pot-stands, and (10) the phonetic use of pictographic characters.

It is by no means certain that all these common features were derived from Sumer. The Sumerian and Egyptian scripts did indeed both start in pictograms, but the individual signs are as different as they well could be; the only concrete agreement is the use of some pictograms as phonograms, in each case first perhaps to represent proper names. The recessed brick-work of the mastabas is completely explicable as a translation into brick of the wooden palace façade. Even the cylinder seals might have developed on the Nile out of carved tubular beads[1] or still better out of carved reeds. There can be no question of civilization being introduced into backward Egypt from precocious Sumer. On the contrary, now that Sumerian chronology has been so deflated that the Royal Tombs of Ur must be equated not with the Abydos cemetery, but with the grave of Hetep-heres or even Vth Dynasty sepulchres, Egyptian civilization appears richer than contemporary Early Dynastic Sumerian.

Even so, Sumer could claim a technical superiority in some respects. The wheeled cart and the potter's wheel, for instance, were

1. Scharff, *Altertümer der Vor- und Frühzeit*, ii, 1929, 96.

current there much earlier than in Egypt.[1] Egyptian metal tools and weapons are quite easily distinguishable from the Sumerian, so that unilateral imitation is excluded. Some cross-fertilization surely took place, but relations were hardly one-sided. To estimate the respective contributions of either partner as well as to weigh the claims of independent evolution versus diffusion, the rise of civilization in the Tigris–Euphrates valley must be examined.

1. No wheeled vehicles were used in Egypt till the New Kingdom, and down to Dynasty III most vases were certainly made without the wheel, though Myers (*Cemeteries of Armant*, 177) claims to observe wheel marks on Gerzean pots.

CHAPTER VI

THE COLONIZATION OF MESOPOTAMIA

THE Tigris–Euphrates valley has far less unity than the valley of the Nile. Its lower reaches, Babylonia proper, roughly from the level of Baghdad to the Persian Gulf, are indeed economically dependent on the rivers; only their waters, by natural inundation or canalized irrigation, make settled life possible in those latitudes. This economic unity had eventually to find its political expression as it did at last under Hammurabi. But further north the lowland plain is traversed by other streams—the Diyala and the two Zabs, flowing into the Tigris, the Khabur and the Balikh, tributaries of the Euphrates—each an economically independent system. And here, too, in Assyria and Syria, the rivers traverse a zone still visited by winter rain-storms from the Atlantic sufficient to make cereal cultivation without irrigation possible if slightly precarious.

There are further differences in climate, and consequently in flora. The southern portion of Babylonia, Sumer, enjoys a relatively mild winter, and here the date-palm is at home. Even in northern Babylonia, the ancient Akkad, the winter is bitterly cold, with heavy frosts every night. In Assyria and Syria snow may fall. Here there grew no date-palms to tie man to the soil, but instead vines and fruit-trees, which are no less efficacious.

Not only is Mesopotamia much less homogeneous geographically than Egypt, she is also much more exposed. Egypt, surrounded by desert, is easily defensible, and from the beginning of the historical period successfully closed her doors against invaders, save for brief interludes like the Hyksos episode, for 2,000 years. To the east of the Tigris lie the valleys of the Zagros Mountains and the Iranian plateau, to the north Kurdistan and Armenia, fertile enough to nourish a prolific population. The overflow of such upon the valley is easy, and the history of Mesopotamia is punctuated with raids from, or periods of domination by, Elam, Gutium, Awan, Hittites, Assyrians, Chaldæans. No natural barrier separates Babylonia from

the Arabian Desert. And there roams a mobile and warlike population, ever liable to be forced by drought on to the irrigated lands.
Some authorities would derive from this quarter both the Akkadians
and the Amorites.

Thirdly, Babylonia is even less self-sufficing than Egypt. The
treeless alluvium stretches for miles on either side of the rivers. There
are, indeed, limestone ridges, providing chert and poor building
stone, but the Mesopotamian desert is not covered with flint nodules
nor are abundant supplies of excellent flint available in accessible
wadis as in Egypt. Hence, not only timber (apart from palm-stems)
and good stone for building, but even the material for the simplest
tools must be imported. Such a situation favours the rise of a
commercial and industrial civilization. At the same time, where for
tool-making even decent stone had to be imported, the superiority
of copper would be quickly appreciated; in view of its greater
durability it would be found relatively cheaper than flint or obsidian,
which give just as sharp a tool for a single operation.

The surviving archæological record contains no evidence of
climatic changes comparable to those implied by the discoveries at
Tasa and in the Fayum; the flora and fauna depicted on the earliest
figured monuments are those appropriate to an arid climate such as
rules to-day. Such advantages as the pluvial period conferred on
Mesopotamia had already passed away before the graphic record
begins; but after all its beginning is long after the earliest settlement
in the valley. The land, in any case, has changed considerably even in
historical times. The deposit from the two rivers is still silting up
the head of the Persian Gulf so rapidly that on one estimate the
coastline advances about $1\frac{1}{2}$ miles a century. In the seventh century
B.C. the Kerkha, which now loses itself in the sands and marshes
above Basra, debouched directly into the Persian Gulf; Sennacherib
had to sail 160 km. from the mouth of the Euphrates to reach its
estuary. At the beginning of historical times a series of tidal lagoons
extended inland almost to the foot of the limestone ridge on which
stand the ruins of Eridu, the first royal city of Sumerian tradition.
The land of Sumer must have been a region of swamps such as
subsists to-day round Basra, where date palms grew wild. Since then
the deposit left by the inundation has been steadily raising the level
of the land till to-day, even at Kish, the surface of the plain lies
25 feet above 'virgin soil'.

It was precisely in this newest land of Mesopotamia that written
history began. Here were created that peculiar civilization termed

Sumerian, the social, religious, and legal ideas, the epigraphic and artistic conventions that dominated the whole valley of the two rivers for three millennia; long after the Sumerians had lost their national identity and their language was dead, the cultural edifice they had reared was imposed upon and adopted by their conquerors and neighbours in Hither Asia, just as Roman ideas, law and speech were accepted throughout medieval Europe. But Sumer cannot have been the scene of the 'Neolithic Revolution'; links with the Old Stone Age cannot be expected in this new land. Its first inhabitants must have come from elsewhere, from older land, perhaps the steppe zone to the north-west or the mountains to the east, where urial, mouflon, and goat roam wild and where cereals reputedly grow spontaneously. Now the culture of the earliest agricultural colonists of Sumer is, in fact, duplicated in many farming villages from the foothills of Assyria westward across the steppe to the Euphrates. But in the north these villages occupy the sites of earlier settlements, disclosing a culture that is presumably prior in time, if not ancestral, to the oldest culture of Sumer. It is accordingly legitimate to begin our survey of Mesopotamian origins in Assyria and Syria. That region is at least a possible cradle for stock-breeding and agriculture. In the fifth and fourth millennia it was certainly no desert nor treeless steppe but rather a parkland; even in the IInd millennium plenty of trees grew there. Perennial streams and springs were relatively abundant, but not unlimited as in temperate Europe. So permanent settlements were restricted and remained continuously occupied from prehistoric to historic times.

Perhaps, however, the earliest farming hamlets of all should be sought, not on the plain itself, but on foot-hills and spurs overlooking it. On a spur of the Kurdish uplands, Qalat Jarmo, above the valley of the Touq Chae, a tributary of the Tigris, Braidwood,[1] in 1950, began the excavation of a series of superimposed hamlets, that looks very near the beginning of food-production. The rural economy permitted permanent occupation of the site. Grains of wheat or barley, querns and sickle-teeth prove agriculture while 95 per cent of the animal bones belong to domestic or domesticable species—sheep (or goat), oxen, pig, and dog. Oblate perforated stones might be mace-heads, but the excavator regards them rather as weights for digging-sticks, and no other relics unambiguously served as weapons. The farmers built simple houses of compacted clay—

---

1. *Antiquity*, xxiv, 1950, 190–6; cf. *AJA.*, liii, 1949, 50–1.

pisé—with floors of reeds, the ruins of which eventually formed a small tell, some 5 m. high, in which eight levels were distinguished.

Stone celts, sharpened by grinding, were used as axe or adze blades. Blades of chert and obsidian, mostly 'microlithic' in size but scarcely retouched, served as knives and sickle-teeth or might have armed darts or arrows. Chaff-tempered sherds were found only in the uppermost level. Previously pottery had been unknown though clay-lined basins, scooped in the floor, were sometimes given an internal skin of pottery by lighting fires in them (cf. p. 227). On the other hand, vessels were already manufactured out of variegated stones. Finally, figurines of animals and a seated female were modelled in clay, but less than a third of these were fired.

The flint-work is not stated to link Jarmo either to the Upper Palæolithic Gravettian, represented in the cave of Zarzi only fifteen miles away, nor to the western Natufian, and so gives no clue to the settlers' origin nor an upper date for their arrival. Conversely, the pottery from the uppermost level has not yet been equated with any one of the stratified wares of the valley. Hence, no archæologist can say that Jarmo reveals the starting point of the established sequence of Mesopotamian cultures nor even that it is earlier than Hassuna or Samarra. It might, theoretically, be a retarded highland contemporary of even the Halafian culture of the plain. On the other hand, the quantity of radio-active carbon (C14) contained in a shell from Jarmo points to an absolute date for the occupation round about 5000 B.C.

The first cultivators of Mesopotamian soil, in the strict sense, are therefore known in 1950 almost exclusively from Hassuna,[1] in Assyria, west of the Tigris. There, on a plain where Atlantic rains even to-day suffice to water the corn of Kurdish villages, but at the junction of two perennial streams, the first recognized farmers settled or at least encamped. Of houses nothing remains. But large jars of coarse pottery, generously tempered with chaff and imperfectly fired to a pale pink, were sunk in the virgin soil presumably for the storage of food. That they held grain may be inferred from the discovery of rough saddle querns. Moreover, heavy, flaked implements of quartzite and sandstone (Fig. 56, 1–2) may have been used as hoe-blades in tilling the soil; they were somehow mounted with the aid of bitumen, but may really have been adzes. Bones of cattle and sheep or goats presumably belong to domestic stock.

1. Seton Lloyd and Fuad Safar, *JNES.*, iv, 1945, 257–280.

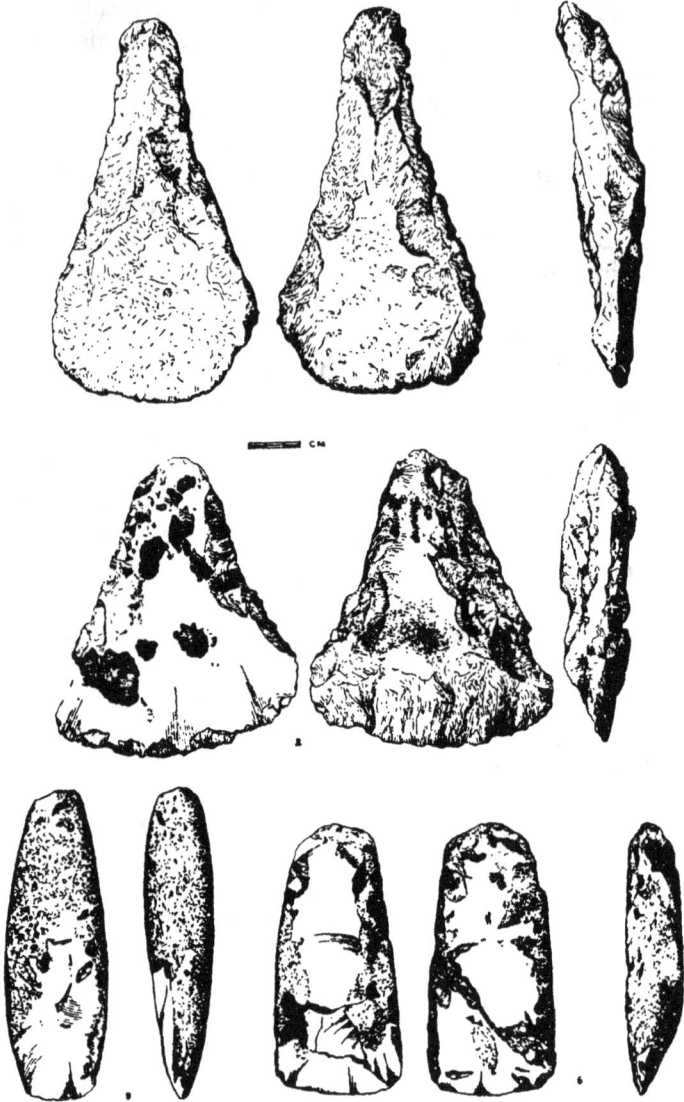

FIG. 56. Flaked stone 'hoe blades' and ground stone celts, Hassuna, after Lloyd and Safar.

Gazelles and asses, or rather onager, were hunted. The huntsman's normal weapon was the sling as ammunition for which clay bullets were baked in the standard form, familiar several thousand years later in lead. But a few beautifully worked points of obsidian,

9 cm. or more long, may have armed reed darts. Typical arrow-heads are conspicuously absent. For carpentry celts of fine-grained rock with polished edges served as axes or perhaps only as adzes (Fig. 56, 3). The settlement seems typically neolithic in that all essential equipment could be supplied from local materials. But in fact obsidian was already imported from Armenia or some still unlocated nearer source.

This first, and apparently transitory settlement, Ia, does not indeed illustrate the very first steps in food production, though certainly nearer thereto than anything yet known in the Tigris–Euphrates valley. But it may well represent the lineal precursor of the completely sedentary peasant villages that succeeded it on the same site. Ruins of six superimposed villages of substantial adobe houses—Ib to II termed 'Archaic' and III to V, 'Standard'—overlie the 'Neolithic' encampment of Hassuna Ia. They must represent a long period during which the site was continuously inhabited so that their builders must have elaborated some system of fallowing to preserve the soil's fertility.

While from the earliest village only fragmentary curvilinear walls survive, level II already boasts rectangular houses, apparently divided into several rooms. In the Standard villages the houses

FIG. 57. Isometric view of Hassuna Standard farm after Lloyd and Safar.

consisted of three or four modest rooms, probably grouped around a court (Fig. 57). The wooden doors of the houses were already pivoted on socketed stones, in the manner customary throughout historical times. Round clay ovens for baking bread stood in the courtyards or sometimes indoors. Grain was stored in the compounds in bins, shaped at first just like the 'Neolithic' jars, but made now of unbaked mud, mixed with straw and externally coated with bitumen.

The grain was now reaped with curved wooden sickles, armed with stumpy flint flakes fixed in bitumen so as to overlap. The 'hoes'— of chert—were less carefully shaped than the 'neolithic', but ground stone celts and obsidian blades were still used, but not the finely worked dart-heads. The only weapon attested is, indeed, the sling. The most distinctive novelty is the manufacture of well-fired painted vases. The ware is now generally tempered with grit rather than chaff and fired to a pale buff hue. Vases are normally flat-bottomed, but the repertory of shapes is small—globular vases with short straight necks and open bowls, sometimes oval in plan. On the clear clay surface, sometimes slipped or burnished, simple rectilinear patterns were painted in warm black. Then in the 'Standard Ware' the painted strokes were combined with incised lines, herring-bones or triangles, or the whole design was incised on the pale wet clay without painted embellishment (Pl. XIV). Together with the Hassuna Standard vases appear a few vessels in another style and fabric that is more widely distributed and is conventionally known as Samarra ware from the site where it was first identified.[1] Samarra pottery is always slipped, fired to a pale pink or more often to a greenish hue and decorated with 'basketry' patterns—i.e. such as could easily be produced in plaiting coloured straw. The arrangement of the patterns in zones is likewise proper to basketry and even such shapes as the 'beaker' of Plate XVIII, *b*, a form already encountered in Egypt, are inspired by the same art. With the geometrical basketry patterns are combined amusing animal figures which are deliberately stylized and translated into angular, 'basketry' shapes (Fig. 58). Though found from Sakçe gözü, west of the Euphrates, to beyond the Tigris in Assyria, Samarra[2] ware seems always mixed with distinct local fabrics and so cannot be used to define a culture.

There is no direct evidence that the Hassuna villagers used copper

1. Herzfeld, *Die vorgeschichtlichen Töpfereien von Samarra*, Berlin, 1930. Note that the copper and iron objects here described have subsequently been dismissed by the excavators as Islamic intrusions (Herzfeld, 'Steinzeitlicher Hügel bei Persepolis,' *Iranische Denkmäler*, i, 1932).

2. Braidwood, *JNES.*, iii, 1944, 48–68. At Baghouz, nearly opposite Mari, on the Middle Euphrates, Samarra ware seems unmixed with other fabrics, but no details are known as to its non-ceramic associations.

in any form, though Lloyd and Safar term the phase 'proto-chalcolithic'. But they did import, besides obsidian, turquoise and possibly amethyst and perforated these and other stones for use as beads. Like most other early peasant societies, the people of Hassuna

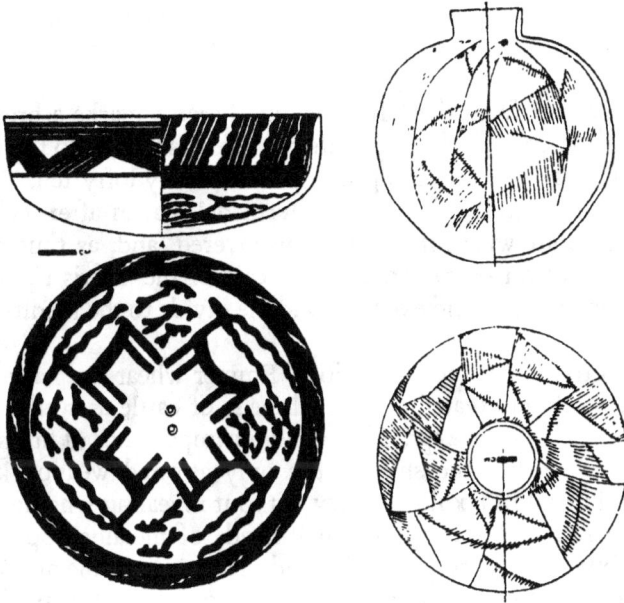

FIG. 58. Samarra bowl and Hassuna-incised jar after Lloyd and Safar.

modelled female figurines in clay. Infants were buried among the houses at Hassuna, but at Samarra there was a regular cemetery of contracted or flexed skeletons.

There is no reason to believe that the culture of Hassuna was brought to Assyria ready made. It might have developed there when, in that favourable environment, primitive farmers had worked out a rural economy compatible with sedentary village life. And when they had, the consequent multiplication of population would compel the occupation of new land. It is true that painted pottery vaguely like Hassuna archaic turns up even west of the Euphrates basin at Sakçe gözü and Mersin and again in Palestine, while the incised herring bone patterns of the Standard ware remind us even of Merimde. Conversely, a few sherds of black burnished ware technically akin to those found alone in the lower 'neolithic' levels of Sakçe-gözü[1] and Mersin but persisting there in later phases, have been found at Hassuna. That does not, of course, mean that the neolithic culture of the Levant coasts lies at the basis of agricultural life east of the watershed. But the wide distribution of clear and painted wares means that the Hassuna cultures have as much relation to the west as to the east; if not domesticated in Assyria, their cereals and sheep are as likely to come from Amanus or Carmel as from the Iranian plateau.

The pottery from the VIth level at Hassuna marks a break with old traditions, and in the sequel the village was moved to the western flank of what was becoming an inconveniently lofty tell. The new culture is defined by the pottery, termed Halafian after Tel Halaf[2] on the Khabur where it was first discovered, and, as thus defined, it extends from the Iranian foothills east of the Tigris right across the parkland steppe and even beyond the divide to the Mediterranean coast.

An all round advance is obvious. Emmer wheat and barley[3] were now certainly cultivated and two breeds of cattle as well as sheep, goats, and pigs[4] were kept. The economic importance of hunting was undiminished, but the sling is the only attested weapon. Spindle whorls illustrate a textile industry without revealing whether it were wool or flax that was spun. Small beads of metallic copper[5] now occur, but these were probably made from native metal. Obsidian and chert remained the normal materials for knives and sickle-teeth; ground stone celts mounted in knee-shafts served as adzes[6]; chert was still flaked for heavy 'hoe-blades' as before. But indirectly the industrial use of metal might be inferred from the scene on the vase shown in Plate XIX, if this really represent a wheeled vehicle; for a wheel can hardly be made without a metal saw. But this interpretation is unlikely. Halafian potters did not employ the wheel, and spoked wheels are otherwise unknown before 2000 B.C.

1. Christian, *Altertumskunde der Zweistromländer*, 92, wished perversely to start the whole Mesopotamian sequence with a 'Sakçe-gözü culture', which is in reality foreign to Mesopotamia.
2. Von Oppenheim, *Der Tell Halaf*, Berlin, 1943. For points not otherwise documented below see Perkins, *CAEM*.
3. *Iraq*, ii, 15.
4. *Iraq*, viii, 124.
5. *Iraq*, iii, 26.
6. Mallowan, *Iraq*, ii, 102, found only the stain left by the haft on the earth, which naturally did not show the relation of the edge to the haft.

Still really beautiful and technically excellent pottery is the outstanding product of the culture and period. The ware is fine, creamy buff, covered with a slip and generally polished. The vases are decorated with elaborate patterns in red and warm black, sometimes with white superadded, in a true glaze paint, owing its lustre to the fusion of alkali silicates. The varied shapes reveal a masterly appreciation of the potentialities of clay. Vessels have usually flat, sometimes even concave bases while some stand upon hollow pedestals. Angular, carinated forms were popular, notably the beautiful Arpachiya milk bowl that looks like a copy of a beaten metal dish. Stippling was a favourite decorative technique; chequers and scale patterns and—in the centres of dishes—rosettes or Maltese squares —were common motives (Pl. XVI, *a*). But these geometric themes are combined with conventionalized bulls' heads—*bucrania*—or with stylized equids and cervids, as in Samarra ware. Naturally, this rich and varied repertory of shapes was not achieved all at once; at Arpachiya Mallowan could trace through five or six superimposed occupations a development culminating in the gorgeous polychromy of the topmost stratum.

Of course, this admirable pottery was fired in proper kilns fragmentary remains of which have been found at Arpachiya and Carchemish[1]; a firing temperature as high as 1200° was sometimes attained. Indeed, such is the technical and artistic perfection of Halafian pottery that some think it must have been produced by professional craftsmen. Perhaps these authorities underestimate the high general level attained in domestic arts and crafts, like embroidery, among peasant societies to-day and would have to conclude that 'Persian rugs' were manufactured by full-time specialists who bought their food in shops. Still a building in the latest Halafian level at Arpachiya, regarded by the excavator as a potter's workshop, was more richly furnished with other commodities than the remaining houses.

The Halafians were skilled at working obsidian and other hard stones for the manufacture of vases and also of beads and amulets. The talismans include bulls heads, birds, double-axes, crescents, a gabled house roof, stone versions of Natufian winged beads (Fig. 105), . . . all very skilfully carved and all, of course, perforated for suspension and fashioned, towards the end of the period, even in obsidian, but at first perhaps only in soft stone or shell. At the same

1. *Iraq*, i, 1934, 148; for the temperature see Tobler, *Gawra*, ii, 160.

time simpler pendants were engraved with geometrical designs, like those painted on the vases, and then used as 'seals': the pattern was multiplied by impressing the carved pendant on a lump of soft clay. Doubtless the patterns were symbols endowed with a magic potency. In historical times, however, in Mesopotamia as in Egypt, the impression of a seal on a lump of clay, affixed to the cord fastening a jar-stopper or a packet, marked the contents as the property of the seal's owner. So even in Halafian times the transfer of a magic pattern to such a clay sealing may have had the effect of 'putting a tabu on' the contents and so enforcing recognition of 'proprietary rights' therein. If so, the acquisition of 'riches' and exchange of commodities would be practicable and socially commended activities.

Exchange of goods between communities, i.e. external trade, is certainly illustrated not only by the extensive use of obsidian in all Halafian villages but most strikingly by the discovery at Chagar Bazar[1] on the Khabur of a shell of *Cypræa vitellus*, brought thither from the Persian Gulf. Indeed, some measure of intercommunal specialization may be inferred from a reputedly Halafian community, engaged in quarrying obsidian at Shamiramalti, near Lake Van.[2]

Few details are available as to Halafian domestic architecture or town planning, but organized communal works are illustrated by cobbled streets joining up the houses of Arpachiya. Here, as also at Gawra—XX, were built mysterious circular buildings with a very low, domed roof, that are usually termed *tholoi*; some have long rectangular chambers attached to them. The foundations for the adobe walls and vault were sometimes of stone, sometimes of stone and clay and sometimes of adobe alone, while the *tholoi* vary in internal diameter from 4 m. to 6.5 m. Mallowan and most subsequent writers attribute to the *tholoi* some unknown ritual function, but use as store-houses or granaries would seem theoretically possible.

More convincingly classified as ritual are the female figurines that the Halafians, like their Hassunan precursors and the Merimdians and Badarians of Egypt, modelled in clay and, towards the end of the period, even carved in soft stone. Rough animal models may also fall within the same category. Finally, the dead were interred, normally in the flexed position, and apparently among the houses rather than in regular cemeteries outside the villages.

1. *Iraq*, iii, 10.
2. *BASOR.*, 78, 1940, 32.

In Assyria the development of Halafian industry and art can be followed thourgh several stratigraphical and typological phases. In the Khabur-Balikh basin such development is not so clearly documented; beyond the Euphrates at Hama or Ugarit the Halafian culture seems to arrive fully formed and mature to replace or mingle with cultures characterized by quite different self-coloured pottery and by bows-and-arrows instead of slings. In Iran no close analogue is known though we shall meet some similar decorative motives at least in Sumer. Hence, Dr. Perkins reasonably concludes that the Halafian culture developed in Assyria. But even there, after the long development leading up to the polychrome phase in ceramic art, it was eventually replaced by another culture named after al'Ubaid in Sumer, which from the æsthetic and architectural standpoint seems inferior.

The Ubaid culture in northern Mesopotamia thus appears not only to mark a break with the Halafian tradition but also a decline: the distinctive pottery is no longer slipped and polished and has been so highly fired that the surface is generally greenish. It is still decorated with painted patterns, but no longer in polychromy, while the repertory of motives is poorer and the patterns themselves less pleasing. Again, reed huts appear to have replaced adobe buildings at Nineveh and some other sites.

But even in these domains and in the north the appearance of decline is quite deceptive. The Ubaid potters displayed a fuller mastery over their material than the Halafians and turned out a wider variety of shapes—including vases with spouts or handles and many vessels standing on a ring foot. Though reeds were used in architecture, clay was not neglected; on the contrary it was now mixed with straw and moulded to form bricks, and from these handy units really monumental buildings were soon erected. Moreover, the 'northern Ubaid', even in Assyria, seems but a retarded and provincial version of a culture that appeared most typically and probably earliest in Sumer where it was first recognized.

There this Ubaid culture wears a rather different aspect from that manifested in Assyria and Syria. Indeed, at the oldest settlement yet detected—at Eridu, the first city of royalty in Sumerian tradition (p. 11), the oldest pottery diverges, even from the South Babylonian standard, and its decorative patterns are more reminiscent of Halafian art.[1] Only by level—XIII (that is, XIII counted from the top) does the classical 'southern' Ubaid style replace the

1. Lloyd and Safar, 'Eridu, 1947–8,' *Sumer*, iv, 1948, 115–125.

proto-Ubaid or Eridu ware current in the underlying five layers. The ceramic and other differences between northern and southern Ubaid must be due not only to discrepancies in age but also to the more challenging environment to which the latter is the response.

The new land, laid down by the Tigris–Euphrates at the head of the Persian Gulf, where the Ubaid culture is first detectable, was indeed enormously fertile and refertilized every year by alluvial silt. The many channels and lagoons teemed with fish; wild fowl and game swarmed in the reed brakes; date palms grew wild. But the exploitation of this natural paradise, the original Eden, required intensive labour and the organized co-operation of large bodies of men. Arable land had literally to be created out of a chaos of swamps and sand-banks by a 'separation' of land from water; the swamps must be drained; the floods controlled; the lifegiving waters led to the rainless desert by artificial canals.

The requisite social solidarity was apparently guaranteed not so much by a belief in common descent from a mythical totemic ancestor as by a feeling of dependence on a more personal deity. As in historical times, each group of the first colonists of Sumer felt themselves 'the people', the servants, or perhaps the children, of a god upon whose continued favour their prosperity depended. In any case, the oldest building yet detected on the soil of Sumer is a shrine at Eridu, occupying the site of a series of later sacred edifices that was crowned in the early IIIrd millennium B.C. by a veritable cathedral, dedicated to Enki. The first peasant settlers at Eridu[1] erected for Enki a square sanctuary (Temple—XVI) measuring only some 3 m. square and built of long prism-shaped mud bricks upon a sandhill among lagoons, close to the sea. Beyond this memorial to their piety nothing is yet known of the first colonists save their painted pottery and some clay beads. Their success in exploiting their environment and the consequent multiplication of their numbers has to be inferred from subsequent reconstructions of the sanctuary on an ever grander scale. By the seventh reconstruction the sanctuary had grown into a spacious temple (Temple—XI), more than 15 m. long and standing on an artificial platform that raised it above the floods and at the same time encased the hallowed remains of the older shrines. But its furniture belongs already to the fully developed Ubaid culture as known from many other sites in Sumer, which at Eridu begins already in Temple—XIII.

The pioneer cultivators of the new Tigris–Euphrates delta land

1. *Ibid.*

are hardly likely to be autochthonous—a band of hunter-fishers (represented by no known mesolithic remains) who had on the spot begun to breed and cultivate wild animals and plants whose existence in the vicinity is unattested. The colonists surely arrived as farmers, bringing at least the rudiments of their culture with them. Both Lloyd and Safar and Ann Perkins[1] infer from their pottery that the peasants had descended from the highlands east of the Tigris. In view of the Sumerians' own traditions of their origin in Dilmun, somewhere on the Persian Gulf, the starting point should perhaps be located further south. Admitted similarities to Halafian and Samarra patterns on their vases should merely indicate that all three groups are sprung from a common ancestral stem. Though the excavators distinguish the builders of Temples −XVIII to −XIV at Eridu from their Ubaid successors, it seems quite likely that the distinctive features of the Ubaid culture represent merely the adaptations of the imported 'Eridu culture' to the peculiar conditions of the Delta.[2]

The Ubaid culture, though spread right across the northern parkland, too, does represent a most perfect adaptation to the environ-ment of lower Mesopotamia. From the monumental size of the buildings they erected it may be inferred that the Ubaid farmers in Sumer had devised a rural economy, based on irrigation, capable of producing enough food to support a growing rural population and also yielding a social surplus usable for non-productive works and trade. But their very success might provoke such a rise in the effective birth-rate that younger sons must emigrate to apply ancestral techniques to new virgin land. Boats were available on which the produce of distant fields could be readily conveyed to a single centre of settlement along the myriad waterways that intersect the delta. Indeed, the winds were already harnessed to propel the boats; a late Ubaid grave at Eridu contained a model of the oldest sailing boat,[3] known anywhere in the world in 1950.

Local materials were ingeniously utilized to the full. The new soil of the Delta provided no stone for knife or axe-blades nor yet good building timber. So angled sickles and nails were made of hard-baked clay and became among the commonest relics of the Ubaid culture in Sumer. The huge reeds of the marshes can be converted

1. *CAEM.*, 74, 81.
2. Perkins, before the appearance of *Sumer*, iv, interpreted the new 'Eridu culture' as just the oldest version of the Ubaid, and in 1950 Mallowan held the same view.
3. *Sumer*, iv, pl. v.

into efficient shelters as they grow and, when cut and tied into bundles or plaited into mats, provide material for commodious dwellings as well as cattle-byres. But by Ubaid times men seem to have learnt to mould lumps of clay in wooden frames to form bricks and could thus initiate a freer sort of construction by putting small units together. Reed huts have been already encountered in the Ubaid villages of Assyria, but at Eridu[1] a complex reed structure was attached to a mud brick house, apparently to form a group of outbuildings as one room contained a large oven, 2 m. in diameter.

Of course, even in Sumer farmers managed to obtain stone for the manufacture of cutting tools. There, as in northern Mesopotamia, ground stone celts were still used as axe or adze blades and chert cores flaked to form 'hoe-blades (Fig. 59), somewhat rougher than

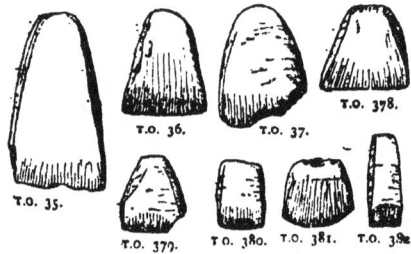

FIG. 59. Stone celts from al 'Ubaid, ¼.

those from Hassuna, while obsidian and chert furnished knives and sickle teeth. But in Sumer these materials had to be imported and paid for from the social surplus. Under such circumstances copper tools that can be resharpened and remelted when worn out would come cheaper in the long run. But copper, if current, was so scarce and therefore so carefully preserved for re-use, that only a couple of metal objects survive[2]—a stout harpoon from Ur and an axe from Arpachiya, both probably very late. Its intelligent use has to be deduced from numerous clay models of copper shaft-hole axes with splayed blades that can only copy cast copper patterns (Fig. 60). Other clay models represent 'battle axes'[3] of a type that must immediately have originated in metal but is more familiar in stone

1. *Sumer*, vi, 1950, 30.
2. *Ant. J*, x, 338; *Iraq*, ii, 104.
3. The best come from T. Uqair, *JNES.*, ii, 1943, 151, pl. xviii; but cf. Tobler, *Gawra*, ii, 167.

both in Europe and western Anatolia. The latter must rank as weapons, and in addition clay sling bullets were still made.

There is no evidence for smiths resident at any Ubaid site. Metal ware was presumably distributed and worked by perambulating smiths, but even that, like the use of obsidian, implies trade with regions outside the valley. But there is little evidence for trade in

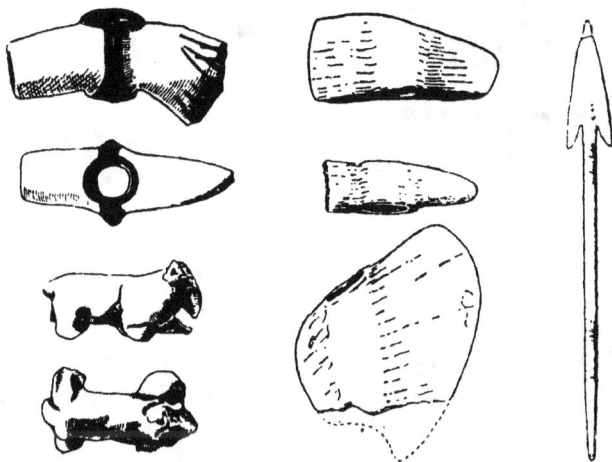

FIG. 60. Clay figurine Uqair; clay battle axes of Ubaid culture, Uqair and Ur; late Ubaid copper 'harpoon', Ur, ¼.

luxury articles, the sources of which can be identified. Beads of amazonite are reported from Ur, and lapis lazuli was imported into Assyria, while the Ubaid culture still flourished there, but only in Gawra — XII that must be contemporary with the Uruk phase further south.

The pottery is all hand-made (reports of wheel-made vases from Erech — XVIII are probably wrong[1]) and generally fired to a greenish hue. On this unburnished surface geometrical designs were painted in slightly lustrous paint. Save at Uqair, in Akkad, and in late strata further north,[2] recognizable representational designs are rare, but some of the geometric patterns may themselves be conventionalized representations of birds, animals or divine symbols. Among the shapes mention should again be made of the popularity of spouted vessels in general and in particular of a very specialized

1. *UVB.*, iv, 1932, 33; Perkins, *CAEM.*, 78.
2. *JNES.*, ii, pl. xix; Tobler, *Gawra*, ii, 146–8.

libation vase (Fig. 61, c) found in the comparatively late Ubaid Temple— VIII at Eridu in Sumer, and in the earliest Ubaid temples in Gawra·—XIX to XVII, in Assyria.[1]

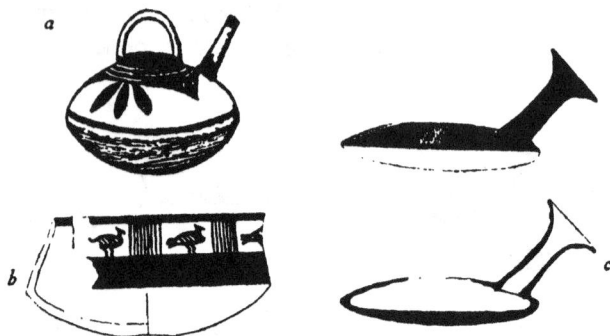

FIG. 61. 'Kettle' from Ur, libation vase from Gawra — XVIII and bowl with painted birds from Uqair, ⅛.

Vessels were also carved in stone, perhaps mainly for ritual purposes. Even obsidian was ground out to form stately tumblers with a tiny button-like foot which resemble somewhat the Amratian form shown in Plate VI, a, 1, while 'kettles', like Fig. 61a, were copied in limestone.[2]

The great achievement of the Ubaid period in Lower Mesopotamia was the creation of a rural economy appropriate to the delta and a social structure and ideology conducive to its efficient exploitation. At the beginning of history most of the land of each community belonged to the temple of a deity and was tilled on behalf of the god by tenants, share-croppers or day-labourers under the superintendance of his servants, the priests.[3] Thereby the maintenance of the canals and the rational utilization of land and water were assured. This system must be rooted in Ubaid times; for already we find the village dominated by a monumental temple.

At Eridu the first complete Ubaid temple, —XII, stood already on

1. Perkins, *CAEM.*, 48, 95; *Sumer*, iv, 119 and pl. vii; *Gawra*, ii, pl. cxxiii, 13.
2. Both types of stone vase are best documented from the casing of the Anu ziggurat at Erech which is of Uruk age. Hence Baumgärtel, *CPE.*, 106, argues that they too are Uruk. But clay versions of both forms are well known in Ubaid strata and the mud of the casing contained many other Ubaid types, cf. Perkins, *CAEM.*, 86.
3. Deimel, 'Sumerische Tempelwirtschaft zur Zeit Urukaginas,' *Analecta Orientalia*, ii, Rome, 1931.

a substantial platform and the bareness of its exterior walls was relieved by regularly spaced projecting buttresses. This feature was repeated in each subsequent reconstruction. For the edifice was rebuilt and enlarged no less than six times during the Ubaid period, till the latest Ubaid temple, —VI,[1] occupied a space 23·5 m. by 12·5 m. and stood on a platform 26·5 m. long and at least 16 m. wide. Temples — VIII, VII, and VI each had the form of a long cella with an altar at one end and a podium or offering table near the other and lateral chambers grouped symmetrically on either side of the nave. Thus, at the traditional site of the oldest fane in Mesopotamia we find the standard plan of the Sumerian temple established by the middle of the Ubaid period.

It seems then reasonable to infer that by this time the temple already played that central role in the community's economy that is attested by the earliest written documents. It must have been the repository where the social surplus of the group was concentrated. Presumably, too, its erection was planned and directed, the ceremonies of cult conducted and the divine household administered by professional ministers of the deity. We may, that is, assume a body of full-time specialist priests, exempted from the absorbing task of growing their own food and supported by the community in order to perform the vital function of ensuring the continued blessing of society's divine patron. Moreover, Ubaid vases from certain sites are painted with symbols subsequently associated with the local deity; thus the crescent occurs at Ur[2] where the Moon-god, Nannar, presided as patron.

If, then, by 'Sumerians' we mean the authors of the distinctive polity and religion of historical Sumer, we might safely follow Frankfort and call the Ubaid farmers 'Sumerians'. But, since nothing is yet known of the language they spoke, the epithet 'Proto-Sumerian' might be safer. At the same time, since the Ubaid temples at Eridu are erected directly over, and encase, the foundations of the earliest shrines, the religious tradition was continuous from the foundation of the settlement. So, despite changes in pottery, it might be legitimate to assume continuity of population too, and accordingly to extend the label, Proto-Sumerian, to the first colonists of Sumer.

Moreover, the distinctive plan of a long central cella, flanked by lateral chambers on either side, detected at Eridu in the extreme

1. *Sumer*, iii, 1947, 103–8.
2. *Ant. J.*, x, 1930, pl. xlv.

south, is repeated, albeit on a smaller scale—overall length 8·15 m.—in the earliest recognizable temple at Gawra −XIX in the north. Hence, even in Assyria the Ubaid colonists should be designated Proto-Sumerians. On the other hand, while their culture is in general the same as that of Sumer, ceramic peculiarities, notably the spouted libation vase of Fig. 61, c, indicate that the earliest Ubaid temple at Gawra (−XIX) is in time contemporary only with the late phase represented by Eridu−VIII in Sumer. It looks, then, as if the Proto-Sumerians had spread only slowly to the parkland steppes and in the delta marshes must have been established while the Halafian culture was still flourishing in the north. At Gawra, as at Eridu, the Ubaid temple was rebuilt and enlarged. By Gawra−XIII[1] the temple complex exceeded in magnitude any Ubaid temple in Sumer and the façades are decorated with niched buttresses and recesses exactly as in the Uruk temples of Sumer (Fig. 63). This and other facts—the importation of lapis—suggest that in time the Ubaid culture of Gawra−XII belongs to the Uruk period as defined in Sumer.

Side by side with the public worship of deities, more personal magic rites may be inferred from the figurines, manufactured by the Proto-Sumerians as by other early cultivators. They also give some hints of the fashions of the Ubaid period. Women (Pl. XVIII, c) wore wigs, like predynastic Egyptians, which were modelled separately in bitumen and stuck on. Black spots and pellets of clay on the shoulders and upper arms have been interpreted as tattoo-marks,[2] but cicatrices would be a more exact description. Some females are nursing infants and thus represent a widespread type, termed the *kourotrophos*. But now male figures, too, occur.[3] Men wore their hair done up in a bun at the back and sometimes dressed in sheepskins; then they give just the same impression as a modern Kurd, silhouetted against the sky.

Amulets were seldom carved into shapes. In the north engraved seal-pendants of Halafian type were still used in Ubaid times. But in the earliest Ubaid levels at Gawra true stamp seals were already current and such are found in the south, too, albeit rarely, at Eridu and Lagash.[4] Most take the form of a round button with a suspension loop on the back while the face, flat or convex, is engraved with

1. Tobler, *Gawra*, ii, 30–5.
2. Woolley, *Ant. J.*, x, 1930, 338.
3. *UVB.*, iii.
4. Perkins, *CAEM.*, 63–4, 87.

a geometrical pattern—most commonly a filled cross, like Fig. 77, 1–2). In the late strata—XIII and XII of Gawra, belonging in time to the Uruk phase, some seals are conical or pyramidal in form and engraved with lively figures of birds, snakes, fishes, ibex or other quadrupeds. Like the engraved Halafian pendants, these Ubaid seals were impressed on clay and presumably served the same magic and economic purposes. In any case, the conoid and button seals, bearing a filled cross, are the oldest relatively dated members of a family that spread eastward all over Iran and westward across the Anatolian plateau to Greece thereafter to be copied in clay in the Balkans and Central Europe. Equally widespread in Europe were ring-pendants such as came into fashion during the final Ubaid period in Assyria.[1]

The normal burial rite in the Ubaid period throughout Sumer was interment in the extended position[2]—an exceptional practice among early peasant societies. Adults were laid to rest in regular cemeteries outside the settlement of the living, but infants might be buried among the houses. The cemetery of Eridu, belonging to the same late phase as Temples—VII and VI, is thought to have comprised a thousand graves. These consisted of brick cists, sealed with a brick platform. Sometimes a secondary burial had been introduced, and occasionally dogs were buried with their masters. But in one grave at Arpachiya, in Assyria, a male and a female had been interred simultaneously, locked in each others' arms.

The Ubaid period must have lasted a long time. A community of simple peasants, virtually neolithic in equipment, are not the least likely to have built a new 'parish church' every generation, hardly every century. Moreover, Delougaz[3] has adduced some positive, though far from conclusive, evidence for believing that later and much better equipped literate communities were content to worship in the same temple for 100, or even 140 years. Now at Eridu, apart from the small 'Proto-Ubaid' shrines, six successive temples were erected. That should occupy six to eight centuries. The seven Ubaid strata at Gawra give figures of the same order for the north though there the last four or five centuries might fall outside the Ubaid period. So even on a conservative estimate 300 to 400 years would seem the minimum duration of the Ubaid period in Sumer.

During that time the Proto-Sumerians had perfected their rural

1. Tobler, *Gawra*, ii, pl. clxiii, 41–2.
2. *Sumer*, iv, 117–18 (Eridu); *Ant. J.*, x, 337 (Ur); *Iraq*, ii (Arpachiya); but at Gawra contracted or flexed burial was commoner (*Gawra*, ii, 113).
3. 'Presargonid Temples of the Diyala Region,' *OIP.*, lviii, 1942, 126–133.

economy and multiplied, probably very fast, in response to the generous food supplies it would yield. The thousand graves of the late Eridu cemetery and the magnitude of the public works executed at the same time document such an expansion of population. But throughout that period the Proto-Sumerians remained simply peasants with no alternative means of livelihood; for only an insignificant number could aspire to become professional priests, metal-workers or even potters. Hence, the sole outlet for the expanding population would be to open up fresh land and, with the existing transport facilities, that must soon mean the foundation of fresh settlements. Perhaps that necessity accounts for the gradual spread of Ubaid farmers right across Mesopotamia to the Mediterranean coasts. (It must, however, be recalled that in 1950 only one Ubaid settlement, T. Uqair, is known between Sumer and Assyria.) In any case, all known Ubaid settlements from Eridu to Gawra and Carchemish remain villages; neither in magnitude nor in functional differentiation do the local agglomerations of population deserve the name of cities. That status was achieved by some in the Uruk period.

CHAPTER VII

THE URBAN REVOLUTION IN MESOPOTAMIA

THE Uruk period has been conventionally defined by the appearance of unpainted red-slipped and grey pottery at level −XIV in a test-pit sunk through some 20 m. of stratified occupation debris from the court of the prehistoric Limestone Temple (−V) in the E-anna at Erech.[1] These plain dark-faced wares, together with an equally plain drab ware, replace the painted Ubaid fabrics and mark a breach with the old ceramic tradition. At the same level appear cups and jugs with handles (Fig. 62) that look

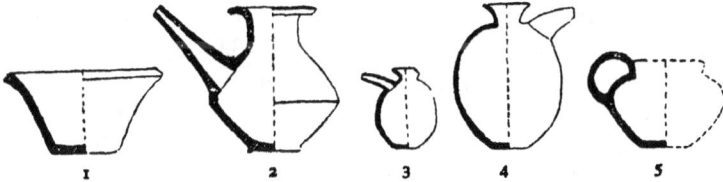

FIG. 62. Uruk pottery from Eanna–VII–V, at Erech, $\frac{1}{10}$.

equally foreign. How far other innovations, such as the use of the bow, certainly observable in the Uruk period, coincide with the change in pottery cannot be decided from the limited material furnished by a narrow test pit. The new ceramic shapes and techniques suffice to prove a profound foreign influence on the culture of Sumer, very probably to be explained by an actual infiltration of a new ethnic element. Since red and grey wares and

1. *UVB.*, iii, 1932, 30; iv, 36; Perkins, *CAEM.*, 97 ff., would restrict the term 'Uruk period' to the contents of levels −XIV to VI in the E-anna at Erech and following Delougaz assigns the subsequent strata, together with Jemdet Nasr, to the 'Proto-literate Period'. Eliot, *EMWI.*, 8, proposed a similar restriction and would even term E-anna −VII to III and Jemdet Nasr 'Early Dynastic I'. I follow the usage of Frankfort (*ASP.*, 1932, 16–18) with the division of Uruk into Early and Late proposed by Lloyd, *Sumer*, iv, 1948, 39–51.

handled vases were long popular in North Syria and Palestine, the new impulse most likely came from the west or north-west. If immigrants be postulated, the most likely candidates would be Semites.

Were the 'foreigners' responsible for the introduction of superior technical devices and a more advanced social structure? Even the earliest Uruk pottery, from Erech—XIV and Eridu—V,[1] includes wheel-made vases. Admittedly the potters' wheel is not only itself an epoch-making invention, but also implies a more articulated economy, the use of metal tools and consequently professional smiths, and is nearly always associated with wheeled vehicles. It does not, however, follow that all or any of these advances were introduced into Sumer, together with the new ceramic fashions and techniques, at the beginning of the Uruk period. On the contrary, indirect evidence for the use of metal in Ubaid times has already been quoted. Nor is any culture known, least of all in the west, that is at once demonstrably as old as the Ubaid culture of Sumer and at the same time likely to have outstripped it technically and socially. On the other hand, the exploitation of the Tigris–Euphrates delta would be calculated to produce just those social and economic conditions in which metallurgy and wheeled vehicles would be serviceable and under which the unit of settlement could and must be relatively large and the social surplus sufficient to support professional potters, smiths, and other full-time specialists.

No doubt the infusion of foreign traditions, evoked by a different, western environment, fertilized the cultural heritage of the marsh-dwelling peasant societies. Nothing proves that a 'higher' culture was imposed upon the latter from without. During the Uruk period peasant villages did grow into cathedral cities, but it is illegitimate to claim that the observed achievements of Sumer were introduced ready made from some unknown centre outside. What we can reasonably infer from the archæological record are the development of an economy to employ and support new classes of specialists, the application of fresh productive techniques and devices, and a consequent expansion of population.

All that is most clearly reflected in temple architecture. And rightly so if, as in historical times, the temple were the centre where the surplus grain or milk or fish, produced by individual peasant families above domestic needs was 'saved' and concentrated to be redistributed to support professional artisans and pay for imported

1. *UVB.*, iv, 1932, 37; *Sumer*, iv, 45–7.

materials. The Early Uruk temples at Eridu (−V and IV)[1] carry on the traditions of the Ubaid temples they replace, though built on a more lavish scale and on ever higher and more spacious platforms. But the platform of Temple −III was eventually faced with limestone blocks.

The same exotic building material was employed in the foundations of a veritable cathedral at the beginning of the Late Uruk phase at Erech. There the earliest preserved temple in the E-anna, the precinct of the goddess Innin, the Limestone Temple of level−V,[2] must have covered an area 76 m. long by 30 m. wide. It consisted of a long cella with niched walls, flanked on either side by lateral chambers symmetrically disposed. It was replaced in level−IVB by a yet more imposing edifice, the Pillar Temple. This stood on a mud brick platform and was apparently approached through a sort of portico, consisting of two rows of four free-standing brick columns, each 2·6 m. in diameter, corresponding to four half-columns in the temple wall. The columns, the walls and the platform face were strengthened and decorated by a mosaic of baked clay cones, hammered into the soft mud plaster. The exposed ends of the cones have been painted red, white or black and are arranged to form diamond and triangle patterns suggesting the palm stems that the columns presumably copied and the mats or rugs that hung between them.

The Pillar Temple, in turn, was replaced by others during the Uruk period. Temple B, in Level−IVA, repeated the plan of the Limestone Temple but presented a façade of rebated buttresses and recesses as elaborate as any First Dynasty mastaba in Egypt.

Meanwhile, in another part of Erech a parallel series of consecutive temples had been erected in honour of the god Anu. Foundations of seven buildings, termed respectively X, G, F, E, D, C, and B, are here superimposed. Each stood on an elevated platform which at every reconstruction was raised—from 9 m. high under X to 13 m. at B—and simultaneously extended till the whole was encased in a great rectangular massive of mud brick, A, which, in turn, must have supported an eighth temple, now vanished. The best preserved temple, B, surnamed the White Temple[3] because of its whitewashed walls, stood on a Z-shaped platform, measuring 70 m. by 66 m. and

1. *Sumer*, iii, 1947, 106–8.
2. *UVB.*, ii, 48; iii, 16; vii, 8; Eliot, *EMWI.*, 4.
3. Lenzen, 'Die Entwicklung der Zikkurat,' *ADFU-W.*, 4, 1941, 11) assigns it to −III (Jemdet Nasr), but Perkins would equate with −VI.

13 m. high. Its well-battered walls were strengthened by evenly-
spaced buttresses and relieved by a horizontal band of pottery flasks,
the bases of which had been hammered into the mud brick and
plaster while still wet. A stairway, 2·5 m. wide, gave access to the

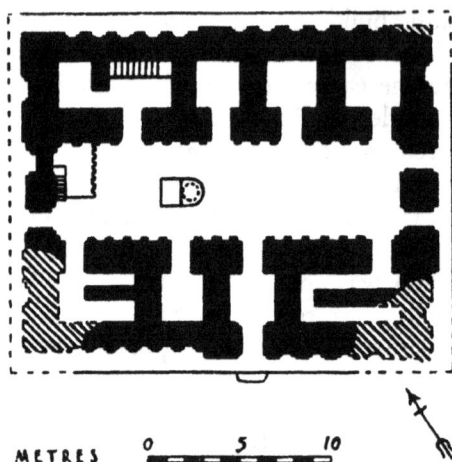

FIG. 63. Plan and Reconstruction of the White Temple at Erech.

summit on which stood the temple, only 17·5 m. long by 22 m.
wide across cella and flanking chambers (Fig. 63). In plan the White
Temple closely resembles Temple −IV of the Ubaid period at
Eridu, but stairs from two of the flanking chambers led up to a

second storey. But, though Ubaid figurines and broken stone vases were found in the mud of zigurrat A filling the chambers of the White Temple, the latter can hardly be older than the Late Uruk phase.

Almost equally imposing temples were built about the same time at Uqair, in Akkad.[1] The second agrees in length, in the crenellation of its outer walls and in plan with the White Temple at Erech. But its interior walls had been decorated with frescoes in red, orange, and black on a white ground. The altar front bears an architectural theme with motives recalling the Pillar Temple at Erech, but leopards and bulls were painted on its sides. In a vestibule panels depict human figures, wearing gaily decorated knee skirts, comparable in cut, but not in material, to the Sumerian kilt or *kaunakes*, familiar in historic times.

The Uqair frescoes show that the Uruk period had developed a new style of representational art and this is confirmed by seal-engravings, sculptured vases, and larger bas-reliefs. Hunters since the Old Stone Age have attempted to portray animals and plants in a lifelike manner and often succeeded. Neolithic and later peasantries have been content to symbolize the idea of ibex or woman by an abstract conventional figure. The painters, engravers, and sculptors of the Uruk period sought once more to depict things or persons as they saw them, but now in accordance with deliberate sophisticated conventions. Their pictures are the principal source of our knowledge of the equipment of lower Mesopotamia in Uruk times since few actual objects of profane use have survived.

Throughout the period stamp seals were in general use, but these are now engraved with lifelike figures of animals in preference to abstract geometrical patterns. But in Late Uruk times they began to give place to the cylinder,[2] a type of seal current in Mesopotamia throughout all later periods and already encountered in Late Gerzean Egypt. Like most early Egyptian examples, many Uruk and Jemdet Nasr seals are not perforated longitudinally but are provided with a transversely bored projection at one end (Pl. XX, *c*). The earliest cylinder impressions come from the monumental temples of Erech, from layers — V and IV in the Inanna and from the White Temple, but can be matched by plenty of cylinders in museums and private collections. Technically and artistically they are masterpieces. But their themes presumably reproduce in miniature scenes depicted on a larger scale in other media, illustrated by the Uqair frescoes and

1. *JNES.*, ii, 1943, 137–145.   2. Frankfort, *Cylinder Seals*, 15–29.

by a monumental vase and a basalt stele[1] depicting a Lion Hunt (Pl. XIII), both found in a Jemdet Nasr layer at Erech, but explicitly Uruk in style.

A third source of information is available. In the latest Uruk temples of Erech —IV have been found clay tablets[2] on which have been scratched conventional numerals and characters. They are the oldest extant written documents and represent temple accounts. The corporations of priests, who must have conducted worship in these vast edifices and administered the equally vast revenues of the deity, have been obliged to record receipts and disbursements in symbols, comprehensible to all their members. Numbers from one to nine are represented by repeating the unit symbol (D); for 10 a new cipher (O) was introduced, repetitions of which indicate 20, 30, ... At 100 a third cipher (big D) was generally introduced, but for certain measures this new sign stands for 60. This is already the 'sexagesimal notation', universally used in Mesopotamia in historical times, to which we owe our divisions of time and of angles.

Most characters of the script are shorthand pictures of objects, but a number in themselves suggest nothing and must have purely conventional meanings. Even the pictorial signs or pictograms are drawn in accordance with a standardized convention, and many of them must have equally conventional meanings. Though we term the script pictographic, it must be also ideographic, and each sign must stand for an idea or even a word. By the succeeding Jemdet Nasr phase there is evidence that some signs could be used as phonograms, too.

Writing is used by sociologists as a convenient criterion to distinguish civilization from barbarism. So we can assert that in Mesopotamia civilization was created in the Uruk period. We can

FIG. 64. Pictographic signs from Uruk tablets.

1. *UVB.*, v, 1933, 11; for the date cf. Basmachi, *Sumer*, v, 1949, 87–90.
2. Falkenstein, 'Archäische Texte aus Uruk' (*ADFU-W.*, 2, 1936).

now term the larger settlements—Eridu, Erech, Ur, Lagash, Uqair—cities and compare the great temples to cathedrals.

The citizens were, of course, supported by the products of fishing, farming, and hunting. The farmers now certainly used ploughs (Fig. 64, 1) for cultivating their fields and possibly metal sickles (Fig. 64, 7) for reaping their crops. They bred cows to provide milk, goats and two kinds of sheep[1] (Pl. XX*b*), one hairy, like the Egyptian but the other carrying a woolly fleece. The huntsmen now used bows and spears tipped with metal; the arrow heads of chert or obsidian were sometimes chisel-ended, sometimes perhaps leaf-shaped.

The surplus of primary production supported specialist crafts-men—metal-workers, sculptors, carpenters, leather workers, potters. The copper-smiths had learned to alloy copper with lead[2] to lower the melting point and could cast *cire perdue*, but there is no evidence for tin bronze. But silver was almost certainly known. Silver and lead were most likely already imported from the Taurus in Anatolia. Trade brought to Sumer also regular supplies of copper, gold, coniferous wood[3] and even lapis lazuli, presumably derived from Badakshan.

Transport by water was effected in boats with high prow and stern, resembling the 'foreign ships' of late Gerzean Egypt (Fig. 64, 2), and on land by sledges and wheeled carts (Fig. 64, 4–5). The vehicles were doubtless drawn by oxen, but perhaps the Asiatic ass or onager had already been tamed to act as a draft animal.

Owing to the absence of graves and the concentration of excavation on temples, craft tools and weapons of the period are scarcely known. Wood, stone, and hard-baked clay were certainly still used side by side with metal. The ceramic industry was thoroughly industrialized by Late Uruk times. Numerous kilns are mentioned in excavation reports, but never adequately described. Professional potters produced vases *en masse* on the wheel, but the finer red and grey wares are rare in Late Uruk times or at least in temples; drab wares predominate; jars with bent spouts (Fig. 62, 3–4) and votive bowls with bevelled rims (Fig. 62, 1) are very characteristic. But red slipped wares were still manufactured.[4]

For cult purposes pots were largely replaced by vessels of metal

1. Hilzheimer, in Heinrich, 'Kleinfunde' (*ADFU-W.*, 1, 1936, 48–54).
2. Heinrich, 'Kleinfunde aus den archäischen Tempelschichten in Uruk' (*ADFU-W.*, 1, 1936, 47); 9 per cent lead was added.
3. *UVB.*, viii, 1936, 32.   4. *UVB.*, iv, 1932, 37.

or stone. Pot forms like the ewer with bent spout perhaps imitate metallic models. The lapidaries not only carved vases with figured designs in relief (Pl. XX) but ingeniously reproduced such traditional ceramic forms as the spouted pot by turning the several parts separately and fitting them together exactly.[1] In technical skill and in artistic taste their products compare favourably with any stone vessels produced in early Egypt. Stone was also carved to represent animals as amulets or weights and similar miniature figures were cast in metal.

Side by side with creative activities, the emergence of civilization in Sumer coincides with the first direct evidence for organized homicide. While the majority of the Uruk seals depict cult scenes, craftsmen at work or heraldic groups of animals, a few sealings from Erech, E-anna —IV, present 'the king on the battlefield'.[2] Bound captives and a war-chariot are explicitly represented. At the same time piriform mace-heads may be regarded as weapons of war. The bound captives may be taken as evidence for slavery; the chariot shows the new wheeled vehicle employed as a military engine. There is no other evidence, such as palaces or royal tombs, to show that 'kingship had descended from the heavens'. The leader in war may then have been an elective office as Jacobsen[3] supposed rather than a permanent hereditary ruler.

The civilization of the Uruk period is known only from Eridu, Erech, Lagash and Ur in Sumer and Uqair in Akkad. Pottery gives indications of contemporary settlements at Kish and Khafaje. Something similar may be expected at Mari and is attested at Susa, in Elam. In northern Mesopotamia, though grey ware and some Uruk ceramic forms occur at Grai Resh, in the Sinjar, and a few other sites there were as yet no cities. Indeed, in some villages the Ubaid culture persisted well into the Uruk period as defined in Sumer.

By Late Uruk times almost all the Mesopotamian features detected in Late Gerzean and Early Pharaonic Egypt (pp. 78, 100) can be matched in Sumer. The most striking document of the parallelism between the two countries is the Lion Hunt stele (Pl. XII) from Erech.[4] Though found in a —III temple in the E-anna, it is plausibly regarded as a votive offering preserved from an older, Uruk, sanctuary. The lion hunters' costume duplicates that of the lion-

1. Heinrich, 'Kleinfunde,' 36.
2. Frankfort, *Cylinder Seals*, 21–5; *UVB.*, iv, 29; v, 46.
3. In Frankfort et al, *Before Philosophy*, London, 1949, 140–2.
4. *UVB.*, v, pl. 12–13.

dompter on the Gebel el-Arak knife-handle, their armament that of the bowmen on the Lion Hunt palette (Pl. XII). The foreign boat of the same ivory resembles those depicted on Uruk seals where the antithetical group also is a favourite theme. The cylinder seal was, of course, in regular use in Sumer by now while the Late Uruk type of jar with bent spout is just that found in Gerzean funerary pottery and depicted on the Narmer palette. If these agreements denote a synchronism between Late Uruk and Late Gerzean, the remaining common features would be older in Sumer than in Egypt. The closest analogies to the crenellated façades of the Early Pharaonic mastabas are indeed provided by the White Temple and contemporary buildings at Erech, but the façades of the latter are just elaborations of the buttressed walls of the early Ubaid (−XII) temple at Eridu (p. 119). Similarly, the use of stamps for sealing packages goes back to Ubaid times. On the other hand, the decisive step of using ideograms as phonograms for writing proper names would have been taken about the same time by Sumerian and Egyptian clerks. This need not mean that the innovations enumerated on p. 100 were all inspired from Sumer. The heroes of the Erech stele and the Egyptian knife-handle are not obviously Sumerians. The cylinder was an innovation of Late Uruk times and might be a translation of carved wood or reed rollers, adapted by Sumerian lapidaries to the needs of temple administrators. It has been suggested that the ceramic novelties of the Early Uruk period and also the use of stone in building might have been prompted by an infiltration of a Semitic element from the west. The Lion Hunt stele certainly gives support to this idea. Semites cradled in the intervening Arabian region might then have acted as intermediaries in the transmission of Mesopotamian devices to Egypt and of some western usages— the bow, self-coloured pottery to Sumer. As both regions shared in the trade in at least one imported material—lapis lazuli—opportunity for the transfer of ideas undoubtedly existed. On the other hand, a comparison of the contemporary cultures of Sumer and Egypt, on the basis of a synchronism between the Uruk and Gerzean periods, shows that the latter was in no position to impose a higher culture on Sumer.

Against the theory of Semitic influence in the Uruk period must be set the appearance of very similar pottery, glyptic and even script at Susa where there is no literary evidence for Semites. Indeed, Speiser[1] argued in 1939 that it was the Sumerians who made themselves master of the Tigris–Euphrates delta in the Uruk period and

1. *JAOS.*, Suppl. 4, 1939, 29–31.

introduced writing, the cylinder seal, sculpture, and monumental architecture. The subsequent discoveries at Eridu have refuted most of his arguments and supplemented generously those advanced by Frankfort[1] in 1932 for identifying the Ubaid culture with Sumerians. In ritual and architecture the continuity between Ubaid and Uruk has proved complete, and there are few achievements of the latter period that cannot reasonably be attributed to the intelligence and piety of the Proto-Sumerians. Their efflorescence was doubtless accelerated by a stimulating infusion of foreign traditions, evoked by different environments. That need not have involved any replacement of population. On the contrary an absolute increase can be deduced from the magnitude of the buildings erected. Falkenstein[2] calculates that it would have taken 1,500 men working a 10-hour day five years to build one of the temple terraces at Erech!

The Uruk period must cover several centuries. Monumental temples were rebuilt at least six times at Erech, five times at Eridu, and thrice at Uqair. That gives time for a considerable expansion of population quite apart from additions due to immigration. By the succeeding Jemdet Nasr period new cities had been built at Shuruppak (Fara),[3] Jemdet Nasr,[4] and Mari[5] while other settlements had attained urban status at Kish and Khafaje. The period is defined by ceramic and glyptic styles.

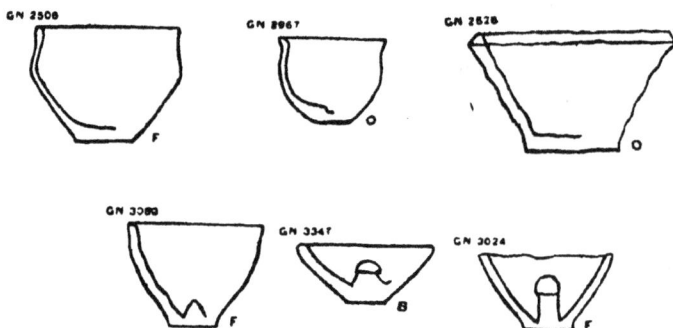

FIG. 65. Bowls and lids from Jemdet Nasr, ⅛, after Mackay.

1. 'Archæology and the Sumerian Problem,' OIS., 4, 1932, 18–23.
2. UVB., x, 1939, 24, n. 2.
3. Mus. J., xxii, 1931, 211 ff.
4. Field Museum Anthropology Memoirs, i, No. 3.
5. Syria, xviii, 1937, 6.

In pottery[1] there was a revival of painted decoration though the usual drab wares and many Uruk shapes persisted (Fig. 66). A notable innovation is the stopper in the form of an inverted cone with a handle on its inner side (Fig. 65, bottom),[2] since it recurs in

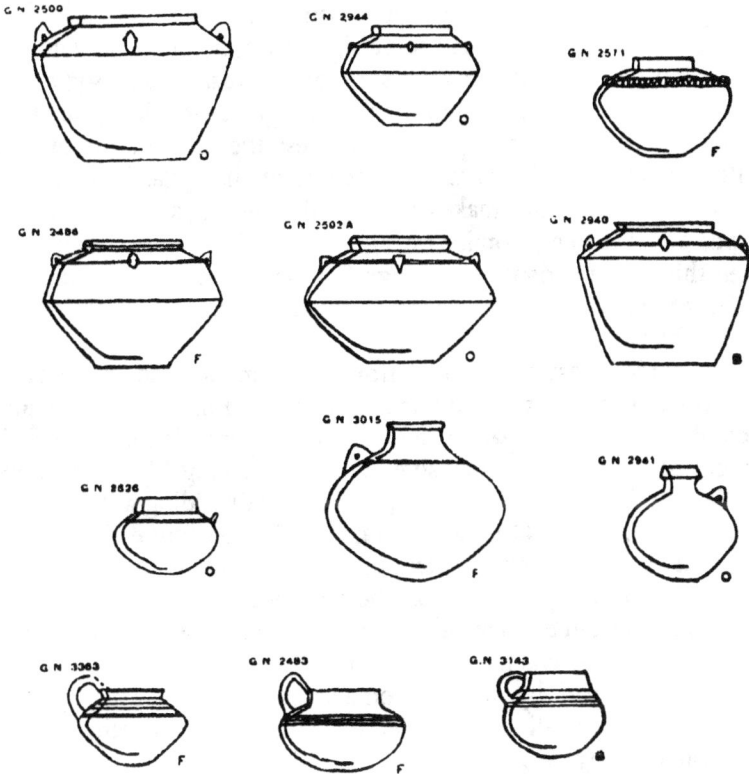

FIG. 66. Jars and jugs from Jemdet Nasr, ⅛, after Mackay.

India. Painting is virtually confined to the keeled jar (Pl. XXI). The vase surface was either covered with a plum red slip save for reserved panels which were outlined and filled with designs in black paint or the panels were outlined and filled with designs in black paint applied directly to the greenish clay.

1. Field, *AJA.*, xxxix, 1935, 310-320, Harden, *Iraq.* i, 1934, 30-44, emphasizes the continuity from Uruk to Early Dynastic as does Eliot, *EMWI.*, *passim.*

2. *Field Museum Anthropology Memoirs*, i, No. 3.

Stamp seals were still in use, including stamps in animal form like Fig. 78, but the cylinders are engraved with rows of stiff, conventional animals, fishes, and birds in contrast to the lively scenes of the Uruk style. Despite the æsthetic deterioration of the glyptic, the script[1] shows a definite advance. The characters remain largely pictographic. But now, instead of devising a new sign for each idea, the clerks have agreed to use some signs with the phonetic value of the object's name and can thus spell out words. As in Egypt, the first use—that we can confidently recognize—of ideograms as phonograms is to write personal names: the symbol for arrow, called in Sumerian 'ti' is used to represent the syllable 'ti' in the name Enlil-ti'—'Enlil-makes-to-live'. But by this and other means it was possible to economize on signs. In the Uruk period there had been thirty-one variants of the sign for sheep, presumably denoting different breeds, ages, and sexes; only four variants occur on Jemdet Nasr tablets.

At Jemdet Nasr itself[2] a platform, 300 m. by 200 m. in area, supported a complicated building measuring 92 m. by 48 m. overall. Langdon called it a palace, and, were that appellation correct, it would be the earliest conclusive evidence for kingship in Mesopotamia. But there is no conclusive proof that the building was occupied by a secular ruler. On the contrary, in it was found the vase of Pl. XXI, *a*, marked with a star, the Sumerian ideogram for 'deity'. At other sites temples carry on the long established tradition. The first temple of Sin at Khafaje[3] is a classic example of the long central cella with lateral chambers albeit of diminutive proportions. The 'Sacred Hut' had by now become a conventional Hut Symbol represented by small stone models in the temples of Erech, Khafaje and Lagash (Fig. 105, 1).

Burial rites can now be illustrated by a cemetery at Ur, attributed by Woolley[4] to the Jemdet Nasr phase, but possibly going back to the Uruk period which had not been recognized when he wrote. The dead were buried in a strictly contracted attitude, contrasted to the extended Ubaid burials and the flexed position normal in Early Dynastic graves.

As tools of production, clay sickles, chert 'hoes', obsidian knives and other stone implements were still in use. Of metal utensils,

1. Cf. Hooke, in *Antiquity*, xi, 1937, 270–6.
2. Langdon, *Der Alte Orient*, 26, 1928, 67–75; Eliot, *EMWI.*, 10.
3. Delougaz, 'Presargonid Temples,' *OIP.*, lviii.
4. *Ant. J.*, x, 327.

a barbed fish-hook (Fig. 67), a chisel with rounded butt[1] like the
Early Pharaonic ones, and a flat dagger tapering to a tang[2] have
survived. But clay models show that copper was used for shaft-hole
axes. Vessels of copper, lead, and silver have been reported from

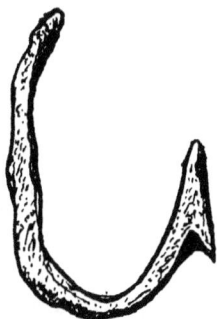

FIG. 67. Copper fish-hook, Jemdet Nasr, $\frac{2}{3}$.

graves and temple treasures. By Jemdet Nasr times Asiatic metallurgists had evidently mastered the complex process of separating
silver from lead.[3] Vessels were made also from fayence, products of
a new industry which produced personal ornaments too. Stone vases
were, of course, still manufactured and sometimes carved, albeit less
tastefully than before. The steatite boar with a hollow or socket in
its back (Pl. XX, a) can, however, compare with Uruk work. And
the superb alabaster head from Erech (Pl. XXXVI) might serve as a
model example of the contrast between civilized naturalism and
barbaric convention!

Personal ornaments include bone pins with perforated shafts,
precursors of the Early Dynastic toggle-pins, beads, and spacers of
fayence, wood, shell, soft stone, carnelian and lapis and various
pendants. These include models of men, doves, fishes and animals
and rings from which project four perforated loops, related perhaps
to the ring pendants of European pre-history but not without
Egyptian analogues.

Though it witnessed four rebuildings of the Sin Temple at
Khafaje, two building phases at Uqair and several drastic reconstructions in the E-anna, at Erech, the Jemdet Nasr period has a
transitional character. Many ceramic forms and architectural devices

1. *Field Museum Anthropology Memoirs*, i, No. 3.
2. *Mus. J.*, xxii, 1931, 211 ff.
3. Cf. Forbes, *Metallurgy in Antiquity*, Leiden, 1950, 210–18.

survived from Uruk times, many were carried over into Early Dynastic I. Yet at Shuruppak and Erech 'flood deposits' intervene between Jemdet Nasr and Early Dynastic layers. They have as good a claim as any others to represent the Deluge of Sumerian tradition.

THE URBAN REVOLUTION IN SUSIANA

At this point it is convenient to interpolate a digression sketching the parallel rise of civilization in Susiana. For that part of Elam belongs geographically to Lower Mesopotamia, being separated from the Tigris drainage by only a very low divide; in historical times relations between Susa and Sumer were close and interaction frequent; in prehistoric times the similarities of archæological cultures are sufficiently close to warrant belief in similar bilateral relations.

The site of Susa is a low spur of gravel and clay, projecting into the alluvial plain of the Kerkha. Naturally raised above normal floods, but conveniently situated for exploiting the fertile plain, Susa soon became a populous centre. The ruins of superimposed villages and towns grew into an imposing tell with three summits, crowned respectively by the Citadel, the Apadana and the Royal Villa of Achæmenid and Sassanid monarchs. Since 1897 a French 'Mission' had been exploring the ruins. Almost at once they distinguished two archaic levels, Susa I and Susa II, characterized by distinct styles of superb painted pottery, and till 1928 this sequence was used as a standard for the classification of cultures with painted pottery that came to light in Mesopotamia after 1919.

In the sequel it has appeared that Susa I and Susa II are separated by as much as 11·2 m. of deposits containing tombs and domestic ruins and relics of a different character. The methods of excavation and publication, however, in which tomb groups are never described as wholes and relics are classified by mere depth below the ill-defined 'Susa II' horizon, allows no opportunity for tracing precisely stages in the advance to civilization. A provisional culture sequence can be established only thanks to the close parallelism with Sumer.

The earliest recognizable settlement, Susa I (A),[1] must have been a populous village, but is known almost exclusively from its cemetery, estimated to comprise over 2,000 graves. According to de Morgan the bodies were interred sometimes extended and sometimes flexed,

1. *MDP.*, i, 17; xiii, 33; xxv, 183, 204; xxx, 193–8; Eliot, *EMWI.*, 28, 25.

but according to de Mecquenem[1] only after the flesh had decayed from the bones. Grave furniture and domestic relics attest a culture technically ahead of the earliest known in Sumer. Though ground stone celts, crescentic stone knives, obsidian blades, perforated stone mace-heads—piriform or pointed oval—and perhaps battle-axes,[2] and even finely-trimmed leaf-shaped and barbed arrow-heads of chert (Fig. 68) were in use, copper was available in sufficient quantity

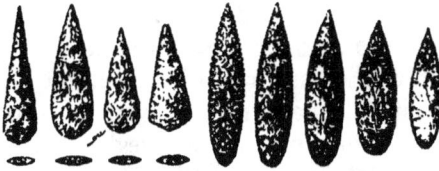

FIG. 68. Flint arrow-heads, Susa.

for the manufacture of flat axes, chisels, needles with eyelets and even mirrors of as much as 19 cm. diameter. Lapis lazuli was also imported as well as copper and obsidian. Fayence, too, was used for the manufacture of beads. The social surplus must therefore have been large enough to support specialist craftsmen. Even the pottery is so fine that though the wheel was not used it may well have been made by full-time specialists. The kilns[3] found at a depth of between 9·1 and 11·2 cm., if not dug down from the next stratum are of highly sophisticated type.

Most of the funerary pottery is of very thin, porous ware, pale green or pink in colour. But burnished black or red slipped wares are also mentioned[4] and some funerary vases, too, were painted in

FIG. 69. Carinated pot and spouted jug, $\frac{1}{3}$, Susa I.

1. *MDP.*, xxix, 5.   2. *MDP.*, xxx, 195, fig. 42; only the butt survives.
3. *MDP.*, xxv, 204.   4. *MDP.*, xxx, 183; Frankfort, *Studies*, i, 38.

black on a red slipped ground. The characteristic funerary vases,[1] however, are made in the clear porous ware. The principal shapes are (1) wide open bowls (Pl. XXII), (2) tall tumblers (Pl. XXIII), (3) ovoid jars with low everted necks, and (4) squat carinated pots with lugs on the shoulder (Fig. 69a), rarely also spouted pots (Fig. 69b) and shallow goblets on a hollow foot. It should be noted that both the bowls and tumblers are normally given stability by an incipient ring base (as at al'Ubaid), a genuinely ceramic device implying a long practice in the potter's craft.

The vases are decorated with splendid designs executed in a warm black paint, applied as a rule directly to the clay without the intervention of a slip. The patterns, which are undoubtedly 'magical' in content, are a blend of geometric motives or symbols—swastikas, even-armed crosses, Maltese squares (Pl. XXII, 2), step patterns, serial triangles, double-axes—and representations—birds, bulls, ibex, mountain goats, dogs, perhaps a horse, more rarely men (Fig. 70),

FIG. 70. Sherds from Susa I, depicting human figures.

quivers, and a lance. But the natural objects represented are so stylized as to become pure decorative designs. Frankfort terms this treatment 'abstract' and regards it as indicative of the abstract mentality of the artist. But W. Bremer[2] has recently shown in detail that the precise form of the stylization has been conditioned by basket-work while many of the vase forms might also be regarded as copying baskets (as at Ubaid). In other words, the Susian potter

1. Frankfort, *Studies*, i, 25 ff.   2. *PZ.*, xvi, 1925, 22.

is copying basketry models, and the peculiar shapes he gives to animals are due to the exigencies of plaiting straw. The modern ethnographic parallels on which Bremer relies are significantly taken from the arid regions of the south-western States which climatically approximate to Elam. At the same time the birds and animals as well as the geometric symbols are the forerunners of divine or magic signs later engraved upon seals and sometimes eventually converted into elements of writing. Stone vessels are represented by a square

FIG. 71. Square vase of alabaster, Susa I, after de Morgan.

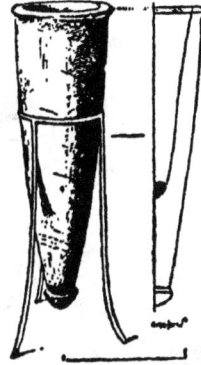

FIG. 72. Stone paint-pot in form of a cornet, Susa, after de Morgan.

vase said to come from the cemetery (Fig. 71) and many little paint-pots termed in French *à cornet* (Fig. 72)—a form also manufactured in bitumen.

Personal ornaments include strings of beads of lapis lazuli, carnelian, shell, and fayence, held together by fayence spacers. Stamp seals of both bead (Fig. 73) and button types were already current.

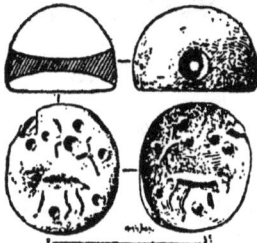

FIG. 73. Bead seal, Susa I (cemetery).

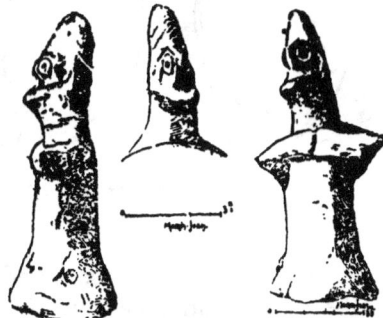

FIG. 74. Female figurine, Susa I.

They were engraved with rather crude animals figures or with the filled cross, already familiar in Sumer. Finally, figurines of women, cows, birds, and snakes were modelled in clay (Fig. 74).

In the later layers of Susa I (A) some vases are painted in black

FIG. 75. Pottery of Uruk forms from Susa B.

on a red ground, like those found below the Eye Temple at Brak on the Khabur and in Gawra—XII (p. 208). But after the accumulation of 2 m. of debris, painted pottery went out of fashion altogether, and a new cultural phase, B, began.[1] It is characterized by red-slipped and drab wares. The vases, now made on the wheel, include familiar Uruk forms; Nos. 3 and 12 on Fig. 75 are distinctively Late Uruk.

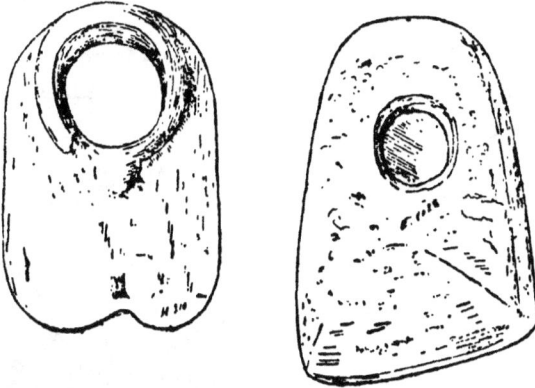

FIG. 76. Shaft-hole adzes of copper and stone, Susa B, ½.

All are obviously products of professional potters. Professional smiths about the same time began casting transverse axes,[2] like Fig. 76, an archaic version of the most distinctive Sumerian type,

FIG. 77. Button and bead seals, Susa B, ¼.

1. Attempts to correlate the several reports on the strata between Susa I and II have been made by McCown and Eliot. The former, *CSEI.*, 43–6, subdivides B into three phases and admits no tablets till C, which is Jemdet Nasr. Eliot, *EMWI.*, 23–30.

2. *Rev. Ass.*, xxvii, 1930, 189; *MDP.*, xx, 104; xxv, 181.

and even double axes. But stone was still employed extensively for tools, and the metal types were imitated in this older material (Fig. 76). Button stamp seals continued in use, but the engraved face is now generally convex (Fig. 77) and not flat as normally in Susa A.[1]

Then in the next phase, C, seals in animal form (theriomorphic seals) (Fig. 78), like those from the Jemdet Nasr hoard in the

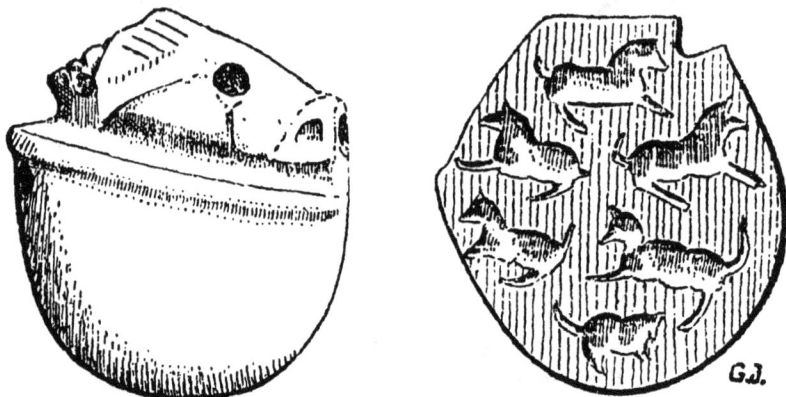

FIG. 78. Theriomorphic seal, Susa C, nat. size.

E-anna, at Erech, came into fashion and still later cylinder seals, at first engraved in the naturalistic Uruk style. To this phase should belong twin vases of alabaster (Fig. 79), related to the block vases

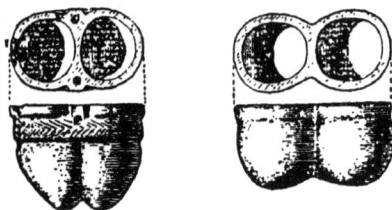

FIG. 79. Twin vases of alabaster, Susa C or D, ¼.

of Early Pharaonic Egypt and Early Dynastic Sumer, and lead vessels that illustrate the same mastery of complex metallurgical processes as do the lead bowls from Jemdet Nasr graves at Ur. Finally stone 'Hut Symbols' like those found all across Mesopotamia and into the Orontes valley (Fig. 105) confirm the partial synchronism between Susa C and the Jemdet Nasr period in Sumer.

1. *MDP.*, xxx, 198.

But during Susa C the urban revolution was completed; the transition to civilization is indicated by the first written documents, account tablets as in Sumer. These so-called 'Proto-Elamite tablets' are inscribed in a 'pictographic' script, comparable to that of the tablets from Erech and Jemdet Nasr. But the characters are far from identical; indeed, the same object, such as a plough, is represented by different shorthand conventions. The numeral system also diverges from the Proto-Sumerian. The Proto-Elamite script continued in use at least till the Empire of Agade, but under the Empire of Ur it was finally replaced by Mesopotamian cuneiform, adapted to the local tongue.[1] Throughout its currency it remained purely ideographic; presumably the clerks managed to distinguish new ideas by modifying existing signs or adding new ones. Hence, it is only a guess to call the language thus expressed Anzanite, the language of the legible later texts. It is equally a guess to suggest that it was a corporation of priests that devized the elaborate system of book-keeping illustrated by the tablets and the conventional symbols used therein. There was, of course, an important temple to Shushinak on the site. At the same time, as we shall see, Proto-Elamite tablets occur as far north as Sialk in a settlement that can hardly pretend to urban status. Their presence there must then be connected with that north–south trade for which Susa is happily situated.

The succeeding phase, D, is conveniently defined by a revival of vase-painting. The wheel-made jars are adorned with panels of designs, outlined in black and filled in with badly-fixed red paint. In technique, composition, and style, but not in form, this pottery agrees exactly with the Scarlet Ware that characterizes Early Dynastic I in the Tigris–Euphrates valley. At the same time the polychrome vases have technical and stylistic analogies in the east—in the Kulli culture of Baluchistan—and humped Indian cattle[2] are sometimes depicted on them. So the pottery documents relations at once with the east and with the west. Agreements with the west are not merely confined to the ceramic domain. The polychrome vases, like those of Susa I, are often derived from tombs. At Susa the excavators[3] failed to determine the form of these tombs. But at provincial settlements on the Mesopotamian border, Tepe Aly Abad

1. Contenau, 'Epigraphie proto-élamite,' *MDP.*, xxxi. The plough is 4452–4501 on pl. lvii.
2. *MDP.*, xx, 105; cf. Frankfort, *ASP.*, 71.
3. Failure frankly admitted in *MDP.*, xxix, 156, but analogies to Musyan tombs suggested, *ib.*, xxv, 218.

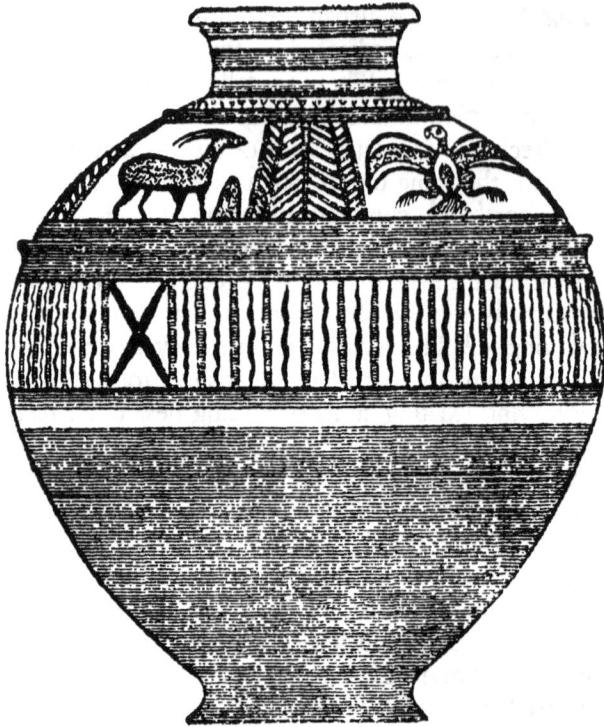

FIG. 80. Jar painted in red and black. Tepe Aly Abad, Musyan, ¼.

FIG. 81. Jar painted in red and black. Tepe Aly Abad, Musyan, ⅛.

and other mounds near Musyan,[1] similar vases are found with extended skeletons in false-vaulted brick chambers (Fig. 82) such

1. *MDP.*, viii, 74–8; but note also the typically Early Dynastic I tumbler (not from a tomb) of p. 136, fig. 270.

as will be found in the next chapter serving as 'royal tombs' in Mesopotamia from Early Dynastic I. The Musyan tombs were, in

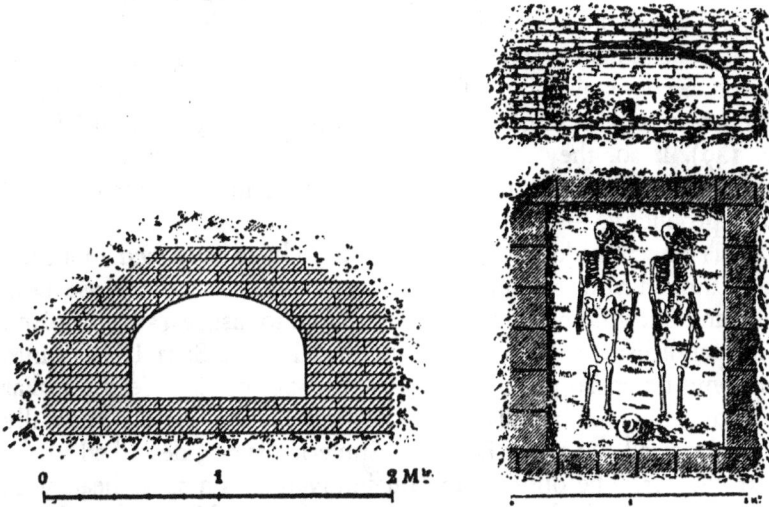

FIG. 82. Brick vaulted tombs, Tepe Aly Abad, near Musyan.

fact, furnished with metal objects—flat chisels, shaft-hole axes, lance-heads, arrow-butts, and pins with lapis heads (Fig. 83)—and inlaid pottery 'offering stands' such as characterize the earlier part

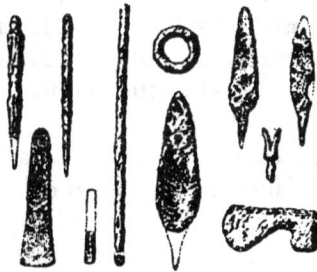

FIG. 83. Copper pin, celt, needle, tubes, ring, spear-head, arrow-heads, arrow-butt, and axe, from tombs near Musyan, ⅙.

of the Early Dynastic period there. Now at Susa itself a rich burial[1] was accompanied by a jar like Fig. 80 painted in black and badly-fixed red with a scene, comparable to that on the Sumerian vase of

1. *Rev. Ass.*, xxxiv, 1937, 150–3; *MDP.*, xxix, 103.

Fig. 84. But this time the vehicle, though carried on the same nail-studded wheels, is drawn by humped oxen instead of equids and is flanked by a deity on a three-staged tower in place of a symposium. Some 8 feet from this rich burial, but possibly in the same tomb, lay the skeletons of two bovids with metal nose-rings and of their driver, accompanied by a few poor gifts. The two groups surely compose a royal tomb, comparable to the 'chariot graves' of Kish Y (p. 149). If so, they symbolize as in Sumer the emergence of an earthly ruler to concentrate the social surplus and utilize it as capital for reproductive—or militaristic—purposes.

This descent of kingship would seem to have happened about the same time in both regions; for the agreements between phase D at Susa and Early Dynastic I are close enough to justify a synchronism. The parallelism can be carried forward in that Susa II lasts into Sargonid times. Its monochrome painted pottery is indeed peculiar to Iran. But the metal work throughout the period faithfully reproduces all the Early Dynastic Sumerian types, described in the next chapter. The only significant innovation is a spear-head with hooked tang,[1] which, if correctly attributed to this horizon, is the first dated example of a type which we shall find widespread towards the end of the IIIrd millennium. Working backward from Susa D, equated with Early Dynastic I in Sumer, the theriomorphic seals and Hut Symbols from C establish a synchronism between that phase and Jemdet Nasr. The pot forms from Susa B suffice to equate it with Late Uruk as defined at Erech and Eridu. Then the relative wealth in copper, the use of the bow, lapis, fayence, and red pottery in Susa I (A) might betoken a substantial overlap in time with the Uruk period.[2] In that case Susa I could hardly be as old as the Ubaid settlement at Eridu.

Accordingly, Susa I cannot to-day be regarded as in any sense standing in parental relation to the Ubaid culture of Sumer. So its inhabitants need not be ancestral Sumerians, even if the Ubaid population deserve that title. But its culture may well be a collateral, Sprung from the same South Iranian stock as the Ubaid. But the Susa I culture was overlaid by that of Uruk or a collateral. Though the break is not really abrupt, there is no evidence that the Uruk features developed directly out of Susa I; at no other time, for example, were handled vases popular in Elam nor do such occur at

1. *MDP.*, xxv, 192.
2. Rutten, *Rev. Ass.*, xliv, 1950, 165, frankly synchronised Susa I (A) with 'the first part of the Uruk period' (our Early Uruk).

all further east. In any case, no system of writing was borrowed ready-made from Sumer. Even if the idea of writing were inspired from that quarter, the Proto-Elamite script was presumably invented at Susa. The economic conditions that made it necessary and their technological bases were certainly developed at a time when the native culture of Susa I was fertilized by the current of fresh traditions, reflected by the Uruk elements of Susa B. If that brought the wheel, it did not demonstrably bring all the new inventions; the cylinder seal seems to arrive later while the bow, metallurgy, and fayence go back to Susa A.

It would be natural to assume that the innovations characterizing Susa B are due to an infiltration of the same western element as promoted the Uruk culture in Sumer. But in that case the new element can hardly be termed Semitic since there is no evidence for Semites in Susiana. An infiltration, perhaps only of specialized craftsmen, from Sumer after the Uruk culture had been established there, might be postulated to avoid this and other difficulties. Finally, the consolidation of Susian civilization in phase D with the establishment of kingship came at a time when Elam was affected by impulses from the east as well as the west. Indeed, it may be found that a 'dynastic period' began earlier in Susiana than in the Tigris–Euphrates valley. The earliest polychrome vases seem to be earlier than the Scarlet Ware of the Diyala and more akin to Jemdet Nasr. But the rise of monarchy there must first be considered.

CHAPTER VIII

THE EARLY DYNASTIC PERIOD

FOR the archæologist the Early Dynastic might be most easily distinguished from the preceding Jemdet Nasr and the succeeding Sargonid periods by a distinctive building method. The rectangular tile-shaped bricks, used in Late Uruk and Jemdet Nasr buildings, were replaced by small *plano-convex* bricks, flat on one face but cushion-shaped on the other. Walls thus built were generally set in a foundation trench, and the bricks themselves are often laid not horizontally but sloping in opposite directions so as to produce a herring-bone effect, which was of course masked by the plaster coating the whole wall. It has been suggested that this type of brickwork was introduced by foreigners, accustomed to build in stone. Be that as it may, herring-bone masonry does occur early at Byblos in Syria, and is distinctive of the earliest settlements at Troy on the Hellespont, Thermi on Lesbos, and in Early Helladic Greece.[1] The name proposed by Christian, 'plano-convex' might then seem a more apposite designation for the period than Early Dynastic.

There is, however, one archæological feature that may justify Frankfort's rather sociological term. From Early Dynastic I on we find a small class of burials that by their peculiar form and ritual may earn the designation 'Royal Tombs'. Private persons in Early Dynastic times were normally buried in a flexed position in simple earth graves or small brick cists roofed by corbelling. The bodies were often wrapped in mats, sometimes enclosed in wicker or pottery coffins (*larnakes*) or even in large jars (*pithoi*). In at least some cities at some periods, for instance at Kish in Early Dynastic I,[2] the dead were buried under house floors, a practice continued in later times and regularly observed in the highlands of Iran and Anatolia throughout prehistory as also in neolithic Lower Egypt.

1. Dunand, *RB.*, lvii, 1950, 591; Childe, *Dawn*, 37, 65.
2. Watelin, *Kish IV*, 1934, 17.

Normally excavators report cemeteries, within the city walls, presumably on open spaces—unless they have just failed to note the flimsy walls of mud brick houses! The graves are always well furnished with vases, doubtless containing food and drink, but metal tools or arms are comparatively rare in private tombs till Early Dynastic III.

The exceptional 'royal' tombs are contrasted with these private graves in structure, ritual, and furniture. The tombs, as in First Dynasty Egypt, are regular subterranean chambers. Three great tombs under the Ishtar Temple at Mari[1] were built of large stone slabs arranged to form a corbelled roof. All had been plundered, but enough was left in tomb 300 to determine the date and the ritual. The vaulted chamber, 6·6 m. long, 2·5 m. wide, and 1·6 m. high, still contained vases of Scarlet Ware and Early Dynastic I form, jewelry of gold, silver, and lapis lazuli, vases, a mirror, and a scalloped axe of type 9 (p. 159), of copper, and parts of a skeleton with two long copper pins still sticking in its neck. It belonged, therefore, not to the tomb's owner, but to an attendant, immolated at this funeral. Such satī burials are, in fact, as characteristic of Royal Tombs in Mesopotamia as in Egypt. The practice is still more clearly documented in three contemporary tombs, of unknown structure and dimensions, in the Y cemetery at Kish.[2] Again each contained several corpses—as many as five were identified—but also another equally distinctive trait, a hearse or chariot with the beasts that drew it. Tombs 237 and 357 each held one four-wheeled wagon; tomb 529 a wagon and a chariot (or possibly three chariots).[2]

Vehicles of similar type are illustrated by several Early Dynastic models, carvings (Pl. XXIV, a), paintings (Fig. 84), and mosaics. All ran on solid wheels, varying in diameter from ·50 m. (Kish Y) to 1·0 m. (Ur, PG 789)[3] and consisting of three planks, clamped together by wooden struts and perhaps bound with leather tyres held in place by copper nails. The projecting heads of these nails are carefully depicted in models and paintings, standing out like cogs, and doubtless served to protect the wheel rims. At Kish, Watelin reports, the wheels turned in one piece with the axle, ·90 m. long, which was attached by leather thongs to the vehicle's body. At Ur

1. *Syria*, xviii, 1937, 60; xix, 4–6.
2. Watelin, *Kish IV*, 1924, 29, 30.
3. Woolley, *Ur Excavations*, ii, *The Royal Cemetery*—for vehicles see especially 64, 108.

FIG. 84. Funerary wagon and other scenes on a Scarlet Ware vase from Khafaje, British Museum.

Woolley[1] found the axle box secured to the body by copper bolts.

The vehicles were sometimes drawn to the tomb by a pair of oxen,[1] as at Susa, but more often by four Asiatic asses or onager.[2]

1. See n. 3 on p. 149.   2. Hilzheimer, *Antiquity*, ix, 1935, 133.

One beast on either side pulled on the yoke that seems to have been fixed firmly to the pole. The outspanners on each side pulled on their neighbours' collars.[1] The reins controlling the draft animals were attached to copper rings passing through the upper lips[2] of onagers as well as of oxen. They were crossed by passing through a metal terret, a pair of rein-rings fixed to the pole in front of the yoke and surmounted by a mascot (Plate XXV). It is obvious that these vehicles and their wheels could only be fashioned with the aid of saws and other metal tools, and it is significant that saws were actually deposited in the 'chariot graves' at Kish.

The four-wheeled ox-carts were naturally used for transport, and even two-wheeled cars figure in pacific scenes. But the celebrated 'standard' from Ur and several other figured documents, including a seal-impression from Erech—IV, show two-, and probably also four-, wheeled vehicles used as engines of war. Even the clumsy Sumerian war-chariot must have been extremely costly, and the 'war-asses' that drew it must have been specially trained. Relative to the meagre total resources of Early Dynastic societies, it was strictly comparable to the tank to-day, an arm that only civilized States and their personal embodiments could afford; against it no barbarian tribe nor rebellious peasantry could compete. The burial of such an engine in the tomb would therefore symbolize the incarnation, as a coercive force, of the State in a human dynast and justify the application of the epithet 'royal' to such a tomb.

The most dramatic expression of the funerary ritual appropriate to kingship is, of course, to be found in the Royal Tombs of Ur discovered in 1928 and now generally assigned to Early Dynastic III.[3] Here again the burial place is an underground house as in the first pharaohs' tombs at Abydos. The chamber was erected at the bottom of a deep shaft entered by a sloping or stepped ramp or dromos such as led to Egyptian tombs from the reign of Udimu. One tomb consisted of three parallel chambers of undressed lime-stone blocks, each roofed with a corbelled barrel vault and originally lined with plaster and embellished with timbering. Another small tomb was covered with a true dome, also of limestone slabs (cf. Fig. 85). Elsewhere brick was used, and in some cases the roof vault was supported by a genuine keystone and illustrates the principle of the true arch, a device met with in the funerary architecture of

1. Frankfort, 'More Sculpture,' *OIP.*, lx, 1943, 13.
2. Schaeffer, *Syria*, xvi, 1935, 136.
3. Woolley, *Ur Excavations*, ii, *The Royal Cemetery*.

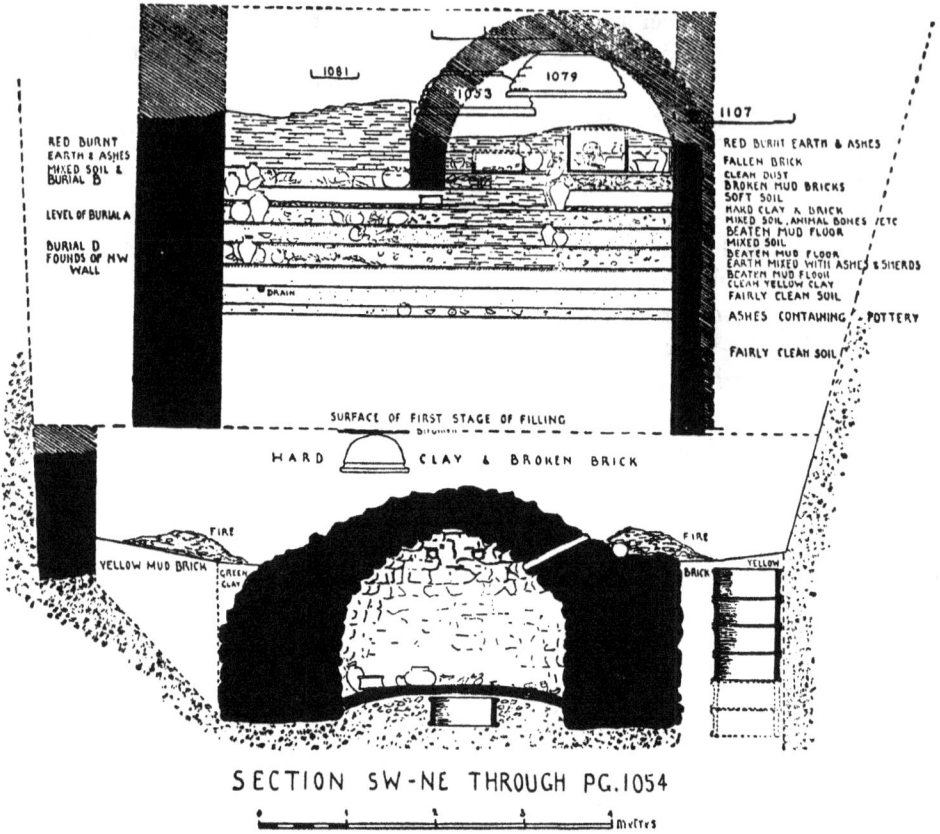

FIG. 85. Section through tomb 1054 in the Royal Cemetery at Ur.

Egypt under Dynasty III, but known in Assyria perhaps even earlier.

At Ur, as at Kish, the ideas implied by the underground house were carried out with the same barbarous logic as at Abydos. The 'royal' dead had been conveyed to the tomb on chariots or sledges clad in full regalia. Not only the draft animals, but drivers, men-at-arms, courtiers, musicians, and ladies of the harem were obliged to follow their sovereign to the future world. In the shaft outside the 'King's Tomb' at Ur lay no less than fifty-nine bodies, including six soldiers in full panoply, and nine women bedizened with costly jewelry (Fig. 86).

After the gruesome ceremonies in the tomb the shaft was filled in but only by stages, each marked by further rituals accompanied by

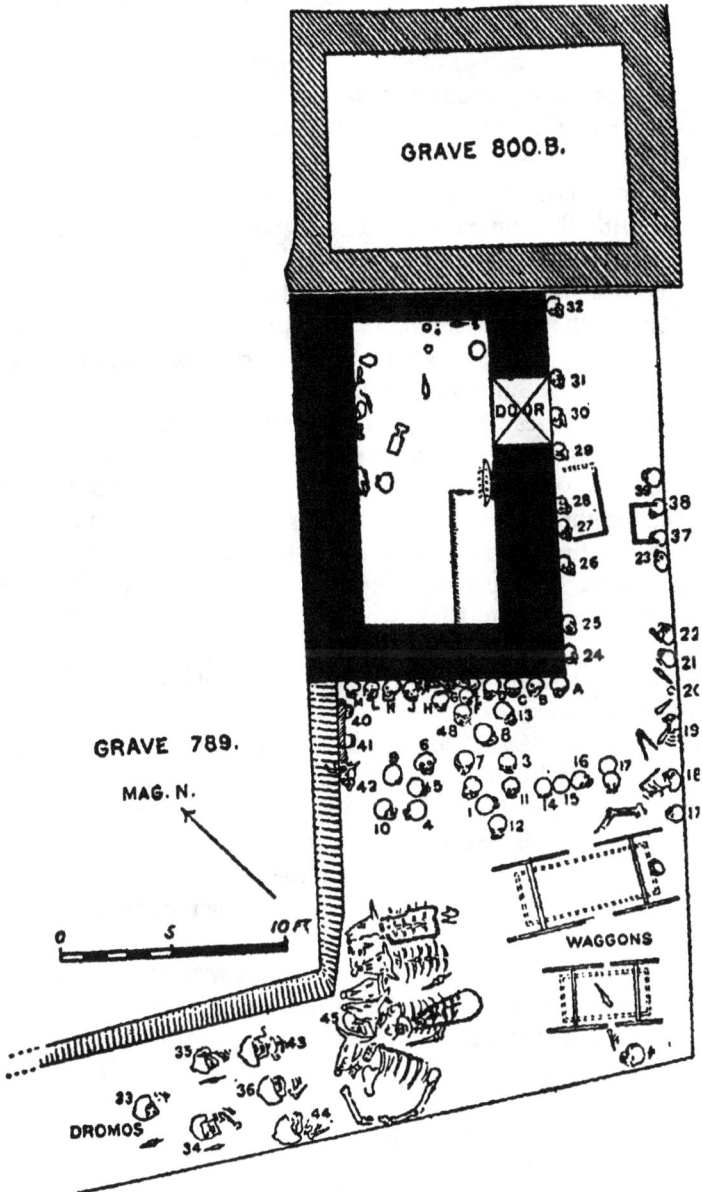

FIG. 86. Plan of two Royal Tombs at Ur, showing disposition of victims in
P G 789.

additional human sacrifices. Eventually some sort of funerary chapel was erected above the tomb, with which it was connected by a pottery funnel (Fig. 85). This, too, might be an approximation to Egyptian practices, though how close we cannot tell, since the supposed chapels have been destroyed. Another hint of Egyptian connections is given by a silver boat, Plate XXIV, *b*, from the 'King's Tomb' and bitumen models from commoners' graves. A comparison with the funerary barques interred in the boat graves of Hor-aha and later pharaohs and of nobles at Helwan is obvious, but perhaps fallacious; for later Babylonian literature gives hints of other functions, such as the removal of sins, for the model boats. The real Egyptian boats might, however, be more aptly compared to the real wagons from the Sumerian tombs.

Some authorities have indeed contended that the persons buried in these tombs at Ur were not secular rulers with their retinue, but the actors in some ritual drama. The arguments are far from conclusive, and the earlier tombs from Kish, Mari, and Susa do seem to provide the first good evidence for kingship in the full sense in Mesopotamia. It is perhaps significant that some of the earliest evidence comes from Kish where the King List places the first dynasty after the Flood and kingship of which was claimed from the dawn of written history by any prince who aspired to more than local sovereignty.[1]

Moreover, at least from Early Dynastic II we can recognize monumental buildings that were admittedly not temples, but the palaces of earthly rulers. The most imposing is the A Palace, at Kish,[2] with a pillared collonade, a 'sublime porte' embodying architectural principles taken from the Pillar Temple at Erech. Significantly situated, too, in view of Sumerian tradition is the palace discovered in 1949 at Eridu.[3]

The introduction of plano-convex bricks was, we saw, attributed to foreign invaders. The vaulted tomb in stone or brick could be interpreted in the same way. Again, several skeletons from Kish Y

1. Among the earliest legible inscriptions is one on a mace, dedicated by 'Mesilim, King of Kish'; he is not mentioned in the King List and probably ruled at Lagash, but possessed sufficient authority outside that city to impose a treaty on its neighbour, Umma.

2. Mackay, in *Field Museum Anthropology Memoirs*, i, 1929; Eliot, *EMWI.*, 20.

3. *Sumer*, vi, 1950, 31.

are described as brachycranial or Armenoid.[1] Men and gods are now often depicted wearing beards and long locks, though the beards may be false and wigs were undoubtedly worn.[2] Contenau[3] and others have stressed the resemblance between the royal burials at Ur and Kish and those of Eurasian nomads described by Herodotus and Marco Polo. Exponents of the 'culture historical school',[4] who believe that civilization is always due to the imposition of a conquering aristocracy of warrior-riders on a settled peasantry, would find here evidence for invaders from Central Asia whom they might even identify with the Sumerians. Some support for this view might conceivably be found in the Susa burials and in the eastern affinities of Scarlet Ware, the new ceramic group that helps to define Early Dynastic I.

On the other hand, just as gory burial practices could be quoted from modern Africa, and the satî burials round the tombs of Zer and his successors at Abydos offer the most apposite analogies to the victims in the tombs of Kish, Mari, and Ur. Moreover, the corbelled vault and other architectural features of these royal tombs have already been encountered in Egypt (p. 88). If then invaders be postulated, these should come from the west, imbued with Nilotic conceptions. If they must have a linguistic label, Semitic would seem the more appropriate, since there were Sumerians in Mesopotamia in the Jemdet Nasr period while Semites would be exposed to influence from Egypt. After all kings of the first dynasty of Kish bear Semitic names in the King List as do Early Dynastic rulers of Mari on their own statues.[5]

Still pottery, art, architecture, glyptic, script, and cult demonstrate very close continuity between Jemdet Nasr and Early Dynastic I.[6]

The form of Mesopotamian royalty and the burial rites of royalties might conceivably be modelled on those of the pharaonic monarchy; in time the unification of Egypt would just precede Early Dynastic I on one possible chronological system. Even its adoption would not make the first kings in Sumer necessarily

---

1. Pennyman, in Watelin, *Kish IV*, 68; others from Kish A are described by Buxton in *JRAI.*, lxi, 57 ff.
2. Cf. Frankfort, 'Sculpture of the IIIrd Millennium,' *OIP*, xliv, 1939, 49.
3. *Manuel*, iii, 1557.
4. E.g., Menghin, *Weltgeschichte der Steinzeit*, 1931, 435, 470.
5. *Rev. Ass.*, xxxi, 1934, 140–2.
6. Eliot, *EMWI.*, 33.

conquerors. Mesopotamian ideas of the Uruk–Jemdet Nasr period influenced Egypt, and the influence might be just reciprocal. Disputes about water rights were almost inevitable between closely juxtaposed communities with expanding populations, and as a result permanent war leaders might be found indispensible. At the same time, increase of wealth is always liable to lead to the differentiation of economic classes within communities. Their conflicting interests can best be reconciled by the subjugation of all to an independent authority more substantial than a mythical deity or rather incarnating the deity in a human embodiment such as Narmer or Aha actually became. An equally plausible chronology would allow the latter to be imitators of the first kings of Kish or Mari.

Whatever actually happened, the mortal 'kings' apparently succeeded better than immortal gods with priestly ministers in guaranteeing security to their followers and in extracting from them tithes or other dues so as to concentrate the social surplus as an effective capital. Though temple-building went on and rituals were continually elaborated, the secular rulers may have used some of this capital for more productive ends. They certainly succeeded better in organizing supplies of metal and other raw materials. A substantial increase of wealth is in any case attested by the more liberal industrial use of metal reflected in the furniture of Early Dynastic graves.

An increase of population, too, can be deduced from the magnitude of the public buildings now erected, from the extent of the cities and the number of graves in the cemeteries. Erech now covered some 1,100 acres, Ur 150. Perhaps, indeed, the population may have been more concentrated. Several prehistoric sites—Meraijib near Ur, Uqair, Jemdet Nasr—seem now to have been virtually abandoned. Improved transport enabled villagers to move their dwellings to the shelter of city walls and still bring home the produce of distant fields. Cities now certainly were walled, but an inner wall encircled the temple precincts, a practice foreshadowed in the Jemdet Nasr period at Erech.

The decisive contribution to civilization of Early Dynastic Mesopotamia was the creation or perfecting of an industrial and military equipment, including a system of writing and ciphering, items from which were borrowed or copied by more barbarous societies throughout Western Asia and even in temperate Europe. This contribution is perhaps most easily recognized in the domain of metallurgy.

The smiths of Mesopotamia now not only secured ample supplies of copper and other metals but also drew their supplies from various sources which would accordingly contain different impurities. They were thus theoretically in a position to discover that certain ores or mixtures of ores, i.e. ores containing tin, yielded a more satisfactory metal. Being further already familiar with lead and even an alloy of lead and copper (p. 129) they might, given the requisite ore, manage to isolate the beneficial impurity and add it to copper deliberately. In any case by Early Dynastic III at latest Sumerian coppersmiths were using bronze containing 6 per cent to 10 per cent tin.[1] It is by no means certain that Sumerian smiths really enjoyed these opportunities, still less that they took advantage of them and actually discovered bronze. Some bronzes from Assyria, Palestine, and even Troy may well exceed the Sumerian in antiquity, but they are still strictly prehistoric.

The Sumerians drew supplies of copper from Oman, from the Iranian plateau, and even from Anatolia, but the source of their tin is unknown. By the time of Sargon of Agade the supplies of tin seem to have been cut off at least from Ur. Even iron was sometimes employed. An object from the Royal Cemetery of Ur turned out to be of meteoric iron. But a dagger blade from Khafaje had been smelted from terrestrial ores.[2] It seems, however, to have been imported ready made, probably from Armenia. There, it can be deduced from later events, some barbarian tribe had discovered an economical method for smelting iron, but kept it secret successfully till the end of the IInd millennium.

The Sumerian coppersmiths had mastered the techniques of casting *cire perdue*, of riveting and brazing and used lead as solder. Whether cultivators benefited directly from their industry may be questioned. In Early Dynastic times the clay sickle was indeed finally abandoned, but its place was taken normally by angled sickles of wood, armed with flint teeth[3]; only a few metal sickles can be recognized[4] in Sumer though they are not rare in Assyria. Craftsmen

1. Desch, 'Reports of the Committee on Sumerian Copper,' in the *Annual Reports of the British Association for the Advancement of Science*, 1928 to 1936; Plenderleith, in Woolley, *Ur Excavations*, ii, 287 ff.; Delougaz, 'The Temple Oval,' *OIP.*, liii, 152.
2. *OIC.*, 17, 1934, 61.
3. Watelin, *Kish IV*.
4. Andrae, *Die archäische Ischtartempel*, 83, fig. 63; Genouillac, *Fouilles de Telloh*, i, 1934, pl. 11, 3b; *Iraq*, ix, 1947, 165. All these specimens may be Sargonid.

and warriors were, however, well equipped with metal tools and weapons. The types manufactured for their use were diffused from

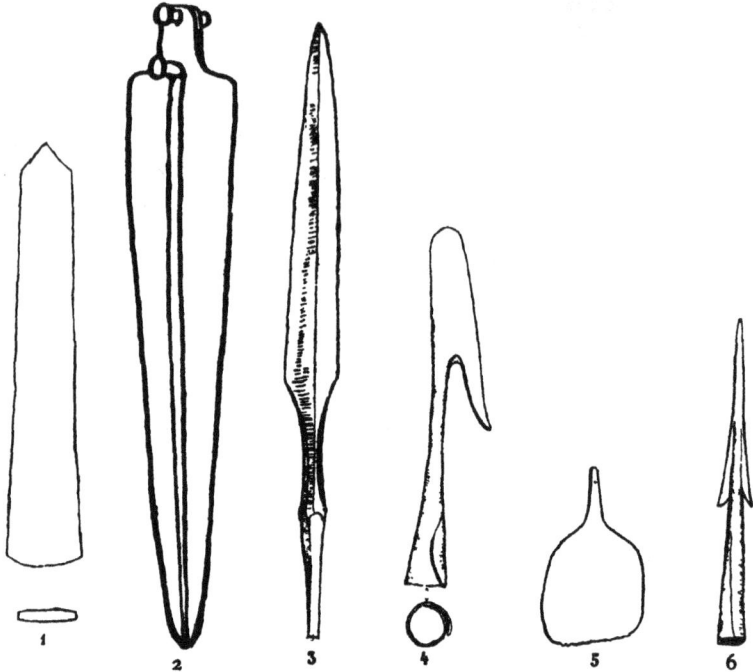

FIG. 87. Flat chisel, dagger blade, poker-butted spear-head, socketed harpoon head, razor, and dart head, Ur, ¼.

Iran to the Levant and admirably illustrate the range of Sumerian commerce and cultural influence. The most important[1] are:—

(1) Chisels—flat celts with pointed butts (Fig. 87, 1); (2) saws with a tang projecting from the centre of the butt (Fig. 88, 1);

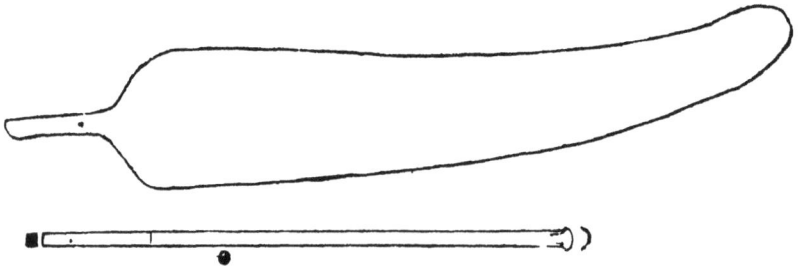

FIG. 88. Saw and gouge (drill-bit), Ur, ¼.

1. A list with references will be found in *MAGW.*, lxii, 1932, 228.

(3) subrectangular tanged 'razors' always found in pairs (Fig. 87, 5); (4) tweezers formed of two strips of metal sweated together; large versions probably served as tongs; the tweezers are often found together with ear-scoops and prickers, all looped like the knŏt-headed pin described on p. 63 and hung on a ring to form toilet sets (Plate XXVI, *b*); (5) fish-spears or flesh-hooks—both bident and trident—with tangs; (6) axes—or battle-axes—with the drooping blade sloping downwards from the shaft-tube (Fig. 89, 1); the back of the shaft-tube may be reinforced with mouldings or ridges or

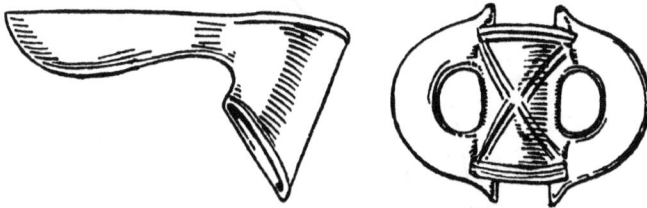

FIG. 89. Axe-heads, Ur, ¼.

studded with spikes; (7) shaft-hole adzes or transverse axes (Fig. 90); (8) ogival daggers strengthened with a midrib and provided with a tang to which the pommel was riveted (Fig. 87, 2); the junction is generally protected by a metal ferrule which always makes a convex line where it overlaps the blade in contrast to the Egyptian

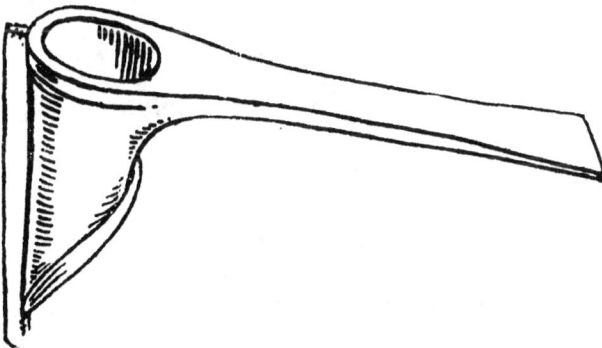

FIG. 90. Transverse axe-head, Ur, ½.

concave junction (Plate XXVI, *a*); (9) crescentic blades scalloped at the back, but generally made of thinner metal than the example shown in Fig. 91; (10) 'poker-butted spearheads' with (*a*) a leaf-shaped or (*b*) a poker-shaped blade, but always with an octagonal

base from which projects a tapering quadrangular tang for insertion
into a reed shaft (Fig. 87, 3); (11) socketed spear-butts formed by
folding a metal sheet into a cone; (12) double-barbed arrow-heads
with a socket similarly folded (Fig. 87, 6); (13) single-barbed dart-
heads, socketed in the same way (Fig. 87, 4); (14) forked arrow

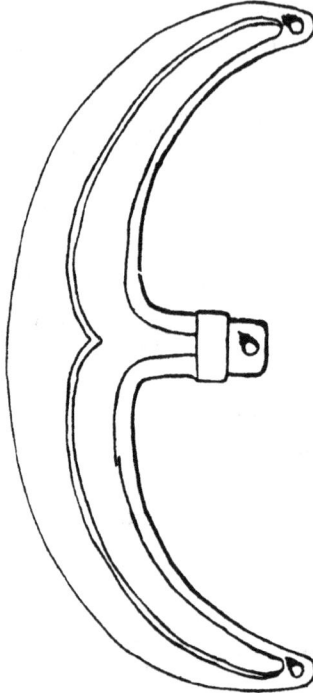

FIG. 91. Scalloped axe-head, Ur, ½.

and spear-butts fitted into the lower end of the reed shafts of arrows
and throwing spears to prevent the string splitting the reed (Fig.
83, 9).

From the published material little progressive change in the
equipment and armament is detectable within the long Early
Dynastic period, and much survived unchanged into Sargonid times.
Admittedly several types are known only from Early Dynastic III,
but that may be due to burial customs or the small number of early
graves published. Types 1, 2, 6, 8, 9, and 14 are, however, attested

by Early Dynastic I[1] while at Susa and Gawra type 7 is foreshadowed in an Uruk horizon.

Personal ornaments make a no less instructive continuation of the series of industrial types. We may mention here: (15) scroll-headed pins (Fig. 92, 5); (16) racquet pins (Fig. 93), probably worn in the

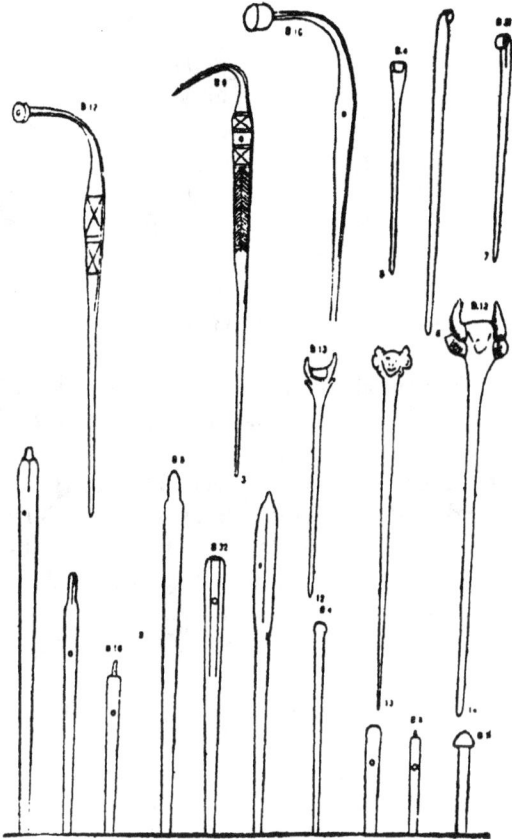

FIG. 92. Copper pins, A Cemetery, Kish, $\frac{1}{4}$.

hair; (17) pins with an eyelet in the flattened neck (Fig. 92, 1–4); (18) pins with small conical heads (Fig. 92, bottom right); (19) pins with animal heads (Fig. 92, 12–14); (20) hand-shaped hairpins with beads at the ends of the 'fingers' (Fig. 93).

1. Watelin, *Kish IV*, 22, 24; Hall and Woolley, *Ur Excavations;* i, *El Obeid*, 204, 210; *Syria*, xix, 4.

The goldsmiths and silversmiths were no less successful than workers in baser metal. They could braze and solder and hence make use of filigree work (Pl. XXVI, *b*) for the ornamentation of their products and at times even of a rather coarse granulation

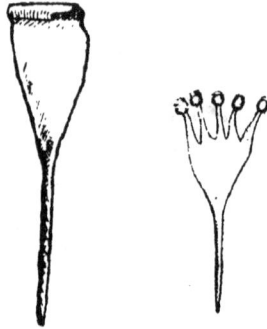

FIG. 93. Raquet and hand pins, Ur, ¼.

(Pl. XXVI, *a*). For royalties not only pins and toilet-sets but even weapons, saws, and chisels were made in gold or silver. Conversely, ornaments created by the jeweller were imitated in copper for poorer classes. Chiefly in the latter material several characteristic products of the Sumerian goldsmiths were diffused as widely as Sumerian types of tools and weapons. Important in this connection are the following: (21) spiral ear-rings with flattened ends developing into the exaggerated boat-shaped type of Pl. XXVII, *c*; (22) helical lock-rings with flattened ends, simple (Pl. XXV, *b*) or recoiled (Pl.

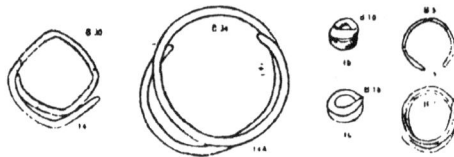

FIG. 94. Copper bracelets and ear-rings with flattened ends, Kish A, ⅛.

XXVII, *a*); (23) pendants in the form of two gold spirals linked together; (24) coiled gold helices singly (Pl. XXVII, *b*) or grouped in fours within a hoop (Pl. XXV, *b*); (25) beads formed of two grooved discs, soldered together so that the grooves unite to form a tube for the string (cf. Pl. XXXI); (26) metal discs ornamented with repoussé designs; a pair from Mari of Early Dynastic I bear six conical bosses grouped around a central boss while the edge of the disc is beaded.

Metal workers also manufactured vessels of various kinds. Apart from cauldrons and buckets, that survive only from tombs of Early Dynastic III, almost every form of vase, familiar in pottery, was reproduced in silver, gold or copper; even wine-skins, shell lamps, and shell paint-pots were copied in metal. Stone vases on the contrary seem less varied and less ornate than in the preceding periods. Still the Royal Cemetery of Ur contained superb vases of lapis lazuli and other semi-precious stones, comparable to those from the Abydos cemetery. For foreign relations block vases, constructed like the specimens from Egypt, mentioned on p. 94, that are common at the cemetery of Shuruppak (Fara), must be mentioned.

Inevitably pottery declined. For the service of the gods and even prosperous citizens, stone, gold, silver, and copper vessels were available; pottery was reserved for menial offices and the tables of

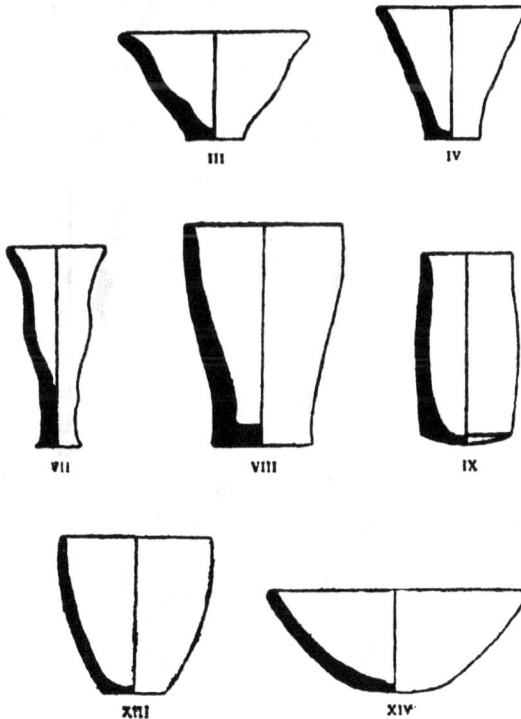

FIG. 95. Beakers and bowls, al 'Ubaid cemetery, ⅒.

the poor. Only during Early Dynastic I and II were any finer wares manufactured. Peculiar to Early Dynastic I is so-called 'Scarlet Ware', found from Mari to Susa.[1] The patterns both geometric motives reminiscent of Jemdet Nasr and favourite scenes of Early Dynastic art (Fig. 84) are outlined in black on the buff clay ground and then filled in with a bright, but ill-fixed, red paint. Plum-slipped ware survives from the Jemdet Nasr phase as late as Early Dynastic II. So does 'reserved slip ware'[2] in which the surface of the vase is completely covered with a brownish slip and parallel stripes of the slip are then removed with a comb—a fabric equivalent to the ' combed ware ' of Egypt and of Syria. But even the common pale drab wares were sometimes decorated with incised patterns although with decreasing frequency.

As in technique, so in form there are many elements of con-

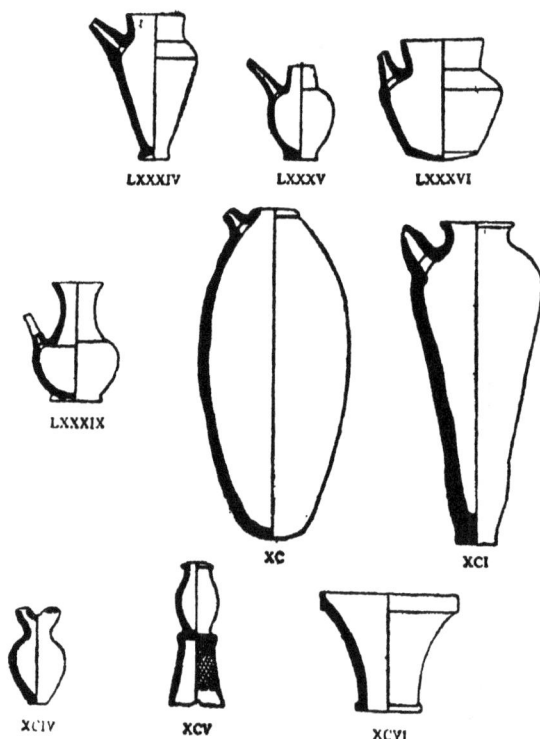

FIG. 96. Spouted jars from the Early Dynastic I (II) cemetery at al'Ubaid, $\frac{1}{5}$.

1. Frankfort, *OIC.*, 20, 65; *Syria*, xix, 5.
2. Frankfort, *OIC.*, 20, 62–5; *Ant. J.*, x, 339; Watelin, *Kish IV*, 14.

tinuity between Jemdet Nasr and Early Dynastic. Peculiar to Early Dynastic I are tall goblets on solid pedestals like Fig. 95, VII. But bell-shaped bowls like III in the same figure, the spouted libation vases and storage jars of Fig. 96 are direct descendants of older forms. Tall 'stands' open at both ends, common in Early Dynastic I and II, may be derived from 'braziers' fashioned already in Ubaid ware at Eridu, but they now carry bowls of metal or stone. In Early Dynastic II bowl and stand may fuse, producing the celebrated pedestalled bowls (Fig. 97) which by Early Dynastic III have

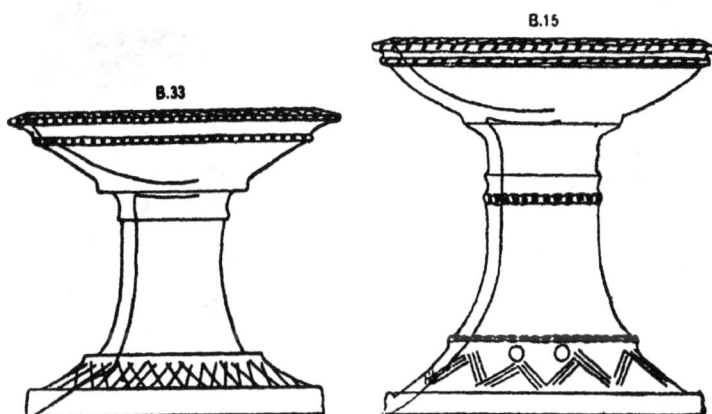

FIG. 97. Pedestalled bowls, A Cemetery, Kish, $\frac{1}{12}$.

replaced the open-ended 'stands' altogether. Loop handles had gone out of fashion by Early Dynastic I, but an upstanding lug handle was attached to the shoulder of carinated jars. By a process of degeneration this lug lost its function as a handle and in Early Dynastic II begins to bear a conventionalized female bust.[1] The result is the so-called 'granny pot' (Fig. 98), exceedingly popular in the A cemetery at Kish during early Dynastic III and recurring in the Royal Cemetery at Ur, at Mari, and at Susa.[2]

From the Sin Temple at Khafaje[3] comes a pedestalled bowl, like Fig. 97, but standing on a model shrine and running on four wheels. It is the oldest example of the wheeled ritual vessels subsequently made famous by the description of Solomon's temple and the

1. Harden in *Iraq*, i, 1934, 30–44.
2. Woolley, *Ur Excavations*, ii, pl. 187; *Antiquity*, v, 1931, 330.
3. *OIC.*, 19, 44.

wheeled cauldrons of Late Bronze Age Europe. In the same connection should be mentioned the metal strainers and bent tubes (straws) used in ceremonial beer-drinking. The symposium, two

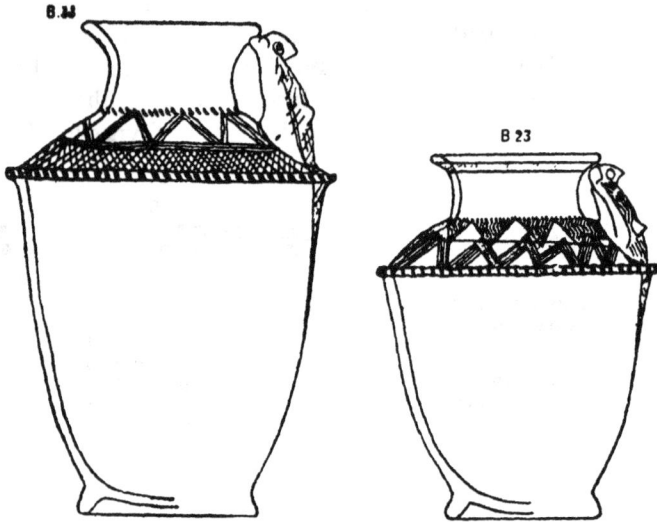

FIG. 98. 'Granary' pots, A Cemetery, Kish, $\frac{1}{12}$.

personages imbibing liquor through such tubes from a large jar, was a favourite theme from the Early Dynastic I vase of Fig. 84 (bottom left) to the 'Standard' and cylinders from the Royal Cemetery at Ur.

Much less use was made of fayence in Early Dynastic Sumer than in Egypt or India, and it was, in fact, confined to beads. True glass was known by the Sargonid period[1]; earlier beads from Fara may be of natural glass. Woodwork is only known indirectly. Apart from the chariots already described, we may mention thrones or couches with the legs carved to represent bull's feet, as in proto-dynastic Egypt. There are also harps and lyres of several types. In Queen Shub-ad's harp, the wooden sounding box was horizontal while an upright was fitted with eleven gold keys to which the strings were attached. In the lyres the sound box is again horizontal, but the nine strings are attached to a second parallel horizontal beam supported by mosaic-encrusted uprights precisely as in the instrument played by the donkey—or man dressed in a donkey's skin shown in Pl. I.

1. *OIC.*, 17, 56.

The favourite medium of the Early Dynastic artists of Babylonia was inlaying with shell, sometimes as in the Standard from Ur, combined with lapis lazuli and red stone, and engraving upon shell. A masterpiece of shell engraving is shown in our Plate I; Gadd[1] believes that the actors in the ritual here represented are really men dressed up in animals' skins such as appear already in palæolithic paintings from France; the combination of the Egyptian sistrum played by the jackal with the typically Sumerian Gilgamesh at the top is in any case amusing. Sculpture in the round—in wood plated with gold—is illustrated already by a bull's head from the same harp to which our engraving was attached, but is far less successful.

Stone sculptures in the round, as well as bas reliefs, were being carved already in Late Uruk times. Early Dynastic sculpture is richly illustrated by statuettes from Lagash, Mari, Khafaje, and Eshnunna.[2] On the whole, this art, like the glyptic, shows a decline from the magnificent vigour of the Uruk period and produced nothing like the masterpieces of Old Kingdom Egypt. In Early Dynastic II Frankfort writes, 'the human body is ruthlessly reduced to abstract plastic forms,' while later in III a more realistic rendering was attempted, not always with great success. Similar tendencies have been observed in seal-engraving.[3] In the Early Dynastic I 'brocade style' the conventionalized animals and fish of Jemdet Nasr have become purely geometric, as devoid of recognizable representational content as the barbarian Halafian stamp designs. Later fashions favoured scenes—generally mythological or ritual, but seldom endowed with the vitality of the best Uruk gems.

The works of art adequately illustrate Sumerian dress. The most familiar garment is a skirt or kilt such as was already worn in Uruk times. In Early Dynastic III it was made of a woollen fabric, covered with tassels which are reproduced in sculpture in the same way as the fleece of a ram. Men are generally depicted as wearing beards and long hair in Early Dynastic I and II, but more often clean shaven in Early Dynastic III. It may be that the earlier portraits depict artificial beards and wigs; bulls are represented as wearing obviously artificial beards and Mes-kalam-dug's grave at Ur contained a golden wig. In no case can fashions in costume nor hairdressing be used to distinguish between Sumerians and Semites as was once believed.

1. Gadd, *History and Monuments of Ur*, 1929, 36.
2. Frankfort, *OIP.*, xliv and lx.
3. Frankfort, *Cylinder Seals.*

The statue of a king of Mari, typically Sumerian in costume, is inscribed with the good Semitic name, Lamgi-Mari.

The uniformity in costume from Eridu to Mari is just one aspect of a comprehensive cultural unity whose authors may be called Sumerians whatever language they happened to talk; for no one is known to have written anything in a Semitic language till the days of Sargon of Agade.

The Sumerians lived in one-storeyed mud brick houses, divided into several rooms which were not normally grouped round an open court. A small private house at Khafaje[1] comprising five rooms occupied a space of only 10 m. by 6·5 m., but a larger dwelling with ten rooms covered an overall area of 30 m. by 20 m. In the latter some doorways were spanned by a genuine arch with keystone, a device illustrated also by some tombs, but were only 5 feet high! Small windows gave light to the rooms. Of course there was a domed bread oven in every house. In temples there were regular 'kitchen ranges',[2] easily mistaken for potters' kilns. The houses were grouped in compact blocks separated by tortuous streets and alleys. But within the city walls, beside the spacious temple courts, there must have been open spaces where cattle could wander as in a modern Indian city. Hence, despite its area, Frankfort[3] estimates the population of Ur, even when it was an imperial capital, as only 24,000 while Khafaje in Early Dynastic times would have held only half as many.

No doubt 'the city, cut off by its encircling wall from raw nature, offered men a purely human environment'. Yet most of the citizens were primary producers who tilled raw land or fished raw waters just outside those walls; tools of primary production, like flint-armed wooden sickles and fishing nets with their clay sinkers[4] turn up in urban residences. But secondary industries were carried on too, and these, like administration and the service of gods, demanded a specialist personnel. They required, too, raw materials imported from abroad; not only metals and gems, but even building timber and stone had to be fetched from outside the alluvial valley.

Some of the requisites may have been secured as booty or tribute. Sumerian princes occasionally boast of 'expeditions' which brought stone and metal for the adornment of temples. Each city had its

---

1. Delougaz, 'The Temple Oval,' *OIP.*, liii, 46; *OIC.*, 17, 10–16.
2. Delougaz, *OIP.*, liii, 130.
3. Frankfort, *Town Planning Review*, xxi, 1950, 104.
4. Delougaz, 'The Temple Oval,' *OIP.*, liii, 30, 54.

militia, trained to fight in phalanx formation, armed with metal pikes and battle-axes protected by helmets of beaten copper and led by chariotry. The best attested use of these armies was against similar armies in the internecine wars between the Sumerian city-states themselves. Doubtless they also served to protect the achievements of civilization against raids by still barbarous mountaineers or desert tribes. For their employment in obtaining raw materials there is no positive evidence before the time of Sargon, and even he is said to have used the forces of the empire to protect the interests of peaceful merchants already established in foreign parts. So the bulk of the supplies for urban industry must have been obtained by 'trade'.

The archæological record alone does not reveal new raw materials, other than tin, nor new sources of supply other than those attested by Uruk times. Nor do durable exports illustrate the expansion of Sumerian commerce. Just after 2000 B.C. written texts disclose that the most important commodities exported to Anatolia in exchange for metals were manufactures, especially fine textiles, that could not survive. The same probably held good of Early Dynastic trade. But in the latter archæologists can detect one striking innovation: the Sumerian cities were then receiving finished articles manufactured in another centre of civilization.

From the Early Dynastic II Temple of Sin at Khafaje,[1] was recovered a cylindrical stone vase, carved with a representation of a wicker house. Isolated examples of the same type have been found at Mari, Ur, and Susa.[2] Quite a number of such vases have been found in sites of the Kulli. culture in Makran where they were manufactured from local stone. From Makran they were exported, not only to the west but also eastward to the great cities of the Indus valley. From the Indus cities, too, manufactures reached Mesopotamia. From Mesopotamian cities and Susa over thirty seals have been collected which are either of Indus manufacture or close copies of Indus types. Only two come from Early Dynastic contexts, seven are Sargonid, three still later.[3] To the Sargonid period belong further shell inlays and other objects of types proper to the Indus cities, all found at Eshnunna on the Diyala.[4]

Such imported manufactures leave no doubt as to the reality of commercial connections between Mesopotamian cities and those in

1. *OIC.*, 19, 53.
2. Woolley, *Ur Excavations*, ii, pl. 178, a; *Syria*, xvi, 1935, pl. xxvii, 3; *Antiquity*, vi, 1932, 356; xvii, 1943, 167.
3. Piggott, *Antiquity*, xvii, 178.   4. *OIC.*, 16, 47–52.

the next great river valley beyond the plateau of Iran. Their concentration on the Diyala suggests that the trade followed an overland route. Moreover, a vase from Tell Agrab, again in the Diyala region, seems to depict an Indus cult scene[1]—a humped bull before a ceremonial manger as repeatedly depicted on Harappa seals. In style the vase is a Sumerian work of Early Dynastic III and was presumably carved in the city by a Sumerian artist. He had therefore presumably seen the Indus cult celebrated in Mesopotamia. That is not in the least surprising if the attested trade was conducted by caravans or flotillas of Indus merchants; for these would have to reside for several months at least at the terminal market to dispose of their wares and collect a return cargo. Indeed, a colony of Indus merchants permanently settled in a suitable Sumerian city would accord with modern practice and what is known of Oriental commerce in the IInd Millennium.

While Indus manufactures thus document direct commercial relations between the Tigris–Euphrates and the Indus valleys, the large consumption of lapis lazuli in Early Dynastic times illustrates no less regular trade north-eastwards towards the Oxus basin; for such quantities of lapis can only have come from Badakshan. But in this traffic at least Egypt also shared. So by 2500 B.C. we have concrete evidence of a network of trade linking up the whole area from the Tigris to the Indus and the Oxus and its extension west of the Euphrates as far as the Nile. While the best evidence for the eastern trade is provided by imports found in Sumerian cities and cemeteries, it was not, of course, unilateral. Apart from copies of Sumerian metal-work to be mentioned in later chapters, a few curiously etched carnelian beads from the Indus valley and Transcaspia are as likely to have been made at Ur as anywhere else.[2]

In any case, this traffic involved movements of persons as well as goods. In particular, skilled artisans could travel about and settle wherever they found a market for their skills as they do in the Orient even to-day. There would thus be ample opportunity for the interchange of ideas. So three civilizations were at this time pooling their cultural capital; for the Indus valley was as fully literate as Mesopotamia and Egypt.

To estimate the relative value of the last-named partners' respective contributions an attempt must be made to define the absolute chronology of the Early Dynastic Mesopotamia. The end of the Early Dynastic period, coinciding with the rise of the Empire of

1. *ILN.*, Sept. 12, 1936. 2. Beck, *Ant. J.*, xiii, 1933, 384.

Agade, has been fixed about 2325 B.C. The earliest ruler mentioned in the King List whose monuments survive is A-anni-padda of Ur; on Jacobsen's arrangement of the King List his accession should be dated about 2550 B.C. By the style of his seals and buildings his reign fell within the latter half of the archæologists' Early Dynastic III. All earlier phases are in practice prehistoric. Still some tablets from Shuruppak bear seal impressions of Early Dynastic II style and names, similar to those of the earliest historical kings of Kish.[1] The latters' reigns on a reconstruction of the King List (which gives no reliable figures for the early kings of Kish) can be put as early as 2800 B.C. So part of Early Dynastic II would fall within the twenty-ninth century or about the time of Menes on the shortest Egyptian chronology.

Some confirmation for these figures has been found in the history of certain temples; for temple building and rebuilding went on as energetically in Early Dynastic as in Uruk and Jemdet Nasr times. At Khafaje no less than ten versions of the Sin temple can be distinguished, five being Early Dynastic and the rest Jemdet Nasr. Delougaz[2] has advanced specific arguments, which are, however, by no means universally accepted, for assigning 100 to 140 years to each temple. Sin Temple VI would on his calculations have been built and Early Dynastic I would begin about 3175 B.C. By the same token the Jemdet Nasr phase should extend back to 3570. It would then be parallel to a large part of the Gerzean phase in Upper Egypt. The foregoing figures, however, are after all just reasoned—and reasonable—guesses. The relatively small changes observable in pot forms,[3] that are reasonably well known, between Jemdet Nasr and Sargonid times could just as well be cited as evidence for a drastically curtailed duration of the intervening period.

Since the Uruk period witnessed more building than did Jemdet Nasr the end of the Ubaid phase at Erech and Eridu would have to be put about 4000 B.C. on the foregoing calculations. The first Ubaid temple would then have been built about 4500 B.C. and be comparable in age to the Fayum neolithic as dated by radio-carbon!

---

1. Jacobsen, *The Sumerian King List*, 188-9; Frankfort, *OIC.*, 20, 'Commentary on the Chronological Table.'

2. Delougaz, 'Pre-Sargonid Temples,' *OIP.*, lviii, 126–133; cf. Frankfort, *OIC.*, 19, 87. (Reducing these figures to agree with new date of Sargon, this makes E.D.II begin about 3000 B.C.!)

3. Eliot, *EMWI.*, 33.

CHAPTER IX

INDIAN CIVILIZATION IN THE THIRD MILLENNIUM B.C.

THE third centre of higher civilization in the Ancient East, the lower valley of the Indus and its tributaries, agrees with Egypt and Babylonia in being an alluvial plain on which, owing to deficiency of rainfall, settled agriculture depends primarily on natural or artificial irrigation. In prehistoric times the analogy to Babylonia would have been still closer; for Sindh was then a real 'Mesopotamia' watered by the Great Mihran (Sarasvati) on the east in addition to the Indus on the west. But the area of natural irrigation is immensely greater than in Mesopotamia, extending right across the southern Punjab and up to the foot-hills; the broad plains along the Sutlej, the Ravi, the Chenab, and the Jhelum, in contrast to the high plains of Assyria, form a genuine continuation of those of Sindh proper. And in appearance the country to-day is very different from Iraq; it is neither mainly a treeless waste, like modern Sumer, nor yet a marsh like prehistoric Sumer and southern Iraq to-day.

Even where the flood waters no longer penetrate owing to dams, the low plains are covered with a regular jungle of trees and scrub nourished by the subsoil water. Though the level of the latter has risen since prehistoric times till it stands now 10 or 15 feet above the ancient ground surface, the relative level of the plain surface and the river bed presumably have remained unaltered. The city of Mohenjo-daro[1] itself was subject to inundations. Though perhaps rather less destructive than recent ones, these ancient floods imply the same facilities for irrigation as subsist to-day. There are, moreover, indications of more bounteous rains then than fall nowadays.

1. Marshall, Mackay and others, *Mohenjo-daro and the Indus Civilization*, London, 1932 (cited *Mohenjo-daro*, i). This work gave also the best general account of the civilization till the appearance of Piggott, *Prehistoric India*, London, 1950.

2. The increased rainfall was due rather to greater precipitation from the monsoon than to an eastward extension of Atlantic cyclones.

The prehistoric documents representa jungle fauna of tiger, elephant, and rhinoceros in contrast to the semi-desert animals of early Sumerian art. The lavish use of baked brick in the prehistoric cities would seem a needless extravagance under modern rainless conditions.

As in Egypt and Babylonia, the conditions of life on an alluvial plain involved organized co-operative effort to control and direct the flood-waters that made life possible and importations on a large scale to make it pleasant. Man's efforts to adjust himself to that environment and subdue it to his will accordingly culminated in the creation of an industrial and commercial urban civilization, but on a vaster scale than on the Nile or on the Euphrates. Only three of the ruined cities have so far been explored, Mohenjo-daro and Chanhu-daro[1] on the Indus and Harappa[2] on the Ravi, but they are already 400 miles apart. Yet the civilization of all three is astonishingly homogeneous; all the specific idiosyncrasies of architecture and town planning, of metal tools and weapons, of ornaments and beads, of art and epigraphy noted at Mohenjo-daro recur at Harappa. The agreement is so complete that every remark in the subsequent description would apply equally to all sites save in a few cases where contrary indications are given. And the agreement is not a simple uniformity explicable by parallel developments under similar environmental conditions, but something much more artificial, expressed, for instance, in the identity of a highly individualized and self-conscious ceramic and glyptic art. This is the sort of uniformity illustrated by the relics of archaic Sumerian civilization from Eridu to Mari. But after all the distance between those cities is only half that separating Chanhu-daro from Harappa; and these points do not mark the extreme limits. Identically the same civilization has been found downstream to Amri and upstream it is reported as far as Rupar on the Upper Sutlej.[3] The area embraced by the Indus civilization in the Harappa period must have been twice that of Old Kingdom Egypt and probably four times that of Sumer and Akkad.

What was the political counterpart of this cultural unity? In Egypt after Menes the cultural unity subsisting from the Delta to the First Cataract corresponded not only to a uniformity of environ-

1. Mackay, *Chanhu-daro Excavations*, 1935–36, New Haven, Conn., 1943.
2. Vats, *Harappa*, New Delhi, 1940.
3. For the distribution of the Harappa civilization as known in 1950 see Piggott, *Prehistoric India*; additional sites were identified in Bikanir State in 1951 and included in map.

ment, traditions, language, and racial stocks but also to political unification under a single sovereign. In Babylonia unity of material culture was accompanied by uniformity in language, religion, and racial types, but subsisted in spite of a multiplicity of independent states. Had the economic unity of the Indus environment found expression in political unification as well as in unity of material culture, religion, script, and presumably speech? No multiplication of weapons of war and battle scenes attests internecine conflicts between city states as in Mesopotamia, nor yet the force whereby a single king, as in Egypt, achieved by conquest internal peace.

At the moment the two cities of Harappa and Mohenjo-daro stand out like twin capitals in a single 'empire' among a number of smaller sites[1]—provincial townships, fortified villages, and possibly frontier posts and factories. The latter vary in area from 60,000 to 700,000 square feet ($1\frac{1}{4}$ to $15\frac{1}{2}$ acres). But at Harappa[2] a century ago the walled area could be seen to measure half a mile on every side. The circuit of Mohenjo-daro cannot have been inferior. But we cannot yet define the nucleus round which accumulated the surplus wealth or capital required for the conversion of the village into the city. Only since 1947 have we learned that each capital was dominated by a lofty citadel, protected by a massive inner rampart of baked brick.[3] That at Harappa covered 460 by 215 yards and immediately controlled a huge granary, covering a total area of 168 by 135 feet and consisting of two blocks of six chambers each. At Mohenjo-daro a comparable granary was discovered in 1950, this time within the citadel enceinte.

That a 'ruler' dwelt in the citadels is clear, and the attachment thereto of great granaries concretely expresses his economic power; like the Sumerian city-god or the divine pharaoh he concentrated the real wealth produced by the city's dependent territories. But was he an imaginary god or a real divine king? A Buddhist stupa and recent graves respectively have prevented such complete excavation of the citadels as should reveal either a temple or a palace.[4] The most imposing building exposed in the citadel of Mohenjo-daro is a public bath. But the efficacy of this still undefined authority can be deduced from the administration attested by the ruins themselves.

1. Piggott, *PI.*, 171–4.   2. Vats, *Harappa*, 4.
3. Wheeler, *Ancient India*, iii, 1947, 61–76.
4. The building termed a 'palace' by Mackay, *Further Excavations at Mohenjo-daro*, New Delhi, 1938 (*Mohenjo-daro*, ii), is just a large merchant's house like the others that surround it.

The cities were carefully laid out on a deliberate plan, and the plan was adhered to strictly during several phases of reconstruction so that the streets were always maintained at a constant width. The cities were provided with elaborate corbelled drains running to sumps which would only function if these pits were periodically cleared out, presumably by public functionaries.

Within the urban population itself architectural remains reveal differences of wealth, amounting almost to class divisions. At Harappa[1] just below the citadel were built rows of two-roomed detached cottages that demonstrably housed artisans. They contrast glaringly with the spacious two-storeyed houses comprising court-yards, bathrooms, many apartments, and often a private well, that accommodated what may be termed the Harappan bourgeoisie. Yet even in these houses rooms on the ground floor served as shops or stores ('go-downs').

Racial differences, too, may have divided the urban population.[2] It was certainly mixed; the skeletal remains and figurines undoubtedly belong to several physically distinct types. At the bottom of the social scale came a primitive 'Australoid' stock; the thick lips and coarse nose of a little bronze statuette (Pl. XXIX) disclose at once the kinship of this group to the surviving aboriginal tribes of Southern India and the position which it, like its modern representatives, occupied in the community. A higher type, long-headed like the last, has been termed Eurafrican or even Mediterranean. It seems to approximate to one of the long-headed Sumerian types and the similarity is accentuated in the portrait statues (Pl. XXVIII) by the beard, shaven upper lip, and long hair done up in a bun behind quite in Sumerian fashion. Thirdly, a brachycephalic Alpine or Armenoid type is represented as at Kish in Akkad. Finally, a single skeleton and several clay figurines belong to undoubted Mongols or Mongoloids, the earliest dated examples of this racial type yet detected, but possibly post-Harappan.

The great cities which sheltered this mixed population were built almost entirely of brick, and most of the bricks were kiln-baked. At Mohenjo-daro mud-brick was hardly ever used except for fillings; at Harappa kiln and mud-bricks sometimes were built in alternate courses of the walls. In the earliest fortifications, however, the bricks were laced with timbers—a device more suitable to mud-brick architecture—and subsequently abandoned. The brickwork

1. Vats, *Harappa*, 63; Piggott, *PI.*, 169.
2. *Mohenjo-daro*, i, 638 ff.; ii, 630; *Anthropos*, xxviii, 1933, 148.

was entirely plain, but there is a little direct evidence that it was faced with mud plaster which, as in Buddhist and modern India, would doubtless be a vehicle for decoration. Timber, local sissoo wood and deodara imported perhaps from the Himalayas, was also employed in building, but stone was scarcely used; stone door-sockets, such a feature of Babylonian architecture, were replaced by brick ones. The larger houses are generally provided with both wells and bathrooms, but unambiguous latrines were found in only one late house.

The Indus economy, like the Egyptian and Babylonian, rested on irrigation farming. A bread-wheat (*Triticum compactum*), barley, dates, peas, and sesame were cultivated; the unit of weight suggests also rice-growing, but direct evidence is lacking. Cotton took the place of flax. Humped Indian cattle (zebus) and a humpless breed (known only from seals and clay models), buffaloes, goat, (urial) sheep, fowls, and elephants were kept domesticated; swine bones, though common, seem to belong to the local wild boar and need not indicate pig-breeding. In the latest layers at Mohenjo-daro bones of camel, ass, and horse occur, but these animals are never represented on seals nor by clay models and may have arrived only after the end of the Harappa civilization.

The cities were inevitably centres of commerce and drew even foodstuffs from a wide area. Transport was facilitated by wheeled vehicles and boats. The wheels were made of three solid planks, as in Sumer and Elam and in modern Sindh, with the hub carved in relief on the central plank.[1] Clay and bronze models[2] illustrate (i) two-wheeled carts, almost identical with modern village carts,[3] (ii) light covered wagons[2] resembling the modern *ekka* and the two-wheeled *arba* of Eurasiatic steppe folk, and (iii) a four-wheeled wagon with high dashboard,[4] recalling the Sumerian chariot on the Standard from Ur. The only draft animal positively attested is the humped ox. The boat, represented on only one seal[5] resembles modern river craft, but looks not unlike the vessel depicted on Uruk tablets and seals (Fig. 64).

Trade was sufficiently well organized to secure regular supplies not only of foodstuffs from the coasts but also of metal from

1. Mackay, *Chanhu-daro*, 162.
2. Vats, *Harappa*, 99–100; *Chanhu-daro*, 163.
3. *Ant. J.*, ix, 26.
4. *Chanhu-daro*, pl. lviii, 9, 13.
5. *Mohenjo-daro*, ii, 1938, pl. lxxxix, A.

Rajputana or Baluchistan, of śank shell from Southern India, and of luxury articles from still further afield—lapis lazuli from Badakshan, jade from China or Burma, amazonite from Gujerat or even the Nilgiri Hills. We have seen Indian manufactures, including even seals and knobbed pottery vases, reaching Mesopotamia during the last half of the IIIrd millennium. Conversely cylinder seals and toilet sets of Sumerian form were occasionally copied in the Indus valley.[1]

The secondary industries of the Harappa cities are parallel to those practised at the same date on the Tigris and the Nile. But the treatment of the material is different, and in some respects the Indus folk were ahead of their Sumerian or Egyptian fellows.

Metallurgists smelted silver, lead, and copper and worked gold too. Coppersmiths employed tin bronze as in Sumer, but also an alloy of copper with from 3·4 to 4·4 per cent of arsenic, an alloy used also at Anau in Transcaspia. They could cast *cire perdue* and rivet, but never seem to have resorted to brazing or soldering. At Harappa metal-workers used furnaces of the 'pot' type, 3 ft. 4 in. in diameter and 3 ft. 8 in. deep into which the blast must have been forced downwards through oblique channels by some sort of efficient bellows.[2] Large pear-shaped furnaces, as much as 8 ft. 3 in. long and partly divided into two by a brick partition projecting from the back wall along the axial line, may have been used rather by potters.

The tools and weapons produced by the Harappan smiths look more primitive than the Sumerian. The most significant types are: (1) flat chisels, wider but flatter towards the butt than lower down (Fig. 99, 3); (2) flat axes with curved, splayed blades; (3) small saws with a straight back like early Egyptian types and agreeing precisely with the iron saws used at present by Indian workers in shell; (4) flat-tanged daggers with a midrib and two very small rivet-holes near the base of the blade, the whole being hammered up from a stout rod (Fig. 99, 2) (these are late or even post-Harappan[3] but technically very 'Indian'); (5) spear-heads with a flat tang and a broad, flat blade, made like the daggers by hammering (Fig. 99, 5); (6) single-edged knives recurving near the point but straight or humped along the back and provided with a short tang but no rivet-holes (Fig. 99, 1); (7) razors with a broad convex blade projecting like an axe from a thin metal shaft and balanced by a semi-

1. *Mohenjo-daro*, ii, 345; *ARSI.*, 1927–28; 73–6; 1928–29, pl. xxviii.
2. Vats, *Harappa*, 470–2.
3. Piggott, *PI.*, 229.

circular projection on the opposite side (Fig. 99, 4); (8) a pruning hook, such as is used in India to-day; (9) an ox-goad; (10) sickles, presumably of the jaw-bone family, but rare; (11) hollow-based arrow-heads without tangs cut out of sheet copper. The whole series

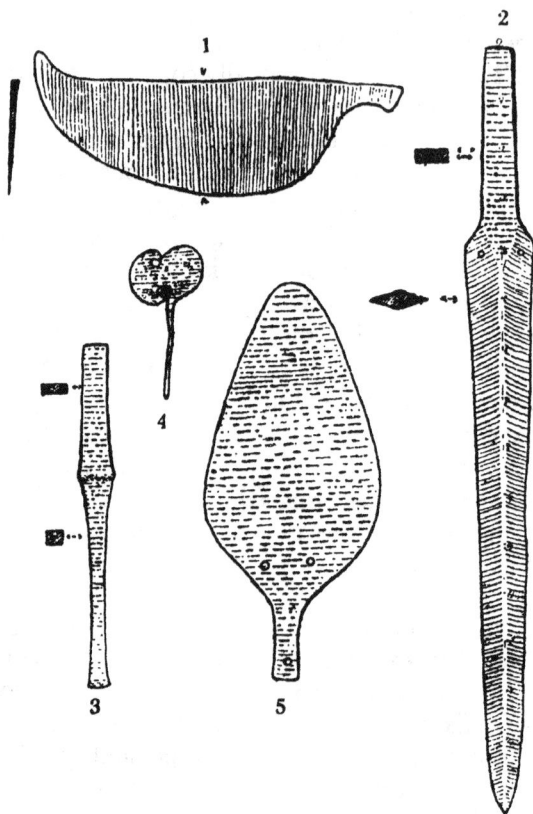

FIG. 99. Copper saw, dagger, chisel, razor, and spear-head, Mohenjo-daro, ¼.

offers striking contrasts to the Sumerian types, listed on p. 158. In particular, the Sumerian method of mounting an axe by a shaft-hole through the blade was never regularly employed. It is true that there is a painted clay model of an axe apparently mounted in this way and one actual axe-adze from Mohenjo-daro.[1] But the former is quite isolated and unrepresented by a single metal specimen while the axe-adze comes from a superficial layer and belongs at best to the last days of the declining Harappa civilization. Pins again were

1. *Mohenjo-daro*, ii, 458–9, pls., cxii, 1; cxx, 27.

not a normal accessory of Harappa costume; an isolated specimen[1] with a double spiral head, as in Hissar II and Sialk III, must have belonged to a foreigner. Similarly, the sole surviving pair of tweezers forms part of a toilet-set,[2] the several implements being attached to a knotted loop precisely as in the Sumerian examples from which the Harappa set was probably copied.

Vessels also were made in copper, silver, or lead, but all the shapes recur in pottery (Fig. 100). The goldsmith made little use of

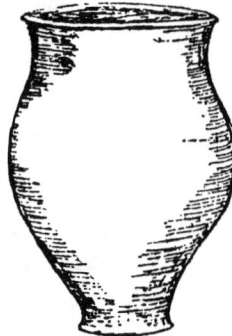

FIG. 100. Copper beaker from Mohenjo-daro, ⅓.

filigree work so popuiar in Sumer, but he could solder and achieved delicate effects by mounting in gold small beads. A silver buckle[3] adorned with a scroll pattern of gold wire and gold-capped beads is a fine specimen of his work. Among other types of gold bead, the disc-shaped form described as No. 25 on p. 162 is noteworthy (Pl. XXXI).

Pottery still occupied a more honourable place in the Indus Valley than in Sumer, and fine wares were produced and sometimes gorgeously decorated. The potter used the fast wheel. Though he normally produced pale or pinkish-red wares, he could control the firing so as to produce a grey fabric like the Uruk ware described on p. 123. The normal technique seems to have been that used to-day by village potters in Sindh;[4] certain articles, notably the tool used for smoothing the vessels and a peculiar stopper, now in daily use by potters in the adjacent villages, have been found in the ruins of Mohenjo-daro. The same type of stopper is that used in Babylonia in the Jemdet Nasr phase and illustrated in Fig. 65.

1. *Chanhu-daro*, 195, pl. lxviii, 9. 2. *RASI.*, 1923–24, 52–5.
3. Vats, *Harappa*, 64, pl. cxxxvii. 4. Mackay, *JRAI.*, lx, 1930, 131–4.

Red or cream slips were used on the finer fabrics and the surface of the red vases might be burnished; even the grey ware was sometimes coated with a dark-grey slip which, as in red ware, owed its colour to iron oxides, this time reduced.[1] The commonest form is a little drinking cup with a curious pointed base, always very rough (Fig. 101); such vessels were probably broken as soon as they

FIG. 101. Drinking cup from Mohenjo-daro and painted sepulchral chalice from Harappa.

had once been used according to contemporary Indian practice. Narrow, almost pointed, bottoms were, however, common in other shapes, particularly in large storage jars. Spouts are confined to shallow feeding-bowls that are far from common, and the only approach to a handle is seen in pierced fanlike ears attached to a rare class of cup. Narrow-necked jars are indeed relatively rare, long-necked bottles or flaring mouths are unknown. On the other hand, the basin on a high foot occurs in red ware, grey ware, and decorated ware and, as in Sumer, is often found in graves (Fig. 101). Another relatively conspicuous type is a cylindrical jar with perforated walls.

The vases might be decorated with the imprint of a cord, by brushing over a thick creamy slip as in Sumerian reserved slip ware, or with little knobs, but the finest were painted. The paint is generally black and applied with a stiff brush over a dark red slip or wash, exceptionally over a creamy slip. In the latest occupation at Mohenjo-daro a polychrome ware appeared: black patterns on a cream ground are filled in with red, green, or yellow pigments applied after firing.

1. *RASI.*, 1928-29, 153.

The black-on-red painted decoration illustrates better than anything else the unity, the originality, and the antiquity of the Indus civilization; for it has a mature, self-conscious style quite unlike anything else, but found with complete uniformity from Amri to Harappa. The essential feature of this style is the use of large surfaces, alternating in broad zones and panels each closely covered either with conventionalized vegetable designs—trees, leafy boughs, or creepers—or with repetition patterns. Under the last term are understood motives that can be repeated indefinitely in any direction. By far the most popular was the intersecting circle (yielding rosettes or, when combined with chequers, the so-called stretched hide motive), then came the scale pattern (based on semicircles) and at a long interval chequers, triangles (the latter always completely alternating so that a blank triangle, for instance, always has a hatched triangle standing on each of its sides) and complicated patterns based on the wavy line, the cross, a T figure, or hearts (Pl. XXXII). Similar patterns were popular also in other arts, such as shell-inlaying. Motives which recur as independent zone patterns in other regions are here used only as borders for the large fields: we find the roundel, the dotted ladder, and more rarely alternating triangles (the hatched guilloche, hatched wavy band, and combinations of hatched triangles and semicircles occur chiefly on the rare pale-slip wares). Figures of animals are quite exceptional; sometimes little peacocks are introduced among the leaves, and a unique sherd from Harappa[1] depicts a farmer's family and livestock. A curious motive, found generally on pale ware from Mohenjo-daro, resembles a large comb but may be a conventionalized version of a bull.

Fayence was extensively manufactured in India. It was used for bracelets (Pl. XXX, d), statuettes (Pl. XXX, c), stamps, and beads, as well as for small vases that imitate common pottery forms. A few sherds of pottery from early and middle levels at Mohenjo-daro are covered with a genuine glaze. Stone vases were on the other hand rare; the most interesting are imports and agree with the carved stone vases imported into Mesopotamia in Early Dynastic II (p. 169).

Weapons, as remarked, were exceedingly rare; the commonest was the sling, round and ovoid sling pellets being quite common. Mace heads also occur, generally spheroid or pear-shaped as in Babylonia, exceptionally disc-shaped. Flint weapons are unknown, and indeed flint and stone tools are represented only by a few quite

1. Vats, *Harappa*, pl. lxix, 3; No. 16 shows a fisherman and nets.

simple blades and a few large chert tools flaked like celts, one being rectangular in cross-section just like a Nordic thick-butted celt.

After the pottery the most distinctive products of the Indus culture and art were the seals (Pl. XXX). The commonest are square tablets of steatite with a boss on the back and engraved on the face; after cutting they were glazed over. They are engraved with legends in an undeciphered script and admirably executed representations of animals—(in order of frequency) 'unicorns', short-horned bulls, Brahmani bulls, elephants, rhinoceros, tigers, buffaloes, crocodiles, and antelopes. Similar designs in the same conscious style are found engraved on flat copper tablets with an 'inscription' on the reverse. There are also long, narrow gable seals, perforated longitudinally and bearing inscriptions only, and rectangular button-shaped stamps of steatite or fayence adorned only with geometrical patterns, including the swastika. Though all these objects have been classed as seals, there is no evidence of their ever having been used to seal anything, whereas in Mesopotamia or Egypt sealings are far commoner than seals. The nearest approach in India is provided by small tablets of baked clay which do bear seal impressions but nothing else and are complete in themselves. The term 'seal' is therefore conventional, and the objects thus denoted must be classed as ritual—a learned way of saying that we have no notion what they were for.

Carefully-shaped stone discs and tetrahedra, as in Sumer, may have been gamesmen. A game with dice was certainly played, the dice being cubical as in Sumer, though rather differently numbered.

Men wore a shawl draped round the shoulders and women some woven garment that needed no pinning. Bangles were very popular in contrast to Egyptian or Mesopotamian fashions; they were made of polished pottery (red or dark grey), metal, shell, or fayence (often decorated with ribs or spiral ridges). The hair was bound with fillets of gold ribbon as in Mesopotamia. Necklaces of several strands were worn round the throat. The terminals, gold or gold-plated, are often semicircular, a type found in Egypt and at Byblos in Old Kingdom times, but represented on painted sherds from Elam that may be earlier (Pl. XXXI, top). In addition to the gold disc beads already mentioned (p. 194) as recurring in Sumer, Egypt, and even Troy, we have gold caps for pendants with a little loop soldered on inside (Pl. XXXI, bottom), a type again found at Troy. Segmented fayence beads seem to belong only to the very latest phase of the

Harappa civilization or to its barbaric successors.[1] Notable, too, are carnelian beads etched with white patterns[2]—rare but imitated in paste—long bicones of carnelian as in the Royal Tombs at Ur and a flattened cylinder of agate precisely like some from Queen Shub-ad's tomb in the same cemetery.[3] The most distinctive Indian bead seems, however, to have been a small disc with milled or notched edge. Amulets are rare. Some miniature animals in fayence might be included here. Rams have their legs doubled under them precisely in the style of lapis rams and bulls from the Royal Tombs at Ur. A fly amulet of bone or ivory is exceptional and presumably copies Egyptian or Sumerian types.

Temple-ornaments or buttons in the shape of plano-convex discs of steatite,[4] perforated on the flat face by two holes, converging to an inverted V, illustrate a type familiar in the prehistoric 'Copper Age' of temperate Europe.

The only burial rite attested in the sole regular Harappa cemetery[5] yet known was inhumation in the extended position, in a long grave pit, the body being accompanied by many vases, personal ornaments, and toilet articles; at least one corpse lay in a wooden coffin wrapped in a reed shroud. But near the coastal settlement of Tharro[6] dry stone chambers, measuring 10 feet by 3 feet and as much as 2 feet high, may have contained burials of the Harappa period. On the other hand, in both the major excavated sites cremation burials and fractional burials in urns[7] have been reported while complete skeletons, isolated or in groups, have been exposed in houses or lanes.[8] But the funerary character of the 'urn burials' is doubtful; the skeletons from lanes and houses do not represent formal interments, and may belong to victims of raids or plagues.

Enough has been said to show that India confronts Egypt and Babylonia by the third millennium with a thoroughly individual and independent civilization of her own, technically the peer of the rest. And plainly it is deeply rooted in Indian soil. The Indus civilization represents a very perfect adjustment of human life to a specific

1. *Anc. India*, iii, 123.
2. *JRAS.*, 1925, 698; *Man*, xxxiii (1933), 150; *Ant. J.*, xiii, 1933, 384.
3. *Antiquity*, v, 1931, 459.
4. *Chanhu-daro*, 197; *Harappa*, 443.
5. *Anc. India*, iii, 1947, 86–9.
6. Piggott, *P.I.*, 207.
7. *Mohenjo-daro*, i, 86 ff., *Harappa*, 161.
8. *Mohenjo-daro*, ii, 94, 117; *Harappa*, 197.

environment, that can only have resulted from years of patient effort. And it has endured; it is already specifically Indian and forms the basis of modern Indian culture. In architecture and industry, still more in dress and religion, Mohenjo-daro reveals features that have always been characteristic of historical India. A few of these may be mentioned here.

In architecture, besides the inferred use of stucco, the number of bathrooms and the virtual absence of latrines, there is a room provided with a well and stands for water-jars which seems the definite forerunner of the *piau* or waterstall, such a distinctive feature of an Indian bazaar. The carts and boats as remarked agree with those still in use in the country to-day. Clay models of couches depict the form now used in India, though paralleled also in ancient Susa and Assyria. The village potters in Sindh seem to have inherited their craft direct from the Indus period. The absence of pins, the love of bangles and of elaborate nose-ornaments are all peculiarly Indian traits. Kohl was used for the eyes as elsewhere, but at Mohenjo-daro it was kept in little flasks and applied with copper rods which seem distinctively Indian. Ivory combs worn in the hair agree exactly with the wooden combs still worn. Stone or rough pottery flesh-rubbers from Mohenjo-daro are similar to toilet articles at present in use in India, though they find parallels also at Kish in Early Dynastic times.

Religion[1] gives the most convincing illustration of the explicitly Indian character of the Indus civilization. Many objects from the ancient cities, otherwise unintelligible, can be satisfactorily explained by reference to Hindu cult. The innumerable clay figurines, indeed, are not without parallels elsewhere. In India the majority represent a female personage, often richly bejewelled and sometimes pregnant or nursing an infant; some may be votive statuettes of deities, but others may represent petitioners, or even dolls. So, too, among clay models of animals the frequent Brahmani bulls may be regarded as sacred, but others, such as oxen provided with a moveable head, are obviously toys like the equally common miniature carts, couches, loaves, and vases. But there are aniconic objects, notably huge stone phalli and rings, often wavy along the edge, that correspond to the lingas and yonis of Hindu fertility cults.

The 'seals' and tablets of stamped clay, engraved copper, or moulded fayence offer more conclusive evidence. A 'seal' from

1. Mohenjo-daro, i, 48–78.

Mohenjo-daro depicts a horned deity with three faces sitting cross-legged in the attitude of ritual meditation between various wild animals; he is obviously the protoype of Śiva, 'three-faced,' 'lord of beasts,' 'prince of yogis,' as Marshall has demonstrated in detail. Several clay tablets depict a male deity; one shows a river gushing out of a goddess's womb. In other cases tree-spirits are clearly indicated. In contrast to such themes, all familiar to Hindu iconography, are isolated motives suggestive of Babylonia—an antithetic group of 'a hero dompting tigers' and a half-human monster like the Sumerian Enkidu grappling with a bull or a tiger. The swastika and the cross, common on stamps and plaques, were religious or magical symbols as in Babylonia and Elam in the earliest prehistoric period, but preserve that character also in modern India as elsewhere.

The religious concepts suggested by the foregoing documents are familiar to modern and post-Vedic Hinduism. But they are conspicuously absent from the oldest of the Hindu sacred books, the Rig-Veda, while scenes illustrative of its hymns may be sought in vain in the Indus period. Siva as depicted at Harappa and Mohenjo-daro is generally regarded as an 'aboriginal' deity taken over by the invading Vedic Aryas and verbally identified with the unimportant Vedic Prajapati. Tree-spirits and female deities played a negligible role in Vedic mythology, and phallicism is unmentioned —all have been regarded by European scholars as post-Vedic accretions in Brahmanism. Conversely, the celestial figures of the Vedic pantheon, like the thunder-wielding Indra, are not detectable in the Indus period. The horse, so prominent in Vedic imagery and a principal sacrificial animal, is never represented on the 'seals', which yet must have had a religious virtue.

For the above reasons alone the Indus civilization may be regarded as non-Aryan and pre-Aryan. In fact, it provides a documentary illustration of the sources, long inferred on comparative grounds, of those 'accretions' which distinguish modern Brahmanism from the religion and ritual illustrated in the Vedas.

The delicate and, as we now see, enduring adaptation to the Indian environment represented in the Indus civilization, can only have been created and spread over a vast area after a long period of incubation on the spot. Yet this civilization, though contrasted to the Egyptian and the Sumerian as specifically Indian, rests upon the same fundamental ideas, discoveries, and inventions as they. The agreements are indeed mostly quite general and abstract—city life, cultivation of cereals, domestication of cattle and sheep, metallurgy, a textile industry, manufacture of bricks and pots, drilling of hard stones for beads, an affection for lapis lazuli, a knowledge of fayence. But even so they can hardly be regarded as independent inventions accumulated in similar environments.

Direct commercial intercourse between the valleys of the Indus and of the Tigris–Euphrates is unimpeachably demonstrated by the actual Harappan manufactures from Mesopotamia, mentioned on p. 170. It may explain some rather superficial agreements between the two civilizations, but not the underlying technological and economic bases, common to both. It does, however, provide a reliable basis for the chronology of a civilization which, though not preliterate is, for us, still prehistoric. The best-dated imports in Mesopotamia, providing a *terminus ante quem* for the Harappa period, belong to the Sargonid age. Only a couple of 'seals' and stone vases imported into both areas from an intermediate centre illustrate trade connections in Early Dynastic times, before 2350 B.C. Other Indus 'seals' from a post-Akkadian context in Mesopotamia imply a persistence of the Harappa civilization down to 2000 B.C. Plainly then the Harappa civilization is not the result of a mere transplantation or imitation of the Early Dynastic Sumerian. Both are based on the same fundamental discoveries and inventions, but these have plainly undergone a long divergent development in the two areas since the latest common elements reached Mesopotamia in Uruk times.

Of the developments in India during that millennium little evidence is available in 1950. The Indus cities were more than once ravaged by disastrous floods. After each catastrophe the building levels were raised; the old ground-floor rooms were filled with clay or brick while the well-shafts were extended upwards, till to-day they tower like factory chimneys over early foundations. The surviving deposits are accordingly enormously deep, but no significant cultural changes can be observed to distinguish successive levels. The Harappa civilization from first to last exhibits no signs of progress in script or art, in metal-work or architecture.

Still beneath the citadel wall at Harappa a few sherds turned up, which, although wheel-made, have no place in the Harappan ceramic series, but suggest a settlement of illiterate villagers[1] with affinities in northern Baluchistan, in a pre-Harappa period. So, too, in the Lower Indus valley, in Sindh, Majumdar[2] found at Amri and

1. Piggott, *P.I.*, 142; *Anc. India*, iii, 91–3.
2. *MASI.*, xlviii, 1934, 25 ff.; cf. Piggott, *P.I.*, 94.

several other sites beneath quite typical Harappan townships, settlements and distinctive pottery belonging to an earlier period. But of this Amri culture nothing but the distinctive pottery is known. Amri ware is normally wheel-made, but is pale in colour and decorated with geometric patterns—serial triangles, 'double-axes,' lozenges, enclosed squares—outlined in black and filled in with reddish-brown paint. Though pottery alone represents the earliest recognized cultures in the Indus basin, it suffices to show that these had already reached the stage of technical development achieved in Mesopotamia first in Uruk times. It shows, too, that these cultures, despite certain similarities in technique and composition between Amri and Jemdet Nasr, are no more outposts or copies of Mesopotamian cultures than is the Harappa civilization.

The end of the latter is better known than its beginnings. The last reconstructions of Harappan cities[1] exhibit every sign of decadence. Old bricks were re-used for building mean houses on the sites formerly occupied by the spacious mansions of the bourgeoisie. The civic authority could no longer enforce the building regulations so strictly observed in more prosperous days so that dwellings encroached upon the streets.

Then the civilization was destroyed by barbarian invaders and the cities reoccupied by illiterate aliens. At Harappa[2] these are represented only by extended and flexed burials in Cemetery H and the queer painted vases that accompany them. At Chanhu-daro and Jhukar, in Sindh,[3] a distinct barbarian culture, the Jhukar culture, replaced the Harappa civilization. Everywhere the literate tradition exemplified in the inscribed 'seals' was extinguished. But judging by the pottery from Cemetery H and Jhukar sites and by metalwork from the latter, some technical traditions were carried over. Presumably potters and smiths survived to work for new customers. Naturally, they produced quite novel objects to suit foreign tastes.

The pottery from Jhukar and Cemetery H is still wheel-made, painted and fired in the old techniques, but shaped quite differently and adorned with new designs. Jhukar smiths made shaft-hole axe-heads and probably axe-adzes and pins with swollen necks. Button or bead seals of stone, fayence or pottery replaced the rectangular glazed steatite 'seals' and were engraved with geometric

1. Mackay, *Mohenjo-daro*, ii, 6; *Chanhu-daro*, 23–5.
2. Vats, *Harappa*, 220 ff.; cf. *Anc. India*, iii, 74, 98.
3. Mackay, *Chanhu-daro*, 24, 103, 144, 188, 208.

designs, including the filled cross, or rarely with conventional beasts, instead of inscriptions and lifelike animals.

The button seal like the shaft-hole axe is plainly a north-western intruder in India. The closest parallels to the Jhukar seals, and an exact parallel to the axe-adze, comes from Hissar III, in northern Iran.[1] Putative intermediate links will be cited later from Makran and Baluchistan. These agreements suggest that the barbarians who destroyed the Harappa civilization included at least invaders from north-western Iran. Wheeler[2] has boldly suggested their identification with the Vedic Aryas. In any case, the rshis sang their Vedic hymns in a prehistoric night; for the invasion completely broke the literary tradition, and there is no fixed point in Indian history till the reign of Darius.

1. Piggott, *Antiquity*, xvii, 1943, 180; *Anc. India*, i, 1946, 17.
2. *Anc. India*, iii, 82.

CHAPTER X

FROM THE TIGRIS TO THE INDUS

A survey of the archæological data gathered during the last twenty years from numerous tells between Mesopotamia and the Indus.basin would be doubly relevant to the purposes of this book. Do they throw any light on the origins of farming, the Neolithic Revolution? How far do they illustrate the diffusion of culture between the two first centres of Asiatic civilization, the twin cradles of the Urban Revolution in Asia?

The intermediate space is occupied by the vast tableland of Iran. Its undrained heart is now desert. But the parallel ranges of high mountains that surround it catch precipitation which feeds perennial springs, permanent rivers and intermittent torrents. These water the fertile soil of oases on the mountain flanks and of valleys between the parallel ranges on the west, south, and east. Two lines of argument have led botanists to expect that once cereals grew wild round the plateau. It is admittedly the home of many fruit-trees—apricots, peaches, perhaps the vine. Wild sheep still graze on the mountain pastures and were depicted on prehistoric vases. The Transcaspian steppe, just north of the plateau, has long been regarded as the home of fast horses while the Bactrian camel should have been at home near by.

So the conditions for the Neolithic Revolution are fulfilled. But the constant menace of drought and the absolute limitations on irrigable land would impose transhumance—seasonal migration from valley to mountain pastures—on farmers who wished to expand flocks and herds. Ultimately the same necessities might drive the younger sons of an expanding peasantry to emigrate in quest of fresh land in another valley. For here there are no large continuous areas dependent on a single river system to encourage or enforce economic and political unification on a grand scale. Nor was there the same penury in raw materials as provided a healthy stimulus in Egypt, Sumer, and Sindh. Many oases could be self-sufficing; bare life was possible without the laborious organization of an industrial and commercial economy. In practice, urban life was long delayed. Persia remained illiterate till the Ist millennium B.C. Baluchistan has never been more than the barbarous dependency of some historical State, broken up into parochial tribal units. On the other hand, the possession of timbers and ores brought visits from agents of civilization. Such contacts did not indeed convert barbarian villages into literate cities, but may have secured to the mountaineers a share in the surplus so easily produced in the great river valleys. It certainly procured them datable imports which provide the modern archæologist with chronological horizons in the tells.

To-day most of the area is relatively thinly populated. But its highland rims are studded with tells that suggest a relatively dense prehistoric population. Please note the word 'relatively'. In the first instance the comparison is with contemporary Belgium or Britain; in the second not with contemporary Iran, but with Belgium or Britain in the IIIrd millennium B.C. No area in the world was 'densely populated' in the modern sense five thousand years ago.

The tells are strung out along most of the valleys and foothills in western Iran and thence spread eastward round the central desert on the one hand along the foothills of the Elburz with spurs into the Turanian basin and probably to the Helmund. On the south the valleys of Fars and Makran are studded with tells while the coast of the Arabian Sea is bare of any trace of prehistoric settlement. The upland valleys of Baluchistan continue one series or the other. All the many tells examined by Sir Aurel Stein have yielded an abundant harvest of painted pottery of a 'prehistoric kind'. But the sherds exhibit very marked local differences and do not really define cultures, comparable in extent or uniformity to Halafian or Ubaid. It is true that the background for the dark paint seems to be more often red in the west and north, in the south and east more often pale buff. McCown,[1] followed by Piggott, accordingly distinguishes a 'Red Ware' and a 'Buff Ware culture'. But even these technical peculiarities are not rigidly distributed in space and by themselves could not suffice to define a 'culture'. One common feature to the whole area can, on the contrary, be detected. Though stone implements are frequently recorded as well as sherds, arrow-heads are fantastically rare and at excavated sites are always late. In revenge, every excavation in north-western and south-western

1. *The Comparative Stratigraphy of Early Iran*, OIS., 23, 1942.

Iran and in Transcaspia, too, brings to light numerous clay sling bullets.

For the rest we are confronted with an embarrassing multiplicity of local cultures and in a few areas with stratigraphically determined sequences of cultures. Fortunately the lapis trade and Indo-Sumerian commerce traversed the settled areas. They have left a few Harappan or Mesopotamian manufactures in the tells, and these provided dated horizons. In a few instances it has proved possible to work back from an horizon thus dated to earlier stages in the lower strata.

At Sialk,[1] in western Iran, a literate outpost of Susian civilization crowns a sequence of stages that began where Jarmo (p. 105) left off, in a neolithic village. At Sialk a perennial spring forms an oasis on the western edge of the desert basin of central Persia. The oasis is still traversed by an artery of north–south trade which was in use during the later days at least of the prehistoric settlement. The ruins of successive villages have formed two adjacent tells.

No architectural remains survive from the earliest settlement, I, 1, at the base of the North Tell; it consisted perhaps of reed huts. But after 3·8 m. of deposit had accumulated, ruins of houses with pisé walls define four successive architectural levels, I, 2, to I, 5. The villagers lived by mixed farming, combined with hunting and fishing. The crops, whatever they were, were reaped with sickles made from grooved rib-bones armed with flint teeth, just like the Natufian. Like them the handles were carved naturalistically, but the most interesting represents a human figure wearing a skirt or kilt, folded and joined at the back (Pl. XXXIII). Oxen and two kinds of sheep were bred for food and perhaps also for wool and milk. Gazelles and other game were hunted. The huntsman used maces and slings, the sling-bullets being made of baked clay. Adze or hoe blades of stone were shaped by flaking, the edge being ground in only one specimen from I, 4. Whorls attest a textile industry.

Four kinds of pottery were current: (1) a coarse dark-faced ware, tempered with chaff and grit; (2) a very rare black ware; (3) a fine red ware, often slipped and burnished and sometimes blotched with black owing to irregularities in firing; and (4) a clear buff ware tempered with chaff. Save in the earliest layers, vases in the last-named fabric were normally, those in the third ware frequently, decorated with basketry patterns in matt black paint (Fig. 102). The forms are relatively simple, but stability was given to flat-bottomed

1. Ghirshman, *Fouilles de Sialk*, i, 1938; for report on animal bones see vol. ii, 1939.

forms occasionally by a concavity or omphalos (Fig. 102, *a*): Simple vases were also made in stone.

Cosmetics were ground in minute clay mortars with tiny clay pestles that resemble the stone nails that in the Ubaid culture and

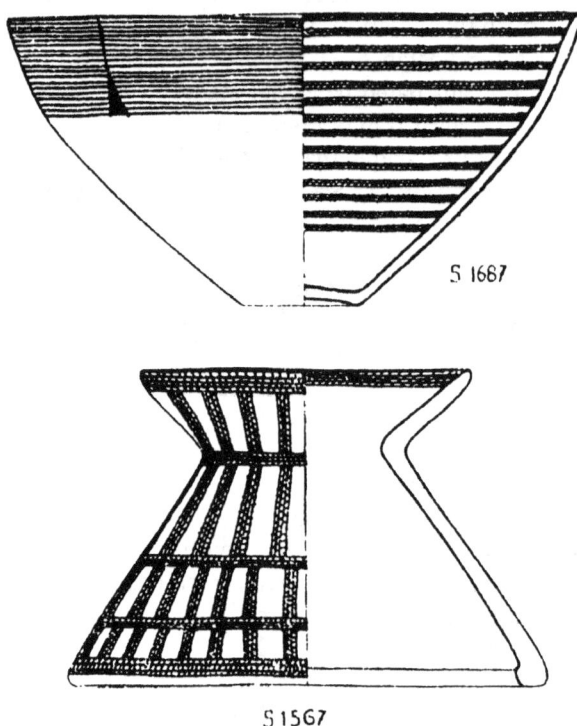

FIG. 102. Painted vases from Sialk I, ¼.

in 'neolithic' Thessaly have been regarded as lip-plugs. The only surviving ornaments are stone bracelets. Though formally neolithic, the villagers did obtain by 'trade' at least one obsidian blade and two or three small awls of copper. The latter were probably made from native metal and certainly were not cast.

No figurines nor amulets were found. But the dead were ritually interred, generally in a flexed attitude, under or between the houses. The bodies had been liberally sprinkled with red ochre so that, when the flesh decayed, the bones were stained. This practice was observed in Europe even during the Old Stone Age and later was regularly followed in north-eastern Europe, South Russia, and China.

The last three occupational levels in the North Tell are sometimes assigned to a distinct culture—Sialk II or Chashmah Aly—that is really only an advanced phase of the Sialk I culture. Distinctive innovations are: the appearance of a very few bones of horse and pig—neither certainly domesticated; a tentative use of mud brick in architecture; more polished edges to adze (or hoe) blades, and an extension of trade which now brought to the oasis turquoise and carnelian, *Pterocera* shells from the Persian Gulf and more copper. The metal was, however, still apparently shaped only by hammering and the shapes remain simple. In pottery red ware was now predominant and by the latest village may have been fired in a proper kiln. Vases are often provided with ring bases or pedestals; the geometric basketry patterns may be enriched so as to suggest schematized animal forms. On the other hand, carving on bone has been abandoned and no more bone sickle-handles are manufactured. Burial rites remain unchanged, and the sling and mace are the only attested weapons.

The culture just described seems confined to northern Persia. The stage distinguished as 'Sialk II' is clearly represented also at Chashmah Aly, a tell close to Rayy.[1] Parallelism, if not some sort of connection, with the first settlement at Anau in the Merv oasis—the only one of many tells in Turkmenia yet explored—may be inferred from resemblances in pottery. Only a couple of fairly simple pottery designs suggest a possible connection with the Halafian culture of Mesopotamia. In the next period the position is different.

After the occupation of the tenth level the North Tell was abandoned and a new village established half a mile further south. Judging by pottery and burial rites the first settlement (Sialk III, 1) in the South Tell represents a development of the culture of Sialk II. But an almost identical culture has come to light in the lowest levels—IA—at Tepe Hissar,[2] near Damghan, to the north-east.

The culture of Sialk III, 1 to 3, and Hissar IA differs from that of Sialk II and Chashmah Aly only in a few points. Pots are still hand-made, but usually fired in a specially constructed kiln (Fig. 103). Though pots and fuel seem to have occupied the same chamber,

1. Unpublished; cf. McCown, *CSEI.*, 3.
2. Schmidt, *Excavations at Tepe Hissar, Damghan,* 1931–33, Philadelphia, 1937, and *Mus. J.*, xxiii, 1933.

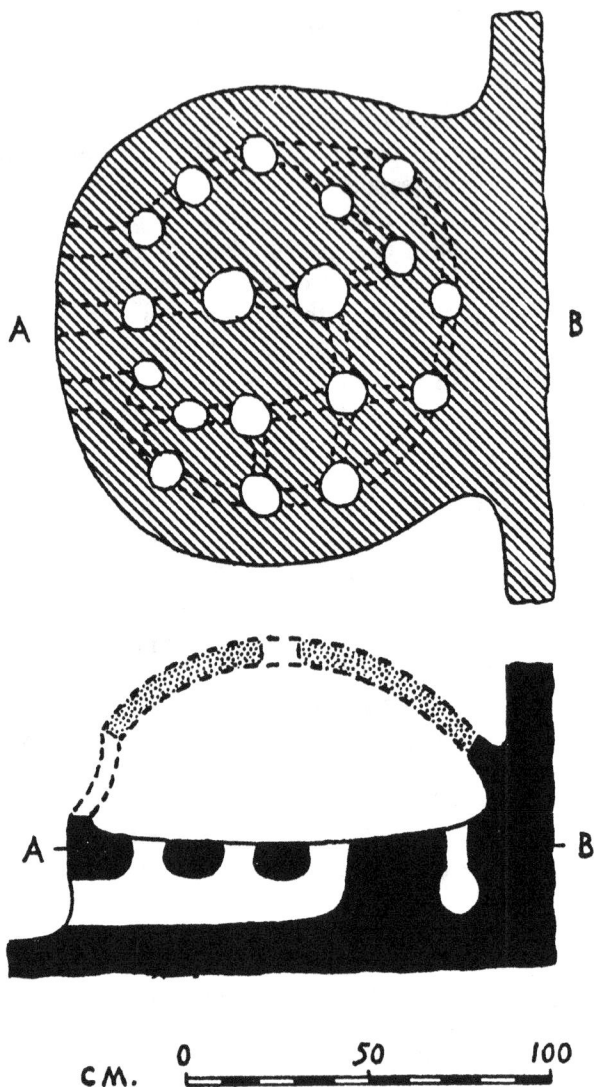

FIG. 103. Potter's kiln, Sialk III, plan and section (reconstructed).

channels in the floor would admit a draught of air to raise the temperature above that of an open fire while the supply could be regulated. The ceramic designs are more varied and include representational elements—notably plant stems with spiral leaves or branches and rows of birds (Pl. XXXIV). Copper becomes slightly commoner—there is even a tanged dagger from Sialk—but it is not demonstrably cast. Clay sling-bullets still represent the normal weapon, but two rough arrow-heads are reported from Hissar. The dead are buried as before, flexed and among the houses, but ochre is applied to the head only and even that not after Sialk III, 1; at Hissar it is never mentioned.

With Sialk III, 4, and Hissar IB comes a dramatic advance, but without any break in cultural continuity. The buildings are oriented as in the earlier villages; the dead buried still among the houses, but of course no longer stained with ochre; the pots preserve the familiar shapes and are painted in the old style, though stylized representations of leopards or other beasts or birds become more popular. But the art of intelligent metallurgy has been grasped; transverse axes or adzes like Fig. 76, a, and midrib daggers were cast in closed moulds. Presumably professional smiths were now established at Sialk and Hissar. Potters became professionals, too; for vases are now made on the wheel. About the same time button seals came into regular use—one had been found in Sialk III, 1, and a few in Hissar IA, but none in Sialk III, 2, or III, 3—and were stamped on clay sealings to transfer thereto the magical design—generally the filled cross. Finally, Sialk III, 6, and Hissar IC have yielded the first relatively dated specimens of a curious type of alabaster weight,[1] apparently used in connection with a horizontal loom and paralleled at Susa B or C and Anau III.[2] Finally, a building in Sialk III, 4, is decorated with buttresses rather in the manner of the façades described on p. 125.

Here in northern Iran, then, metallurgy, the wheel and perhaps even the button seal emerge in the course of a continuous cultural development without any discontinuity of population or break in the architectural, artistic, or funerary tradition. Does that mean that these revolutionary discoveries and inventions were made among the Iranian mountains and adopted by the simple peasants of the oases before they reached the more extensive villages of Mesopotamia? The temperature needed for melting copper could indeed be reached in the Sialk III kiln, and McCown has espoused a relative chronology that would in effect give just this priority to Iran. Its validity can only be judged in the light of reliable synchronisms offered by Sialk IV.

1. *Sialk*, No. S223 on pl. lxxxv; *Hissar*, H2095, p. 58.
2. Pumpelly, *Anau*, ii, 479, fig. 6; the type is said to occur also in Anau I or II; *MDP.*, xxv, 182.

Sialk III, 7, was violently destroyed. Above its ashes rose a settlement of a new type—apparently an outpost of literate Elamite civilization. Account tablets inscribed in the 'proto-Elamite' pictographic script and cylinder seals engraved in the 'Jemdet Nasr' style suggest that Susians had occupied the key position on the highway north to control the commerce in lapis lazuli.

The dead were still buried among the houses, but now in a strictly contracted position and often richly furnished with mirrors and ornaments of copper, gold, and lapis lazuli, and vases of alabaster as well as pottery. Black-on-red painted ware went out of fashion to be replaced by grey wares which are characteristic of Hissar II also. But one vase, partly covered with a red slip so as to leave reserved panels which are outlined in black, recalls the Jemdet Nasr style and technique.[1] Beak-spouted jugs like Fig. 75, 8, and spouted forms suggest Susian or Mesopotamian Late Uruk types, but handled vessels are absent. The ornaments include fly-amulets such as are common in Early Dynastic Mesopotamia, a pin with double scroll head parallel to the double-spiral-headed pins which are distributed from the Indus valley through Anau and Hissar II and III to Troy, the Cyclades and the Balkans[2] and a knot-headed pin such as we met in Gerzean Egypt (Fig. 20).

On the foregoing evidence Sialk IV could well be equated with the Jemdet Nasr phase in the Tigris–Euphrates valley and certainly need not be earlier. In that case only the gratuitous assumption of a period of desertion after the destruction of III, 7, would prevent assigning Sialk III to the Uruk phase. In fact, one of the two spouted pots from Sialk III—layer 6—is a good Early Uruk form.[3] If these agreements be accepted as chronologically significant, the case for assigning Iran, as represented by Sialk III, 4, any priority over Sumer in the development of metallurgy and the use of the wheel looks weak (even rejecting the allegedly wheel-made Ubaid vases from Erech). Even Sialk I need be no older than Archaic Hassuna.

So none of the cultures thus far examined demonstrably stands in parental relation to that of either the first farmers or the first professional smiths of Mesopotamia. But a case can be made out for

1. *Sialk*, S.23, pl. xc; cf. McCown, *CSEI.*, 54.
2. Childe, *LAAA.*, xxiii, 119; *Dawn*, 50, 67, 126.
3. *Sialk*, S.135, pl. lxix; cf. Lloyd, *Sumer*, iv, 1948, table 3, nos. 21, 28, 36, 37. The best parallels are from Nineveh IV and Gawra VII.

such a relation between Sialk II-III-Chashmah Aly-Hissar I and at least one culture on the western border of the Indus valley.

Several large tells in the now arid upland valley of the Zhob in northern Baluchistan have yielded pottery which exhibits really striking analogies in form, technique, and decoration to that of Hissar I B.[1] The vases are made on the wheel. They are sometimes covered with a red slip, though a pale ground was commoner on the Zhob than in northern Iran. Finally, they are decorated with animals, stylized in quite the Hissar manner, albeit bulls were preferred to panthers or ibex. But exactly what assemblage of cultural elements is associated with, and symbolized by, these distinctive vases is rather doubtful. In the great tell of Raṇa-ghuṇḍai[2] they occur in the middle levels—Raṇa-ghuṇḍai II—above the ruins of an earlier and more 'Indian' village.

The people of Raṇa-ghuṇḍai I used unpainted hand-made pots but bred the Indian humped oxen (*Bos indicus*), urial sheep, asses, and possibly even horses as well as cultivating plants. The cattle are explicitly Indian rather than western, the sheep might well be descended from native stocks. In fact, there were neolithic farmers in Baluchistan before unambiguous influence from the west is archæologically detectable. All that must be inferred from the pottery of Raṇa-ghuṇḍai II is the settlement among south-east Asian farmers of a few professional potters bringing their wheels and the artistic tastes of northern Iran.

The upper levels, Raṇa-ghuṇḍai III, then show the development of a local style of polychrome pottery, represented at several other tells in the valley. These mark the sites of villages or even townships composed of mud-brick houses on stone foundations. Trade brought them copper, lapis lazuli, and etched carnelian beads. Flint arrow-heads,[3] on the contrary, may be indicative of warfare. A multitude of bangles, a stone phallos, many clay figurines of a hooded female with 'a grinning skull for face' have Indian rather than Iranian analogies. One of the Zhob sites, Dabar-koṭ, eventually became a Harappan trading post; seals and beads from others denote influence from the Indus cities and an overlap in time with the Harappa period. Nevertheless the polychrome pottery of Raṇa-ghuṇḍai III has close affinities with the earlier Amri ware of Sindh and with that

---

1. Piggott, *Antiquity*, xvii, 1943, 172–3.
2. *JNES.*, v, 1946, 284–316; cf. Piggott, *P.I.*, 121–6.
3. *ASIM.*, No. 37, 1929, 40, 86; Piggott, *P.I.*, 128.

found beneath the citadel wall at Harappa itself. Hence, Piggott[1] considers that the whole Zhob series except the latest phase of Rana-ghundai III must be anterior to the Harappa civilization. Indeed, it might be through the Zhob that a western foundation for the latter reached the Indus valley.

Turning to the southern route we find no stratigraphically attested culture sequence to compare with that revealed at Sialk. In Fars one tell, Bakun B, near Persepolis, is indeed reported[2] to have yielded stone implements and unpainted pottery that may be earlier than Susa I and comparable to Sialk I; further east Stein[3] may have found something comparable in the deepest levels of two mounds near Madavan. No details are available. The richly decorated pottery from all four levels of Bakun A[4] on the other hand, seems already to illustrate the same advanced stage of culture as Susa I. The vases, although hand-made, were fired in regular kilns in which furnace and firing-chamber were apparently separated by a clay floor-plate; some show such ceramic sophistications as ring feet and moulded rims. For their ornamentation animals, stylized to purely decorative patterns, are combined with geometric motives among which the Maltese square is prominent as in Halaf and Samarra. Stone vessels were used too, but only sparingly. No moulded bricks were observed. But buttons were engraved on the convex face with filled crosses and with more complex patterns, recalling Halafian designs, and were employed as seals. Grain was reaped with flint-edged sickles. The only surviving weapons are stone mace-heads and clay sling-bullets. Lapis lazuli and perhaps turquoise were imported for beads. Figures of females and of animals were modelled in clay.

The style of the ceramic art and of the seals justify equating Bakun A with Susa I; the cemetery, if found, would probably contain just as much metal. Further east some sherds and stamps collected by Stein[5] from various tells as far east as the Fasa oasis may document contemporary occupations. Beyond that, stylistic agreements, none too exact, in pottery decoration may indicate contemporary and related settlements in Sistan[6] and round Quetta.[7]

1. P.I., 122–9.
2. McCown, CSEI., 23.
3. Iraq, iii, 1936, 183, 186.
4. Langsdorff and McCown, Tall i Bakun A., OIP., lix, 1942.
5. Iraq., iii, 150, 154.
6. Stein, Innermost Asia, pl. cxiii.
7. Piggott, Anc. India, No. 3, 1947, 131–142; no relics are known that are explicitly associated with this pottery.

The similarities in design between Quetta ware and that of Bakun A might be taken to reflect really early relations between Baluchistan and western Iran but that some sherds at least appear to belong to wheel-made vases. If the artists were really professional potters, manufacturing Quetta wares on the wheel, the stylistic agreements will have to be explained in the same way as those between Susa I and the post-Harappa cemetery of Shahi-tump described below.

Apart from this ambiguous 'Quetta ware', the oldest datable horizon in the high tells along the enclosed valleys of the Bampur River and of Makran is defined by connections with Early Dynastic Sumer and the Harappa civilization of India. In Makran the material is by then sufficiently coherent to justify englobing it under the name 'Kulli culture', coined by Piggott.

The inland valleys, parallel to the waterless coast, now suffer too often from drought to attract many farmers despite the fertility of their soils, but they are studded with tells that have yielded Kulli remains. They represent large and permanent settlements; Mehi,[1] in the Mashkai valley, covers some 250,000 square yards and attains a height of 50 feet! But all remain villages though some, like Shahi-tump,[2] in the Kej valley, may have ended up as outposts of the Harappa civilization. Yet besides farmers the villages housed professional potters, almost certainly resident smiths, and quite probably other specialist craftsmen. Plunder or trade brought the villagers a share in the surplus of the Indus cities and supplies of metal and lapis lazuli. Copper, though represented only by a mirror and a flat axe from Kulli and a few minor objects, was in reality so common that stone was used, as at Harappa itself, only for simple blades; stone axe-heads and flint arrow-heads alike are significantly absent. Among the exports were dancing girls, whose figures were modelled in metal at Harappa (Pl. XXIX, a), and the engraved stone vases[3] that were marketed both in Early Dynastic II Mesopotamia and in the Indus cities; several specimens of the latter were recovered at Mehi and Shahi-tump. Examples from sites in Sistan and Persian Makran mark the route of this trade westward towards Susa and Sumer.

Pottery reflects relations both east and west. The vases, all wheel made, were fired in a kiln to a pinkish hue and then covered generally with a pale slip, but at Mehi more often with a red wash; at Kulli,

1. *ASIM.*, No. 43, 154.
2. *Ibid.*, 88.
3. *Antiquity*, xvii, 176 and n. 15.

however, reduced grey wares were also manufactured. A distinctive style of painted decoration was based on the 'animal with landscape motive': humped cattle or more rarely caprids stand between trees in a landscape with is often crowded with little birds and beasts or geometric figures as if in a frantic endeavour to fill up all vacant spaces (Pl. XXXV, a). Now, though the animals' bodies are hatched in black, and red is used only in a few bands, alternating with black, in the frame, the style is significantly like that of the Scarlet Ware of Mesopotamia and Susa D.[1] On the other hand, at least one vase of Kulli style reached Mohenjo-daro.[2] Conversely, Harappan influence is prominent on all Kulli sites; Harappan motives, like pipal leaves and border-patterns, and Harappan forms like open stands, pedestalled bowls and piriform jars characterize the local ceramic industry. Harappan vases, actually imported from the Indus valley, have been recorded only at Suktagen-dor, a fortified site so near the mouth of the Dasht that it might be a port for coastal trade with that civilization.

In fashions of dress, too, illustrated by a number of clay figurines, the great popularity of bangles and the elaborate jewelry look thoroughly Indian. At the same time it is detailed agreement in ornaments with the Kulli figurines that guarantees the authenticity of the bronze statuette from Harappa[3] shown in Pl. XXIX, a; its antiquity had often been challenged because so lively an attitude was previously unknown in pre-classical statuary. Again, a model cart from Mehi proves not only that the wheel was used for transport as well as pot-making but also that the wainwrights of Makran followed the pattern approved in the Indus valley.

While the later occupations of these Kulli sites are thus contemporary with the Harappa civilization and owe some of their prosperity to its proximity, the deeper levels in the high tells may well go back to an earlier period. But such beginnings of the Kulli culture await exploration. Its end can be more closely defined. Intruded into the ruins of the latest Kulli township at Shahi-tump Stein[4] found graves furnished in a quite alien tradition. The bodies were interred, generally supine, extended or flexed. They were accompanied by flat axes, one shaft-hole axe (Fig. 104, a), and a single-bladed knife of copper, alabaster bowls, beads of lapis lazuli,

1. Frankfort, *ASP.*, 1932, 68–70; cf. pp. 143, 149 above.
2. *Anc. India*, No. 5, 1949, 30, pl. vi, 70.
3. Piggott, *Anc. India*, No. 1, 1946, 16; *P.I.*, 109, 178.
4. *ASIM.*, No. 43, 88–103.

copper stamp seals of Piggott's[1] 'compartmented' type (Fig. 104, *b*) and a whole service of vases, sometimes arranged in nests as in the Susa I cemetery.

The wide open dishes (Pl. XXXVIII), tall tumblers, little squat

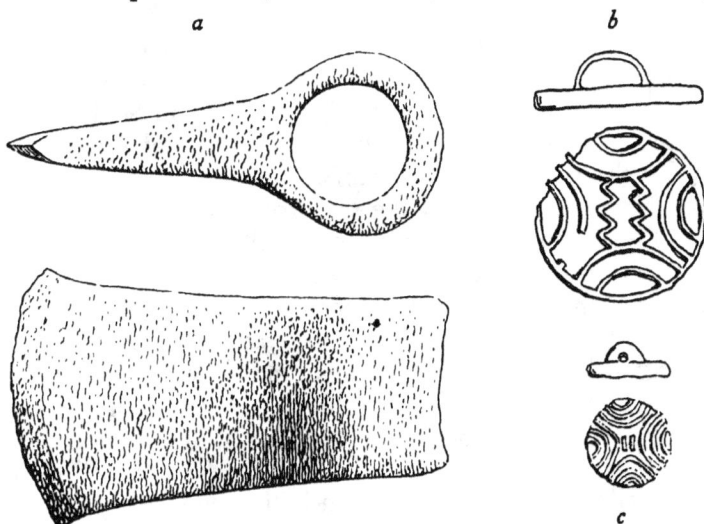

FIG. 104. Axe head and compartmented seals of copper from Shahi-tump cemetery and fayence seal from Chañhudaro II, ½, after Piggott.

pots (no longer angular in outline), and ovoid jars of Susa I are all represented here while a triple vase has parallels only later at that site. The dishes and most of the jars are made in a greyish fabric, so highly fired that it feels like porcelain; other vessels are of an unslipped pink fabric. Both are really the same ware differently fired; all are tempered with chaff. The relation to Susa I is confirmed by the patterns which include the swastika and the Maltese square. At the same time forms and patterns alike show that it was only a late and decadent version of the ceramic tradition of Susa I and Bakun A that inspired the Shahi-tump potters.

An intermediate stage may be recognized in the funerary pottery collected by Stein[2] at Khurab in the Bampur valley. There, however, some graves contained, together with Iranian buff-ware vases intermediate between Bakun and Shahi-tump, red-slipped pedestalled bowls of distinctively Harappan shape, a copper spear-head and dish

1. *Antiquity*, xvii, 180.
2. *An Archaeological Reconnaissance in North-west India and South-east Iran*, 1937, 120.

of Harappan style, and a stone vase of Kulli style. Finally, one burial was accompanied by a copper rod, terminating in a lifelike representation of a camel (Pl. XXIX, *b*), the earliest representation of that beast in the Middle East.

The north-western connections of the intrusive Shahi-tump culture is amply proved by the shaft-hole axe, a type as strange to Baluchistan as to India, the compartmented seals to which there are exact parallels at Hissar II B and III, Anau III and Susa and only a little less exact at Byblos in Syria[1] and in Central Anatolia[2] and finally by the camel from Khurab. A post-Sargonid date can be inferred from the context of the seal from Susa and the probable dating of Hissar and Anau. It is confirmed by the occurrence of a compartmented seal of fayence in the Jhukar settlement at Chanhu-daro. Thus, the Shahi-tump cemetery seems to document the invasion of Makran by barbarous tribes from the west who, while preserving something of the ceramic and funerary traditions of Susiana and Fars, had on the way picked up professional potters and smiths and perhaps camels, but not clerks. They would have destroyed the Kulli culture about the same time as a parallel wave of other barbarians cut short civilization in the Indus valley.

Finally, in the Nal and Nundara valleys of northern Baluchistan, only 150 miles from the Indus, the mounded ruins of large villages illustrate another culture, again partly dependent on the civilization of the valley, but possibly in part preceding it. The chief site, Sohr-damb, near Nal,[3] can hardly rank as a city, yet the ruins of elaborate stone and mud-brick buildings cover an area of 30,000 square yards. Fractional burials in which skulls or a few bones were accompanied by vases were found in several rooms, but complete interments in brick graves were also recognized.

Metal was freely used; the flat celts are long and slender, the saws agree with the Sumerian type, a tanged dagger resembles those of the Indus, but Indus chisels and spear-heads are missing. Figures of humped bulls, stone rings, marble vases, the use of fayence, a shell bangle, long biconical beads of hard stone and a steatite button-seal demonstrate the affinity of Nal to the Indus civilization. But female figurines are absent; the seal is not engraved in Indus style, and another of copper as well as a relative abundance of lapis lazuli suggest rather Shahi-tump.

1. Montet, *Byblos et l'Egypte*, pl. lix, 44.
2. von der Osten, *Alishar Hüyük*, 1930–32, *OIP.*, xxix, no. 1481.
3. *MASI.*, No. 35.

The pottery, in any case, is thoroughly individual. The clay varies from greenish to pinkish in hue and may be covered with a cream or (very rarely) with a dark red slip. The distinctive shapes are bowls with slightly inverted rims, cylindrical pyxides, and squat pots (sometimes keeled) with short collar necks. The vases are decorated with designs outlined in black but often filled in with red, yellow, blue, and green. The last three colours have been applied after the firing, but the red, often of the same plum red tint as at Amri, seems to be fixed in most cases.

The designs are arranged tectonically in broad zones, generally subdivided into panels. The motives include on the one hand superb representations of tigers, bulls, fishes, and leaves realistically rendered, but so stylized as to harmonize with a complex design. On the other hand, we have geometric motives—sigmas, W's, and comb patterns, familiar further west, and incomplete repetition patterns such as the intersecting circles and the motives shown in Pl. XXXV, *b*. These themes, in which the several various parts of the figures are filled in with varying colours, blend to a magnificent decoration, excelling even the Harappa style proper.

Though highly specialized in treatment, many elements in this style and its technique might be derived directly from the Amri phase. Not only do we find there the same slip and plum red paint as at Nal, but even some Nal motives and in particular so highly-specialized a theme as the cross with circular centre. It may then be inferred that the Nal and Amri ceramic styles developed out of a common tradition. In fact, a few vases of Nal manufacture, or at least style, have been found in an Amri context in the Indus valley itself.[1]

Hence, the Nal culture probably began in pre-Harappan times. Quite what should be attributed to this early phase is not yet clear; the culture survived at least till the Harappa civilization was mature and side by side with the Kulli culture. It may even have lasted till the intrusive Shahi-tump culture replaced the latter; for a compartmented seal was found at the type site though its precise context is uncertain. What is certain is that the villages in the Nal and Nundara valleys no more grew into cities than did any others in Baluchistan. Civilization was not achieved in these narrow confines while it flourished in the more spacious valleys of the Indus and the Tigris–Euphrates. That is the most definite conclusion of this survey.

1. *Anc. India*, No. 5, 1949, 16–17.

The foregoing pages contain a very cursory survey of prehistory over a vast area, but ·confined to a very narrow zone of protohistoric twilight interrupting much longer periods of unrelieved gloom. For perhaps five centuries—say 2500 to 2000 B.C.—Indo-Sumerian trade across the area reflected a little historical light from Mesopotamia on the barbarism of Iran, Sistan, and Baluchistan. Then darkness descended again till the days of Darius or rather of Alexander. Of course, darkness did not mean depopulation. Bulky but disorderly collections of documents are already available to fill up those 1500 years; varieties of prehistoric painted pottery have been distinguished in Baluchistan alone. Systematic excavation would no doubt arrange these in the right order and reveal other activities of their makers. In 1950 they may fall anywhere on either side of the twilight band, and the object of this book is not the arrangement of ceramic groups in accordance with *a priori* stylistic principles.

One definite result has already emerged from the survey. The next is even more negative. The beginnings of farming may lie in the unexplored levels at the base of some tell. Scientific excavation should at least provide a sequence descending in that direction on the Indo-Iranian borderlands as it has in western Persia. But it may very well be that the earliest farmers in the Ancient East did not live in permanent villages and are not therefore to be expected at the bottom of the superimposed series of such villages that forms a tell. Inhabited caves may supply the missing information. Dr. C. S. Coon's excavations in a cave south of the Caspian have yielded a sequence beginning with a mesolithic and continued by a neolithic that has not yet been connected on to any historically anchored culture sequence.

One positive affirmation can be made. The earliest food-producing economy detected in the Indus river system, that of Raṇa-ghuṇḍai I, has already a distinctively Indian character. Hence, on the diffusionist postulate assuming that Rana-ghuṇḍai I and Sialk I embody the results of one and the same complex of cultural mutations, ample time must be allowed for divergent specialization as well as for diffusion itself. Both processes lie outside the known section of the archæological record.

That should, however, include the diffusion of a second complex of discoveries and inventions—metallurgy and the wheel. The technical agreements in the application of both mutations afford some justification for the diffusionist postulate. Fixed points of reference at both ends of the area, providing a time scale against which the rate can be measured very roughly, suggest that this process was relatively rapid. At the same time the conditions for the adoption of the potters' wheel or metallurgy and the mechanism of their transmission are different from those governing the diffusion of cereal cultivation and stock-breeding.

The use of the potters' wheel or metal tools does not depend simply on technical knowledge. Mass production of fragile pots is only worth while when the numbers living together in the same village have reached a substantial, but as yet indeterminate, figure. A community can only use metal tools when it is producing an effective social surplus. In each case the threshold is determined by economic and social factors—the efficiency of the rural economy and the concentration, or at least fluidity, of the social surplus. Hand-made pots and stone tools may be indices of the smallness and poverty of a community rather than of its antiquity.

In the second place, metallurgy and the manufacture of pots on the wheel and very likely wagon-building, too, were crafts, exercised by full-time specialists. Such were, at least economically, released from kinship bonds; their mysterious skills could earn them a livelihood wherever the requisite social surplus was available. After all, a normal farming village requires and can afford the services of only one or two smiths and potters. The younger children of such a village artisan had better seek employment and sustenance in some neighbouring settlement not yet provided. Accordingly at this stage the diffusion of ceramic techniques and even forms need not mean a folk-migration, but only the immigration of specialist potters. The similarities and differences between, for instance, Zhob and Hissar pots can quite well be explained by the assumption of potters, trained in one technical tradition, but working to satisfy the demands of distinct social traditions in art and table manners.[1] As between Jemdet Nasr and Harappa vases the techniques and tools of the craftsmen seem almost identical in Mesopotamia and the Indus valley.[2]

Now, in Mesopotamia metallurgy and the wheel were well established by Uruk times, say x centuries before 3000 B.C. They

1. Mallowan, 'The Legacy of Asia,' London University Institute of Archæology *Annual Report IV*, 1948, 33 ff., illustrates how to-day oriental craftsmen while maintaining the continuity of the technical tradition vary styles to suit their customers' tastes.

2. Mackay, *JRAI.*, xxx, 1930, 130–5.

had reached the Indus valley in the Amri phase y centuries before 2500 B.C. Certain considerations may help to define a little more closely the orders of magnitude represented by x and y. In the case of pottery there is little evidence for divergent technical developments in either extreme region. In metallurgy, on the contrary, by the time contemporary products can be compared the divergence is substantial. Much of the contrast between the Sumerian types enumerated or illustrated in Chapter VIII and the Indus types of Chapter IX might indeed be explained away as due to mere differences of fashion. The mounting of axes by a shaft-hole through the head is, however, more than a local trick; its superiority has been demonstrated by its universal adoption. Yet this rational device reached India—and also the Caspian steppes—only belatedly during the IIIrd millennium when metallurgy was already long established. It cannot therefore have been diffused with the art of metallurgy itself.

But since it is attested in Sialk III, 4, and Susa B and indirectly even in Ubaid Sumer the primary diffusion of metallurgy in the Middle East must have begun before the period thus defined. The shaft-hole axe itself must be the result of a secondary diffusion eastwards. Those that did eventually reach Shahi-tump and Chanhu-daro are not Early Dynastic Mesopotamian forms, but must be derived from more archaic types, illustrated perhaps by clay models of Ubaid age from Ur and Uqair. If then shaft-hole axes be admitted in Ubaid times, Sumer was not the primary cradle of metallurgy, but only a secondary centre where perhaps the shaft-hole axe was invented. It need not follow that the postulated primary focus lay east, rather than west, of the Tigris. For no more shaft-hole axes reached the Nile than they did the Indus. At the same time one of the earliest specialized metal types—the knot-headed pin—is common to Gerzean Egypt and to Sialk IV.

CHAPTER XI

BETWEEN THE HORNS OF THE FERTILE CRESCENT

TURNING, in conclusion, to the centre of the Fertile Crescent itself, we encounter difficulties similar to those that impeded our survey of the lands east of the Tigris. The area falls into three provinces, very unequally explored—(1) the parkland steppe of Northern Mesopotamia comprising Assyria and North Syria; (2) the hill country immediately to the west of the Euphrates including the Orontes valley and the Phœnician coastlands; and (3) Palestine. All enjoy natural resources—rainfall, rivers, stones suitable for tools, timber—denied to the Sumerian and Egyptian horns and favourable to the divergent development of preliterate cultures. In all literate civilization and written history began late. The three provinces are all related in different degrees to one or both of the oldest urban civilizations, but adjacent provinces are more closely interlocked with one another. It will therefore be convenient to survey each separately.

(1)

The steppe zone, north of the Sinjar range, was throughout historical times a main artery of communication between east and west. But a relatively reliable rainfall, adequate supplies of permanent water, of stone and of timber and proximity to deposits of obsidian and ores permitted the survival of small but viable economic units, exempt from the pressure to concentration of population and economic consolidation that had operated so urgently in Egypt, Sumer, and the Indus valley. Urbanization and literacy were long delayed and were eventually imposed from the south. The written record begins seven centuries later than in Egypt and Sumer, when Manishtusu, Sargon's grandson, built or rebuilt the Ishtar Temple at Nineveh[1] and Narâm-Sin established a palace at Brak on the

1. *LAAA.*, xix, 1932, 59.

Khabur.[1] Even at Assur, further south, the earliest Ishtar Temple,[2] denoting the conversion of a provincial village into a cathedral city, was not built before Early Dynastic III and looks like the foundation of civilized 'Sumerians' from Lower Mesopotamia.

A similar retardation as compared to Lower Mesopotamia is discoverable in prehistoric times, too. North Syria and Assyria shared, as shown in Chapter VI, the Ubaid culture with Sumer, but it was also shown that the lower Ubaid settlements of Gawra —XVIII and —XVII in Assyria must be contemporary with the upper Ubaid temple —VIII at Eridu. In the last Ubaid level, Gawra —XII, a relative abundance of imported materials including copper, lapis lazuli, and 'paste' (? fayence), the frequent use of button seals and ring-pendants and even a clay Hut-Symbol are phenomena appropriate already to the Uruk period. Even the pottery, while preserving Ubaid traditions in forms and technique, is sometimes decorated with conventional beasts or birds, foreign to the southern Ubaid tradition save at Uqair in Akkad. And this Ubaid ware is moreover associated with a red-slipped ware painted with simple designs in black that is known also at Brak on the Khabur.[3]

Nor is the Ubaid culture succeeded by a Uruk culture as in Lower Mesopotamia. Only at Grai Resh, situated significantly on the southern slopes of the Sinjar range, does 'grey Uruk ware' characterize a group of strata (—II to —V) interposed between Ubaid and Early Dynastic or Ninevite levels.[4] But even here the grey ware appears to be hand-made, red ware is missing and other ceramic products and imports establish synchronisms with only the latest phase of the Uruk period in Mesopotamia. In fact, Grai Resh —V–II illustrates one facies of the culture, or series of interrelated cultures, that flourished in northern Mesopotamia immediately after the Ubaid phase. The contemporaneity of all can be more easily established than their relation to the Lower Mesopotamian sequence. The period thus defined is best termed the Gawra period,[5] since its content is illustrated by settlements —XIA to —VIIIB at Tepe Gawra; the term avoids prejudging the absolute age of an assemblage of contemporary relics and monuments.

1. *Iraq*, ix, 1947, 26.
2. Andrae, *Die archäischen Ischtartempel in Assur*, Leipzig, 1922; cf. Frankfort, *OIC.*, 20, 'Comment on the Chronological Table' at end.
3. Tobler, *Gawra*, ii, 46–7.
4. *Iraq*, vii, 1940, 15–19.
5. Perkins, *CAEM.*

In the Gawra period metal, though certainly known, was everywhere rare. Stone celts were still normally used for axe or adze heads. A decline in their numbers from fifty in Gawra —XII to twelve in —IX[1] might be taken to indicate a gradual replacement of stone by metal but that in Gawra —VIII the number rose again to forty-one![2] However, a perforated stone adze from Gawra —IX[3] resembles Fig. 76 from Susa B and, like it, must copy a metal tool. By the very end of the period metal was indeed used for the manufacture of even agricultural implements—a copper sickle blade is reported from Gawra —VIII—and as much as 5·6 per cent of tin might occasionally be alloyed with copper.[4]

Maces and slings remained the favourite weapons. Clay sling bullets are very common, arrowheads missing from Grai Resh and Gawra, though two are reported from Nineveh. A double-edged stone mace-head from Gawra —XI[5] is absurdly like Late Neolithic boat-axes from Denmark and Sweden and funnily enough occurs in the same horizon as ring-pendants of shell or fayence[6] which again are 'Late Neolithic' in Scandinavia.

The pottery of the period is predominantly plain. Hand-made grey ware was popular at Grai Resh —V–II and in Nineveh 3, red ware only in Nineveh 4. Bevel-rimmed bowls occur at Grai Resh, Nineveh 3–4, and Brak. But bowls or chalices on high hollow pedestals with slightly inverted rims are found at Gawra —IX and Grai Resh. Most of this pottery was hand-made. Only towards the close of the Gawra period did professional potters begin to settle in Assyrian villages; four wheel-made vases alone came from Gawra —IX,[7] but there were perhaps more at Nineveh.

Nor are wheeled vehicles reliably attested earlier.[8] A single clay disc with a central 'hub' from Gawra —XIII is certainly very like later model wheels, but there are none from —XII to —IX and fourteen from —VIII. In the latter settlement, but not before, clay models show that both four-wheeled and two-wheeled carts—or chariots—were in use for transport. As no model horses or asses are known so early, they were presumably drawn by oxen. The cylinder seal, too, remained unknown during the Gawra period in Assyria, but stamp seals of bead, button, or gabled type are well represented as are their impressions on clay sealings. They were engraved with the

1. Tobler, 202.
2. Speiser, *Gawra*, i, 85.
3. *Ibid.*, 88.
4. Speiser, 192–5.
5. Tobler, pl. xciv, d and f.
6. *Ibid.*, 89, 195, pl. clxxiii, 41, 42.
7. Tobler, 154.
8. Tobler, 167; Speiser, 74–5.

filled cross or other geometric designs, but also with lively animals—
in Gawra —XI sometimes grouped tête-bêche[1]—and even human
figures.

In the foregoing respects then Assyria in the Gawra period was
behind Lower Mesopotamia in the Uruk phase. The religious architecture of Gawra affords a basis for quantitative comparison with
Sumer and a rough measure of the period's length. In Gawra —XIA
the summit of the tell, by now quite a lofty acropolis, was occupied
by a circular citadel, 18 m. to 19 m. in diameter, contained in a stout
mud-brick wall. But in Gawra —XI the central area, once hallowed
by the Ubaid temples of —XIX, —XVIII and —XIII returned to its
former religious use and became the site of a small temple, measuring
only 9·5 m. square. After four building periods its successor in
Gawra —VIIIB measured 16·5 m. by 13 m. and was associated, as in
the late Ubaid level —XIII, with two other sanctuaries. Since the
several temples did not occupy the same spot, the four 'building
periods' do not represent as many reconstructions of the same
temple as do the superimposed temples at Eridu or Khafaje, and need
not correspond to more than a couple of centuries.

The existence in Assyria of secular chiefs, competing with the
deities in concentrating the social surplus, may perhaps be deduced
from certain tombs discovered in the acropolis area at Gawra.
Besides numerous burials of infants and children, possibly sacrifices,
there occurred in strata —X to —VIII adult burials in brick cists,
some richly furnished with gold ornaments, stone vases, and in four
cases with stone mace-heads.[2] These weapons, two carved with
projecting knobs, seem more appropriate to war-chiefs than to
religious dignitaries despite the location of the tombs in or near the
temple courts.

Finally, the spiritual life of the Gawra period was characterized by
the popular use of curious pottery and stone objects, variously
described as 'weights', 'spectacle idols', and 'symbols' of the hut
sacred to the fertility goddess, Inanna or her Semitic counterpart,
Ishtar[3] (Fig. 105). Found in clay in Grai Resh —V–II and the final
Ubaid stratum —XII at Gawra, the stone version is well represented
in Gawra —XIA to —VIII C and at Brak. Isolated specimens from the

1. Tobler, 188.
2. Tobler, 78, 84, 92.
3. The latest account of their significance and distribution is given by van
Buren, *Iraq*, xii, 1950, 139 ff. Cf. Mallowan, *ibid.*, ix, 1947, 34, and Frankfort,
JNES., viii, 1949, 194 ff.

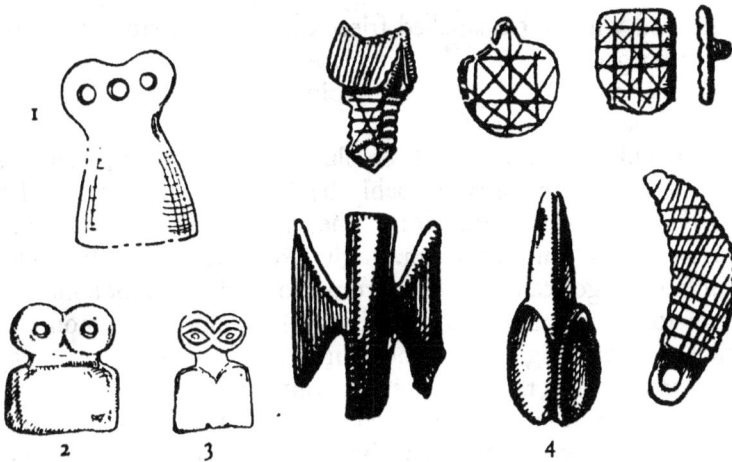

FIG. 105. 1–2, Hut symbols. 1, clay, Hama K, $\frac{2}{15}$; 2, stone, Brak C, $\frac{2}{5}$; 3, Eye idol, stone, Brak, $\frac{2}{5}$; 4, Halafian amulets and seal pendants, $\frac{1}{4}$ Arpachiya.

'hoard' in the Jemdet Nasr stratum —III under the E-anna at Erech and from Sin Temple IV at Khafaje date the series, and so the Gawra period, to Jemdet Nasr and perhaps Late Uruk times in the Lower Mesopotamian sequence. We shall meet the same ritual object in Hama K on the Orontes while Frankfort has shown that a final version of the same symbol is preserved in 'pot-covers' from the IVth settlement at Thermi on Lesbos.

While the Hut Symbols were still in vogue, Brak, on the Khabur, formerly a village where black-on-red painted ware similar to that of Gawra —XII had been used, became the site of a quite monumental temple.[1] Judging from its magnitude and plan and from the cylinder seals found in it, the first recorded from the steppe zone, the temple might have been designed and founded by civilized colonists from Lower Mesopotamia. It seems to have been reconstructed three times, but only the latest temple, A, has escaped destruction by ancient robbers' tunnels.

Temple A stood on a brick platform, 6 m. high, which presumably encased the foundations of earlier temples —B, C, and D, lettered in descending order. The central shrine, 18 m. long by 6 m. wide inside, agrees both in proportions and absolute dimensions with Anu Temples —D and —E, the early precursors of the White Temple at Erech. But the whole edifice must have covered an area of 25 m. by 27 m. The podium or altar at one end of the sanctuary was

1. *Iraq*, ix, 1947.

embellished with an empanelled frieze of white limestone and grey shale with a gold surround, held in place by gold-headed silver nails. A mosaic of coloured clay cones combined with eight-petalled stone rosettes decked the inner walls.

The temple had, of course, been plundered, as had its precursors, but some minor treasures, probably belonging to temple —C, had escaped the robbers' attention. The most striking were three alabaster heads, one 17·5 cm. high (Pl. XXXVII), the oldest example of large-scale sculpture from Northern Mesopotamia but inferior to the splendid head from Erech. Much more common were small Eye Idols (Fig. 105, 3) and Hut Symbols of alabaster or clay. Mallowan considers that the latter are conventional degenerations of the Eye Idols and terms them Spectacle Idols, but Frankfort would reverse the typology. Other surviving votives comprise numerous animal amulets stylistically indistinguishable from those of the E-anna —III hoard at Erech, and again including monkeys, seals in the shape of animals and kidneys, round and rectangular stamp seals, cylinders in Jemdet Nasr style, and thousands of beads, including segmented fayence beads.[1]

The cylinders and the exact agreement of amulets and animal seals with those from the Erech hoard put together in Jemdet Nasr times, prove that Eye Temple C goes back well into that period. The excavator plausibly suggests that Temple D might be Late Uruk. The association on the Khabur of Hut Symbols and seals of the Gawra period with objects appropriate to the Jemdet Nasr period as defined in Sumer is welcome confirmation of the partial equation between the Jemdet Nasr and the Gawra periods, even if we accept Frankfort's view that Eye Idols are typologically later than Hut Symbols.

The succeeding period in Northern Mesopotamia is conveniently defined by a very distinctive kind of wheel-made painted pottery and may be named, after the site where this ware was first identified, the Ninevite period.[2] This pottery is very abundant, and was perhaps manufactured only, in Nineveh 5[3] and the first settlement (—7) under Tell Billa[4] and perhaps Grai Resh I,[5] but a few vases in it at least were exported not only to neighbouring villages like Gawra —VII and —VIIIA,[6] but also to the Khabur basin[7] and even to Eshnunna[8]

1. *Ibid.*, 254. 2. Perkins, *CAENM.*, 185.
3. *LAAA.*, xix, 1932, 252. 4. *Mus. J.*, xxiii, 252.
5. *Iraq*, vii, 15. 6. Speiser, 41, 47.
7. *Iraq*, iii, 1936, 38; iv, 95. 8. *OIC.*, No. 19, p. 21; No. 20, pl. vii, 26–7.

and Kish,[1] in Akkad. The imports at Eshnunna are assigned to Early Dynastic I which gives a date for the Ninevite period confirmed by the cylinder seals.

Nineveh 5 ware is a greenish fabric resembling Ubaid ware, but the vases are always wheel-made and slipped, the paint is lustrous purple-black, the forms and patterns quite novel. Favourite shapes are chalices on solid pedestals (Fig. 106) and keeled cups with a

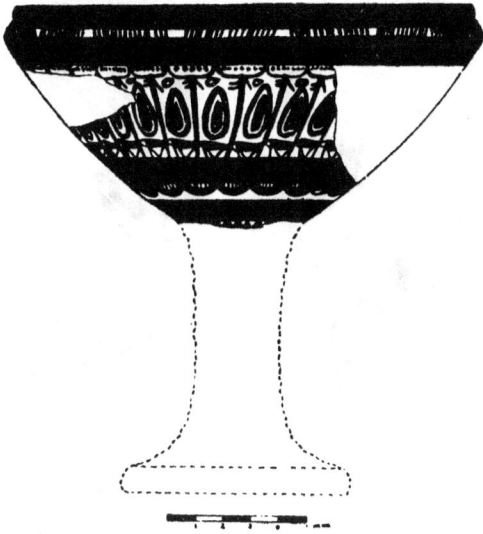

FIG. 106. Painted chalice, Nineveh V.

rounded base (Fig. 107). The designs include the sigma, the double-axe, and other old motives but also birds and beasts deliberately stylized with elongated necks in a manner that recalls Hissar I or even Kulli. With the painted ware goes a pale grey or straw coloured fabric adorned with incised, excised, or relief patterns (Fig. 108). It is best known from Billa —7–6 and therefore termed Billa ware,[2] but is represented also at Gawra and at Chagar Bazar on the Khabur. Chalices and some other forms are related to those of Nineveh 5, but some designs suggest comparison with those carved on stone vases imported into Sumer from Makran (p. 169).

For the rest the Ninevite period shows few really significant advances on the latest Gawra phase. The wheel was of course in

1. Sherds in the Ashmolean Museum, Oxford.
2. *Mus. J.*, xxiii, 1934.

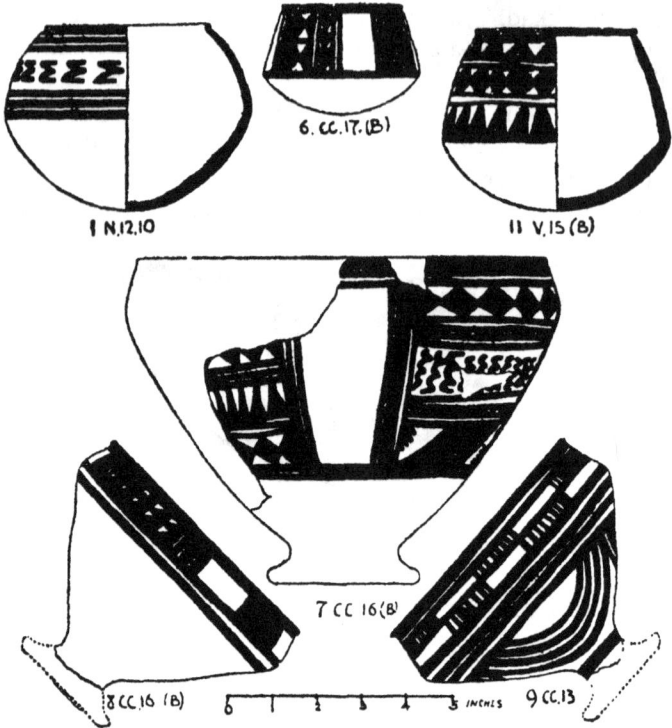

FIG. 107. Painted cups and chalices, Nineveh V.

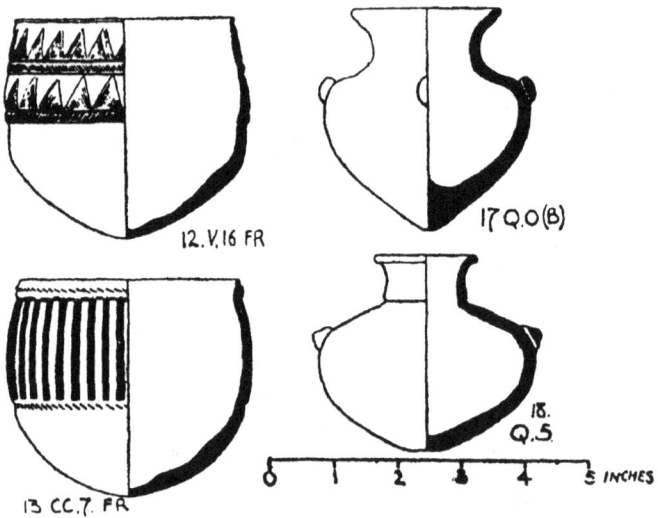

FIG. 108. Incised vases of Billa ware from Nineveh V.

regular use both in transport and the ceramic industry. Arrow-heads are at last relatively plentiful, metal commoner; Gawra —VII yielded forty-two metal objects as against twenty-two from —VIII and 334 from —VI. Notable are a pair of tweezers of the distinctive Sumerian type 4 and toggle pins the perforated swelling on whose necks is cast not hammered.

Nowhere on the parkland steppe is there yet any trace of literacy, but cylinder seals were competing with stamps in Gawra —VII and Nineveh 5. Most of the impressions from Nineveh 5 are classed as 'Jemdet Nasr' in style, but an actual cylinder should be Early Dynastic III! Two seals from Gawra —VII are classified as Jemdet Nasr, two as Early Dynastic II, and one as later than Jemdet Nasr.[1] The evidence of glyptic thus confirms that of pottery: the Ninevite period on the Middle Tigris and the Khabur corresponds to the very end of Jemdet Nasr and Early Dynastic I–II in Lower Mesopotamia.

Literacy and city life did not immediately follow. Some brick vaulted tombs below the Ishtar Temple at Nineveh may, like similar tombs in Kish or Ur, belong to local 'kings', but ancient robbers had emptied the tombs. Gawra —VI and Chagar Bazar —3 remained illiterate villages. Still Gawra, and probably all the rest, now supported resident smiths and benefited at least indirectly from

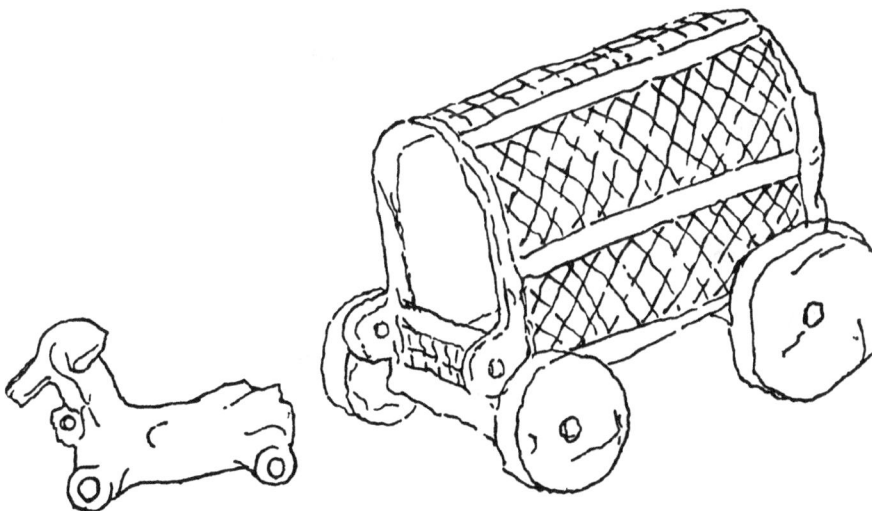

FIG. 109. Models of a covered wagon, ¹⁄₁, and of a quadruped, ²⁄₃, Gawra –VI, after Speiser.

1. Perkins, *CAEM.*, 185.

Sumerian commercial organization for the supply of metal. The local smiths reproduced all the classical Sumerian types enumerated on p. 159 and metal sickles and tongs, constructed just like the normal Sumerian tweezers, that only by chance have not yet been reported from Lower Mesopotamia. Toy wheels, chariots, and carts were now very popular; the covered wagon of Fig. 109 refutes any suggestion that wheeled vehicles were employed principally as arms. A fiddle-shaped stone figurine from Gawra —VI is notable for analogies in Hissar III, in Anatolia, and the Aegean, a double-headed animal for Early Pharaonic parallels. Replicas of both were found in an Early Dynastic II context at Eshnunna.[1] They thus provide some evidence that the beginning of Gawra VI must go beyond Early Dynastic III in Sumer. But Schaeffer would put it later than Sargon!

No doubt 'Early Sumerian' types of tool and weapon were still current in the backwoods of Northern Mesopotamia in Sargonid times. At Brak, on the Khabur,[2] spear-heads exactly like Fig. 87, 3, were still in use then. Similarly, on the Upper Euphrates,[3] round and below Carchemish, Early Sumerian types of rein-ring and weapons and toilet articles of types 3, 6, 9, 10*a* and 10*b* were still being made with only minor modifications in the 'Cist Grave period' that must begin just after or just before the Syrian campaigns of Sargon and Narâm-Sin. The well-furnished cists of slabs were laid beneath the houses of sizable towns or villages; at Til-Barsib a vaulted tomb, built of great stone blocks, like the Early Dynastic I tombs of Mari, must have held the remains of a petty king. Models prove the use of chariots, carts, and covered wagons with two or four solid wheels, and professional potters manufactured red ware vases on the wheel. Resident smiths not only copied Early Sumerian models, but introduced specific variants, notably by providing spear-heads with hooked tangs and enriched their repertory with 'Phœnician' types like flat celts with an eyelet in the butt. Even cylinder seals were engraved locally with rather clumsy imitations of older Sumerian designs, but not inscribed. For there is no

1. Speiser, *Gawra*, i, pl. liii, b, and liv, a; *OIC.*, No. 19, figs 24 and 28.
2. *Iraq*, ix, 121, and pl. 32, 11.
3. Schaeffer, *Stratigraphie comparée*, 80–4, and figs. 9, 79–82, 104–5, summarizes most of the material. But cf. also Woolley, *LAAA.*, vi, 1914, 87 ff., and Thureau-Dangin and Dunand, *Til-Barsib*, Paris, 1936, 96–112, and for wheeled vehicles, also *Berytus*, ii, 132; *Syria*, xi, pl. xxxiv, and *C.A.H.*, pls. vol. i, 1927, pl. 248b. For a slightly higher chronology see Mallowan, *Antiquity*, xi, 1937, 235, whose absolute dates must, of course, be reduced by 200 years to allow for the subsequent deflation of Mesopotamian chronology.

evidence that the local kings felt the need of clerks to look after their revenues. Indeed, the local population had not quite reached the stage attained by the Sumerians a thousand years earlier. Nor is there as yet any record of autonomous local development since Halafian and Ubaid farmers had first colonized the region. Yet we shall find that it was precisely the metal types, most consistently represented in the 'cist graves', that seem most obviously to have been diffused to the Aegean and to temperate Europe.

(2)

But as soon as we cross the narrow belt of high ground that divides the Euphrates from the Mediterranean drainage the whole picture changes. The Amanus and Lebanon ranges tap the moisture-laden depressions from the west. So in Phœnicia and its hinterlands reliable and generous winter rains water cereal crops, fruit trees, and vines and feed perennial rivers and springs. With these resources the Orontes valley and the coastal plains could support a substantial population on a basis of fishing, corn-growing, and stock-breeding, especially when combined with orchard husbandry, but would not demand any concentration of the population. Test pits at Hama,[1] on the Orontes, at Tell esh-Sheikh[2] and Judeideh,[3] in the Amuq plain, and in the upland valley of the Kara Su at Sakçe-gözü (Coba Hüyük)[4] further north seem to prove that Mesopotamian farmers with slings and gaily painted pots colonized the Orontes valley; indeed, they penetrated right to the Mediterranean coasts at least at Ugarit (Ras Shamra).[5] All these sites have yielded sling bullets and Halafian sherds in substantial quantities. Samarra and possibly Hassunan sherds from Sakçe-gözü and elsewhere may well indicate a still earlier colonization.

But in all cases the 'Chalcolithic' settlements with painted pottery are superimposed upon older 'Neolithic' villages—Hama —M, Judeideh —XIV, Ugarit —V—distinguished by self-coloured pottery and arrow-heads. Unfortunately little besides potsherds has been discovered in these deep levels. Common to the whole area are

1. Ingholt, 'Rapport préliminaire,' K. Danske Videnskabs Selskabs *Skrifter*, 1940.
2. *A.J.A.*, liv, 1950, 62.
3. *A.J.A.*, xli, 1937, 10.
4. *LAAA.*, xxiv, 120–140; *Iraq*, xii, 1950, 53–158.
5. *Syria*, xvi, 1935, 162; *Ugaritica*, i,

dark-faced fabrics, designed to have a black, or more rarely a red, surface. These were often ornamented, but the patterns and even the techniques vary from site to site. Decoration might be effected by incision before or after firing, by the imprint of a shell-edge yielding a 'rocker pattern' (a zig-zag of curved serrated lines) or with the burnishing tool itself. The tool is so applied as to leave stripes of shiny black or red on a dull grey or pink ground. The resultant 'stroke burnished' or 'burnish decorated' ware is found in Judeideh —XIV and Ugarit —V, but at Sakçe-gözü only with the first painted ware in the 'Protochalcolithic' level. The same highly specialized technique recurs in 'neolithic' sites on Samos,[1] in the Troad, in northern Greece and at Vinča on the Middle Danube.[2] But it is applied to vases of different shapes in the 'Pyrgos ware' of Early Minoan Crete[3] and to 'grey Uruk ware' at Kish[4] and, finally, in the grey wares of Hissar II, and over a red wash or paint in the lattice burnished wares of Phœnicia and Palestine.

Judging by the great depths of its deposits, especially at Mersin, which belongs to the same general culture, this Levantine neolithic culture must have lasted a very long time and must rival in antiquity anything known in the Nile valley or Mesopotamia. It may indeed prove to be descended from the Natufian or some other local mesolithic culture; for its province offers the botanical and zoological conditions for the neolithic revolution. But links with a pre-neolithic stage remain to be discovered. That the local tradition was very persistent is in any case proved by the survival of the Levantine dark-faced wares in the chalcolithic levels of Sakçe-gözü, Judeideh —XIII, and Ugarit —IV. In the sequel fresh impulses from Northern Mesopotamia must have brought to the Orontes valley at least the Northern Ubaid traditions in ceramic art and promoted the development in the Amuq plain of a local style of painting, best known from Tell esh-Sheik, but traceable as far away as Mersin,[5] in Cilicia. But eventually even the Amuq-Ubaid pottery gave place to unpainted fabrics, some reminiscent of Mesopotamian grey Uruk ware.[6]

Hama (Hamath), well placed for communications with the east and south as well as with the west offers the best material yet

1. *Athenische Mitteilungen*, lx, 1935–36, 129.
2. Childe, *Dawn*, s.v. 'stroke-burnished ware.'
3. Evans, *Palace of Minos*, i, 1921, 59.
4. In Ashmolean Museum, Oxford, Nos. 1930, 239a and 238b.
5. *AJA.*, liv, 63; *LAAA.*, xxvi, 51.
6. Sakçe-gözü, *Iraq*, xii, 100; Tabara, *Anatolian Studies*, i, 1951.

published for establishing connections between the two first regions. Though Halafian as well as Ubaid sherds were found in Hama —L as well as a clay imitation of a stamp seal, sherds related to the Billa ware of Northern Mesopotamia imply the settlement lasted nearly down to the Ninevite period. On the other hand, Hut-Symbols (Fig. 105, 1), bevel-rimmed bowls, and a couple of fayence cylinders of Jemdet Nasr style from the succeeding level, K, should indicate an overlap between it and the Gawra period. So in art a stone head from K is a stage further removed from the naturalism of the sculpture from Erech (Pl. XXXVI) than those from Brak (Pl. XXXVII) and indeed stands midway between them and the quite barbaric marble statuettes of the Cyclades. The design on a clay stamp again might be a conventionalized version of the animals on a Gawra seal, but stone bead-seals bore the familiar filled cross. Funerary practices, burial in large jars or pithoi, accord with those observed at Carchemish on the Upper Euphrates before the Cist Grave period and at Byblos II on the coast. The pottery includes wheel-made red-slipped and lattice-burnished vases and—but only in the last phase of a long occupation—hand-made particoloured black and red vases of 'Khirbet Kerak ware'.

Both groups recur in Palestine, the former in E.B. II, Khirbet Kerak ware only in E.B. III which we shall find equivalent to the Pyramid Age in Egypt. Now, as Hood[1] showed in 1951, this hand-made pottery, widespread in North Syria and Palestine, reflects an incursion of barbarous tribes, coming perhaps from Georgia, into regions advanced enough to support professional potters. This pottery, certainly equates the last phase of Hama —K with Judeideh —XI. Its earlier phases should, on the other hand, comprise Judeideh —XIII and —XII.

In the sequel, Hama J saw a revival of wheel-made pottery and the inclusion of the Orontes basin in the same cultural province as the Upper Euphrates in the Cist Grave period, with the wheeled carts, eyelet celts, and stamped vases appropriate thereto. If then the earlier part of Hama K just overlaps with the late Jemdet Nasr period in Mesopotamia and comprises the first two dynasties in Egypt, its end might roughly coincide with the campaigns of Sargon of Agade and the accession of the VIth Dynasty on the Nile. But unfortunately the correlations with Mesopotamia and still more with Egypt are ambiguous. Better evidence should be obtainable from Byblos on the coast.

1. *Anatolian Studies*, i, 1951, 117.

This port, the natural outlet for the cedar-wood and other products of Lebanon, was from the dawn of history the goal of Egyptian maritime trade and, according to a very late myth, would have been the birthplace of Osiris and Egyptian agriculture. Unluckily, direct evidence of Mesopotamian connections is lacking, and the available reports on the French excavations leave many doubts unresolved.

The origins of Byblos[1] can be traced to a village of farmers and presumably fishers of the usual Levantine neolithic culture. Flint celts, polished on the edges, served as chisels and gouges, leaf-shaped arrow-heads and javelin-heads of triangular section as weapons. The vases, predominantly dark-faced, might be covered with irregular groups of comb impressions as if clawed by some beast, with the imprints of cords or cordage baskets[2] with incised herring-bone patterns or with incised and punctured ribbons and triangles. The last-named designs are strikingly like those on neolithic pottery from Knossos in Crete,[3] while the herring-bone motive recalls on the one hand Hassuna, on the other the neolithic and chalcolithic of Palestine and Merimde.

The Levantine neolithic of Byblos I was not, however, succeeded like Ugarit —V, by a Halafian colony. Instead Byblos II[4] was a village of curvilinear or rectilinear houses grouped along cobbled streets, which covered more than 3 hectares and is allied culturally rather to Hama —K. So the dead[5] were again buried in large jars or pithoi, sometimes crouched, sometimes disarticulated, and sometimes allegedly after cremation. The urns were interred within the inhabited area, often in artificial caves cut in the rock. These rock-cut tombs were regular family vaults that might contain as many as twenty-six adult skeletons. They thus offer the first dated example of collective burial since the Natufians had observed the same practice in a natural cave in Mt. Carmel—a practice repeated all round the Mediterranean in the earliest metal age.

Physically,[6] the chalcolithic Giblites are described as small, dark long-heads of the Mediterranean race, comparable to the Natufians,

1. *RB.*, lvii, 1940, 584–8.
2. Better seen at Hammâm between Byblos and Ugarit, *Syria*, xxi, 1940, 200.
3. *LAAA.*, x, 1923, 39.
4. *RB.*, lvii, 588–591.
5. Dunand, *Fouilles de Byblos* (Paris, 1939), 365, 373–381, 434–445.
6. *Bul. Mus. Beyrouth*, i, 1937, 23–33; Dunand, *Biblia Grammata* (Beyrouth, 1945), 4, n. 1.

but a round-headed admixture is reported, too. Economically, they lived by cultivating olives as well as barley, breeding goats, sheep, and cattle, snaring pigeons and doubtless fishing. Flint was extensively used for the manufacture of tools including undenticulated sickle-blades, fan-shaped scrapers like the Maadian and—allegedly—knives[1] of the distinctive pharaonic family shown in Fig. 32, 6, but more exactly resembling the later Old Kingdom variety. A pear-shaped stone mace was a favourite weapon.

At the same time the tomb furniture discloses a flourishing school of metallurgy, though the organization of supplies was still imperfect. Silver rings were relatively common and imply a mastery of the difficult art of refining. Copper daggers (Pl. XXXIX, *b*, 2) were found in only five of the 850 tombs examined. The stout blades with midribs and two or three rivets do not look the least Mesopotamian nor yet Nilotic. They must be products of a distinct Syro-Phœnician metal industry that may have supplied also Hama and other Orontes villages and even inspired Early Aegean metallurgy.

On the other hand, the wheel was not in use. Free-hand the local potter produced pithoi as much as 1·40 m. high, a variety of two-handled and one-handled jugs and mugs, twin vases, inter-communicating and joined by basket handles, and tripod bowls. Most are dark faced and generally self-coloured; a few vases from the tombs are said to be covered with a leather-coloured or reddish brown lustrous slip which it would be tempting to compare with the 'urfirnis' pottery of Greece. Decoration is confined to impressed circles made with a reed and incised herring-bone patterns.

Nor did the Giblites use seals in the manner associated with painted pottery on and beyond the Euphrates. On the other hand, some thirty vases had been impressed before firing with seals or rather stamps.[2] The stamps were probably made of wood, but a copper 'compartmented seal'[3] found loose in the tell would yield an impression that can be matched on the vases. The motives include, besides the ubiquitous filled cross, so-called pictographic signs and complicated patterns that, as on the clay stamp from Hama —K, look like attempts to reproduce in carving the animal designs engraved on seals of the Gawra period; sometimes the wood-carver has even imitated the effect of the lapidaries' drill. This practice of stamping

1. Dunand, *Fouilles*, pl. cxii.
2. Dunand, *B.G.*, 25–46.
3. Montet, *Byblos et l'Égypte* (Paris, 1928), pl. lix, 44.

unfired vases has, of course, nothing in common with the Mesopotamian custom of sealing blobs of clay attached to finished and
filled vessels. Stylistic comparisons between the stamp designs and
those on Jemdet Nasr cylinders have little chronological significance.
The plausible derivation of some of the motives at Byblos and at
Hama from seal designs of the Gawra period should, however,
indicate that Byblos II is no older than that phase of North Mesopotamian culture.

Dunand's phase III[1] is not separated from II by any sharp break.
But burial within the settlement area was given up; house-plans
were changed and the wall foundations might be built in herring-
bone masonry as at Troy and in Early Helladic Greece. The tradition
of flint working continued uninterrupted, and for a time at least pots
were being made by hand. But now professional potters settled at
Byblos introducing the potters' wheel and kiln and manufacturing
fine red-slipped and combed wares. Among their products were
spindle shaped flasks comparable to those found as imports in First
Dynasty tombs in Egypt (Fig. 53) where, of course, combed ware
is also found.[2] So presumably commercial contacts had already been
established with the Nile valley. Byblos III was in fact well on the
way to urbanization, but it remained an open township for perhaps
a century.

Then Byblos IV[3] was girt with a stout stone wall. Dressed sandstone blocks began to replace split slabs of local rock even in
domestic architecture, and wooden pillars supplemented masonry in
supporting roofs or second storeys to the houses. The local smith
now cast distinctive axe-heads in the form of an elongated flat celt
with a splayed blade and an eyelet in the narrow butt (Pl. XXXIX,
b, 1) as in the Cist Grave period on the Upper Euphrates.

No more pots were made by hand, but the local specialists now
began to decorate vases with lattice burnishing. Some such vases
were stamped, again before firing, with impressions but this time of
cylinders.[4] The latter were probably still made of wood, but were
carved with conventionalized animal files. The designs have been
compared to products of the Jemdet Nasr style in Lower Meso-

1. *RB.*, lvii, 591–2, 600.
2. 'Combed ware' is, however, also known in Sumer during the Early
Dynastic; cf. Ehrich, 'Early Pottery of the Jebeleh Region,' *Mem. Amer. Phil.
Society*, 1939, 30.
3. *RB.*, lvii, 593–6.
4. Dunand, *B.G.*, 59–68.

potamia, but, though an actual Jemdet Nasr cylinder was found unstratified at the site, comparison with Early Dynastic II cylinders would be equally legitimate. In any case, the chronological value of these impressions need be no greater than of those from Byblos II.

Dunand terms Byblos IV 'la première installation urbaine'. But no palace nor temple reveals any concentration of wealth in what must have been a prosperous trading port. And, after flourishing for a considerable time, this first walled town was destroyed by fire.

In Byblos V[1] rose the first recognizable temple to Ba'alat Gebal ('bâtiment XL'), built of limestone block and compared in plan to the Early Dynastic II temple of Abu, at Eshnunna. After a comparatively short time the town was replanned.

In Byblos VI[2] an enlarged temple of Ba'alat (bâtiment II) measured 28 m. by 20 m. overall, and a new temple was erected in another quarter. In bâtiment II were found inscribed alabaster vases offered to Ba'alat Gebal by Egyptian pharaohs from Khasekemui to Pepi II. They are valuable documents for the mechanism of Egyptian trade with a foreign state, but naturally such votive gifts would be jealously preserved and need not have been offered in the temple in which they were found. Ignoring this possibility, Dunand suggests that Byblos VI lasted from 2700 to 2200 B.C.[3]

Even if the oldest inscribed vases dedicated by Khasekemui be not accepted as evidence that the temple of Byblos VI was built under the IInd Egyptian Dynasty, Byblos III and even IV should coincide with the Ist Dynasty. For it is quite likely that some of the flasks and vessels of combed and lattice burnished pottery then imported into Egypt had been filled in Phœnicia and shipped from Byblos. So the social surplus, concentrated by the first pharaohs, could have supplied the capital for the incipient urbanization that is revealed in the first walled town. On the other hand, the professional potters who were already numbered among the townsfolk cannot have been Egyptians. Nor can the wheel have reached Sumer from Phœnicia— nor its North Syrian hinterland; even if the cylinder impressions on vases justified a synchronism between Byblos IV and the Jemdet Nasr phase in Lower Mesopotamia, the wheel had already been in use

1. *RB.*, lvii, 596, 601.
2. *RB.*, lvii; 597–9.
3. Braidwood (*Amer. J. Sem. Lang.*, lviii, 254–8) in 1941 questioned Dunand's evidence for dating the foundation of 'bâtiment II' to the reign of Khasekemui, and his queries had not been altogether answered 20 years later. Cf. also Schaeffer, *Strat. comp.*, 53–5.

there for a long time before the latter period. On the contrary, the labour-saving device must have been diffused to Phœnicia from Sumer and with it doubtless came such technical devices as reserve slip ware.

But metallurgy was by then already well established on the Levant coast. The silver ornaments and copper weapons from the tombs of Byblos II show no trace of Mesopotamian inspiration, but are products of an independent metallurgical industry from which even Aegean metal-work, too, might be derived. So in the sequel the standard bronzes containing 10 per cent tin, reported from Byblos VI, may, despite the uncertain chronology of this phase, be as old as those from the Royal Cemetery at Ur and illustrate a further achievement of the Levantine industry.

But do the handled flint knives, attributed to Byblos II, really represent Egyptian imports and thus prove the survival of the chalcolithic village into Early Pharaonic times? It would have been odd if the Egyptians, as soon as they began making this distinctively pharaonic type, should have exported them to Phœnicia, and in any case the figured specimens all look later than Dynasty II. On the other hand, can the type have originated in Phœnicia where good flint is as plentiful as in Egypt? Can its adoption in Egypt at the beginning of Dynasty I be an archæological counterpart of a pre-historic event allegorized in the late Osiris myth? Is it not after all more likely that the knives were discovered at Byblos out of place and had really been imported from Egypt under the Old Kingdom at the same time as the votive vases?

The chalcolithic village of Byblos II may then be parallel to Maadi and the Gerzean phase on the Nile which would agree well with its equation through Hama —K with the Gawra period in Northern Mesopotamia. Even if there be no hiatus between Byblos I and Byblos II, the Levantine neolithic can claim a respectable antiquity, and Dunand's comparison with Badari is not chronologically impossible. But the archæological record from Phœnicia is still too incomplete for an objective evaluation of the region's claims to be considered a centre of the neolithic revolution.

(3)

Palestine is better situated. Besides the botanical and zoological resources requisite for food-production, it offers two special advantages to archæologists. Its hills are riddled with natural caves where farmers, not yet tied to one spot by fruit-trees and irrigation works, might, like their hunter ancestors, take shelter and leave relics for excavators to find. Secondly, ample supplies of excellent flint are available for the manufacture of tools and weapons. The superficial occurrence of such may disclose settlements so transitory that no tell has accumulated on the site and in which indeed no pots were used nor broken. Since 1935 excavation in Palestine has brought to light long and reliable sequences of cultures at various sites which reach far back from horizons historically dated by contacts with Egypt. Correlations of the several sequences, however, are exposed to the danger of inflation by arranging in consecutive periods distinct, but contemporary, local cultures. For small though it be, Palestine is not an homogeneous cultural province. The broad coastal plain is contrasted with the mountainous hinterland and the rift valley of the Jordan beyond it, while Mount Carmel and the fertile valley of Esdraelon north of it cut across these east–west zones. Palestinian specialists have further complicated the correlation of local sequences into a general frame of reference by divergent, but always arbitrary, uses of the terms 'Neolithic', 'Chalcolithic' and 'Early Bronze Age'. In using these terms it is as well to state that 'Early Bronze' implies nothing as to the use and chemical composition of metal objects, but as a precaution the abbreviation E.B. will be generally used.

By 1934 assemblages of flints from caves and surface sites had enabled Neuville[1] to define a 'Tahunian' industry which could be classified as neolithic. It was characterized by gravers, sickle-blades, and arrow-heads that could be derived from the late Natufian (Fig. 110), together with flint celts sharpened by a transverse, tranchet blow. The sites suggested temporary occupations by semi-nomadic groups practising shifting cultivation and stock breeding combined with hunting, fishing, and collecting. Then Garstang's[2] excavations brought to light similar flints at the base of the stratified tell of Jericho.

Neolithic Jericho was already a permanent village beside a perennial spring where orchard husbandry may have supplemented corn-growing and stock-breeding. Stock-breeding can be deduced only from rough unbaked clay figures of animals, cereal cultivation from sickle-blades and saddle querns and eventually from clay-lined grain-bins or silos. The villagers built houses with walls of clay, plastered inside with lime and sometimes painted, but wooden posts

1. *RB.*, xliii, 1934, 255.   2. *LAAA.*, xxii and xxiii.

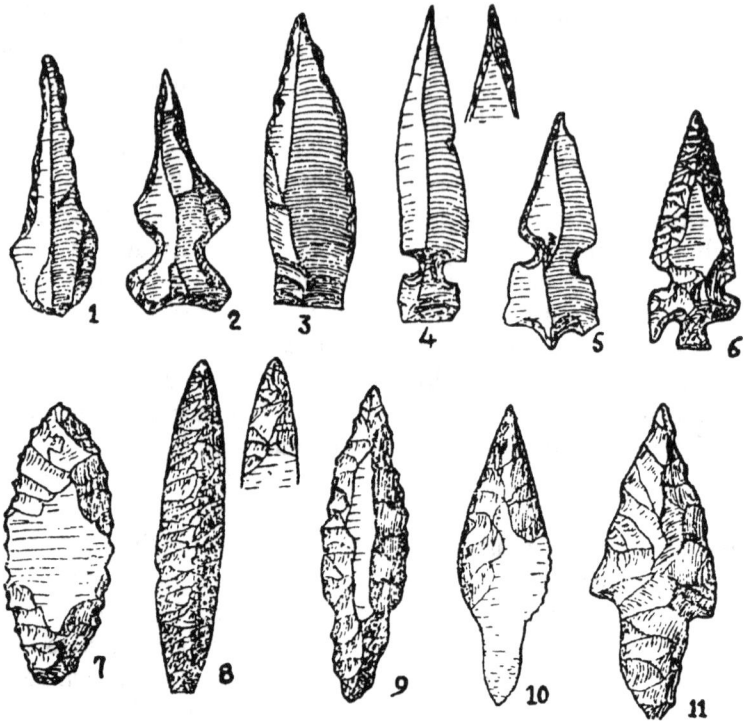

Fig. 110. Late Natufian (1–5) and Tahunian (6–11) arrow-heads after Neuville, ¼.

helped to support the roofs. As wood-working tools polished celts of fine-grained rock were used besides flaked flint celts. Pottery was apparently unknown, but bowls were carved out of calcite and mortars from basalt and limestone blocks. Trade[1] is revealed by obsidian from all neolithic levels and even below, Mediterranean shells, and a fragment of malachite. One house of two rooms behind a portico of wooden posts may have been a sanctuary; many mud figures of animals were found in or near it and under the floor of an adjacent building the skeletons of two males, one apparently slain with violence.[2]

Despite doubts expressed by Braidwood[3] the Jerichoan neolithic could be derived from the Natufian mesolithic. In any case, if not autochthonous, it is not obviously derived from Egypt; for the sickle blades and arrow-heads are quite different from the Merimdian and Tasian.

1. *LAAA.*, xxii, 184, 181.   2. *LAAA.*, xxiii, 70.
3. *Antiquity*, xxiv, 1950, 190.

After an accumulation of 4·5 m. of debris, the first potsherds appeared in Jericho —IX. In this one level Garstang[1] reports silos lined with unbaked clay, unbaked models of clay mixed with chaff or sand, and quite well-fired vases of chaff-tempered pottery. The vases are already provided with small lug-handles generally horizontally pierced while the pale drab surface is sometimes covered with a reddish slip. From a shrine in the same level[2] came a triad of statuettes of unbaked clay—a bearded man, a woman, and a child, the eyes in each case being represented by shells—and a model of a two-storeyed granary or sanctuary, also unbaked. So it looks as if society in neolithic Jericho was organized round the cult of a trinity, already celebrated, as in Sumer, in a sort of rudimentary temple.

In the succeeding layer, —VIII, termed 'Chalcolithic' at Jericho, chaff becomes less common than grit temper in the paste, and the vase surfaces may be decorated with lines of glossy reddish paint on the pale ground or with incised herring-bone and other patterns or with a combination of painting and incision that recalls on the one hand Hassuna, in Mesopotamia, on the other Merimde, in Lower Egypt. But by this time material, that should be more or less coeval with the neolithic or chalcolithic of Jericho, collected from 'tells' on the Wadi Ghazzeh, near Gaza,[3] in southern Palestine, from Umm Qatafa and other caves in the Jordan valley[4] and a site on the Yamuq River, in northern Palestine, reveals the existence of other cultures, or at least ceramic styles, that may be classified as neolithic.

Along the Yarmuq[5] actual bones attest the breeding of sheep and goats, and the pursuit of gazelles, wild boars, wild asses, and apparently camels, while cereals were reaped with denticulated sickle-blades worked on both faces. Flint arrow-heads and tanged javelin-heads were used by hunters. For wood-working flint celts were sharpened either by grinding the edges or by a tranchet blow. Flint nodules, flaked to a point at one end while the cortex was retained on the butt, recall picks from Merimde (Fig. 111, 4). Vases were made from clay tempered with chaff and coarse grits. The surface is pale but may be partly covered with a reddish wash and decorated with incised herring-bone bands. For ritual purposes

1. *LAAA.*, xxiii, 71, 77, 87.
2. *LAAA.*, xxiii, 71.
3. Macdonald, *Beth Pelet II*, 1932, 2–7.
4. Umm Qatafa, *Syria*, xii, 1931, 29–32; Uzba, *BASOR.*, 86, 7, and 89, 22.
5. Stekelis, *Israel Exploration Journal*, i, 1950, 2–18.

pebbles were curiously engraved to suggest a human figure or a phallos.

The varieties of pottery and other artifacts at this stage may well be due as much to local as to chronological differences. The pottery,

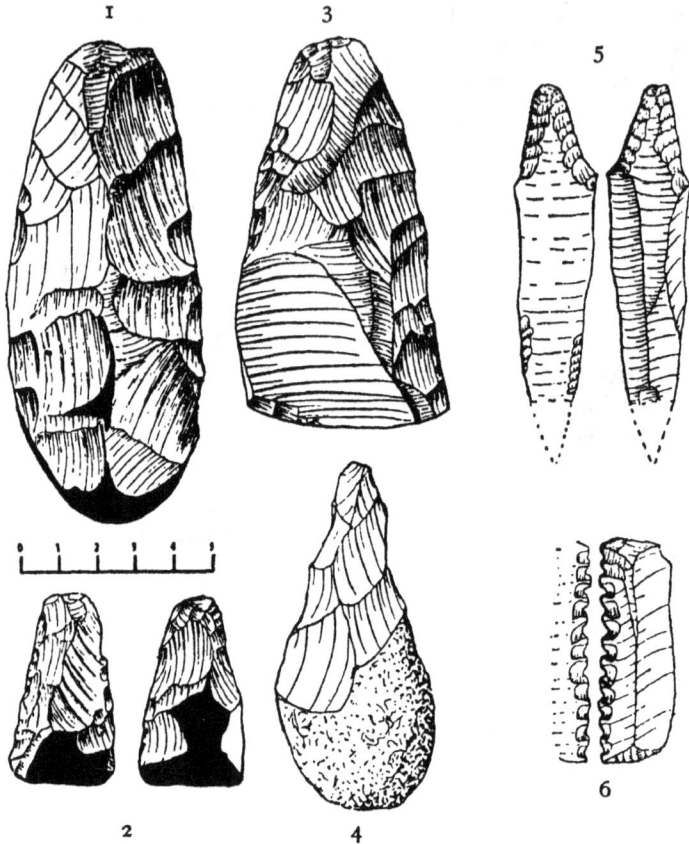

FIG. 111. Yarmuqian axes with ground edges 1–2, tranchet 3, pick 4, sickle blade 5, and javelin head 6, after Stekelis.

however, everywhere shows rather vague affinities to Merimde on the one hand, to that of Hassuna on the other, and more explicitly to the Levantine neolithic of Phœnicia as illustrated in Byblos I and, even better, in Hammâm.[1] But during the Chalcolithic a well-defined culture crystallized out perhaps east of the Jordan though it spread

1. *Syria*, xxi, 1940, 199, and pl. xxii, 2, f.

as far north as the valley of Esdraelon[1] and as far south as the Wadi Ghazzeh. It is termed Ghassulian after Teleilat Ghassul, 5·5 km. east of the Jordan, where it was first identified.

The tell[2] is really a group of mounds, not more than 2 m. high, covering an area of 800 m. by 400 m. They mark the site of a compact village of mud-brick houses. The walls were built of lumps of mud, not formed in a mould but shaped by hand and resting on a stone foundation. Some interiors were decorated with elaborate paintings. Adzes and chisels were sharpened by longitudinal flaking followed by grinding of the edges rather than by a tranchet blow. An exceedingly popular tool was a fan-shaped scraper of tabular flint, similar to those from Maadi and Byblos II. Flint arrow-heads are absent. So perhaps the sling replaced the bow, but pear-shaped and discoid stone mace-heads were also used as weapons.

Pottery vessels were hardly ever painted, but were decorated with applied cordons and digital impressions. The wheel was not in use, but some vessels are said to have been shaped on a 'tournette', and perforated stone discs have been described as the implement used. Easily recognizable shapes are 'cornets'—beakers with long pointed bases—and lugged bowls on high pedestals. The vases are provided with lugs or simple loop handles and include a simple sort of amphoriskos. Bowls were also made out of basalt and other stones. A favourite personal ornament was a pendant of shell in the form of a crescent or the arc of a circle perforated at both ends. An axe amulet recalls Merimde, Crete, and Atlantic Europe, while a fiddle-shaped stone figurine again finds northern analogies.

The Ghassulians in Transjordan were buried individually in stone cists, sometimes covered by round barrows supported by a circular kerb of boulders.[3] The cists, formed of seven or eight upright slabs with two or three cover-stones, do not exceed 1·5 m. in length, 1 m. by ·70 m. by ·50 m. being the average size. Such cists have nothing to do with the megalithic tombs of western Europe, while larger structures of similar shape in Judaea and Galilee have yielded no relics to indicate their age or use. The Ghassulian cists should rather be compared with the so-called 'dolmens' of North Africa

1. Sukenik, *Arch. Investigations at 'Affula* (Jerusalem, 1948); *RB.*, liv, 1947, 395–400.
2. Mallon, *Teleilat Ghassul*, Pontifical Biblical Institute, Rome, i, 1934; ii, 1940.
3. Stekelis, 'Les Monuments mégalithiques de Palestine,' *IPH. Mem.*, 15, 1935.

and the Bronze Age short cists under round cairns of the Highland Zone of Britain. In the Vale of Sharon, on the other hand, the bones of dead Ghassulians after the flesh had decayed were placed in rectangular pottery ossuaries.[1] These imitate the flat-roofed or gabled houses of the living right down to the catches for the bar that fastened the door.

Four occupational layers are superimposed at Ghassul, and some rather suspicious ledge-handles are figured from the site. Hence, though at two sites Ghassulian remains are stratified beneath those of E.B.I., the occupation of the patent station may have lasted into that period. From its latest level come a pair of bronze celts, one of which contained 7 per cent tin. Whatever its exact position in the Palestinian sequence, this bronze compares favourably in absolute age with those from Gawra —VIII.

In the succeeding period Palestine is divided into two contrasted cultural provinces. In the north rules the Esdraelon culture, classified by Shipton and Wright as Upper Chalcolithic and classically represented in Megiddo —XIX,[2] Beth Shan —XVI[3] and T. Farah (Naplouse).[4] It is distinguished by a fine burnished grey ware used chiefly for the manufacture of carinated bowls. But pale drab wares were still made in the old tradition and now often covered with a reddish wash and from them were made many of the new pot forms that are classed as E.B.I. further south. The grey ware is certainly intrusive in Palestine. It is doubtless derived in the last resort from the Levantine neolithic of Judeideh XIV, but is more immediately allied to the 'Uruk grey ware' of the hand-made kind found at Grai Resh in Assyria in the Gawra period and in a similar context at Tabara in the Amuq plain. Its makers doubtless entered Palestine from the north, but if they initiated the 'Bronze Age', they did not introduce the wheel.

The distinctive grey ware does not occur in Judaea where, on the contrary, vases were often painted. But many of the innovations distinctive of Jericho —VII, Ai I, and similar settlements—jars with ledge-handles, spouted pots, amphoriskoi—recur in the native pale wares of Megiddo —XIX and cognate sites of the Esdraelon culture. Now the southern sites are frankly assigned to E.B.I. Since, however, the major social and economic features characterizing that phase and

1. *J. Pal. Oriental Soc.*, Jerusalem, xvii, 1937, 15–30.
2. 'Stages' —VII–V of Engberg and Shipton, *OIS.*, No. 10, 1934.
3. *Mus. J.*, xxiv,
4. *RB.*, liv, 1947, 395–400.

many ceramic innovations are common to both provinces, it seems likely that the distinction between 'Upper Chalcolithic' and 'Early Bronze Age' is more local than chronological and it is convenient to treat the two periods together as a first division of the Palestinian Early Bronze Age, E.B.I*a*.[1] The period thus initiated is undoubtedly a long one, but we shall summarize as a continuous process the development of culture during E.B.I*a*, E.B.I*b*, and E.B.II, though, in fact, the series is punctuated by catastrophes; Ai, for instance, was twice ravaged by fire.

By the beginning of the 'Bronze Age' the cultivation of vines and almonds,[2] in addition to wheat, barley, millet, and lentils,[3] tied the husbandman to the land while asses were available for transport. Settlements therefore tended to be little walled towns: Jericho — VII[4] covered seven to eight acres girt with a mud-brick wall on stone foundations. Ai[5] and the citadel of Megiddo[6] were protected by stone ramparts, 6·5 and 4·5 m. thick respectively and supplemented round parts of Ai by two outer tiers, perhaps as a defence against sling tactics.[7]

Within such enceintes a little shrine would symbolize the union of all the villagers in the service of the local baal. That in Megiddo — XIX was 12 m. long and 4 m. wide. At Ai the oldest sanctuary was undivided, but by E.B.II it was divided into an outer court, a *hekal* and a *debir* (Holy of Holies)[8] on the plan of the standard Semitic temple. Palaces for secular rulers are not certainly recognizable before E.B.II. Then the palace of Ai with its wood-pillared portico— or verandah—vaguely recalls the A palace at Kish and more closely the *hillani* palaces of later Hittite rulers. Peasants, of course, still lived in houses built of mud-bricks, often still only hand moulded. But even within town walls natural caves were adapted and inhabited.

The dead throughout the 'Bronze Age' were accorded collective burial and 'slept with their fathers' in natural or artificial caves

1. Discrepant correlations of the various sites have been offered by Albright (*Arch. Pal.*, 194, 70–1, and *A.J.A.*, liii, 1949, 213), Shipton (*OIS.*, No. 17, 1939, and *OIP.*, xxxiii, 1938, 143–7), and Wright (*BASOR.*, 63, 1936, 63).
2. *LAAA.*, xxii, 161.
3. Macdonald, *Beth. Pelet II*, 14.
4. *LAAA.*, xxii, 151.
5. Marquet-Krause, *Les Fouilles d'Ay*, Paris, 1949.
6. Loud, *Megiddo II, OIP.*, lxii, 1948, 66.
7. As in Iron Age Britain, Wheeler, *Maiden Castle, Dorset*, 1943, 48–51.
8. Dussaud, *Syria*, xvi, 1935, 345.

	EGYPT		PALESTINE	SYRIA
				C I S T P E
	DYNASTY VI	OLD KINGDOM		HAMA J
2325 >	V		E.B. III ><	
	IV			
	III			
	II	EARLY PHARAONIC	E.B. II	
	I		E.B. Ib	HAMA K
2850) 3200)				
3550	GERZEAN	MAADIAN	E.B. Ia	
3950			GHASSULIAN	HAMA L
	AMRATIAN BADARIAN			
4400	TASIAN	MERIMDE	YAMUQIAN	
			TAHUNIAN JERICHO	HAMA M
5000		HELWAN	NATUFIAN	

NORTH MESOPOTAMIA	SUMER	SUSA	IRAN	INDUS
G R A V E R I O D	UR III		HISSAR III	JHUKAR
S A R G O N I D				
EARLY DYNASTIC	EARLY DYNASTIC III			HARAPPA
VI (GAWRA)	III	II		
VII	II		SIALK IV,2	
NINEVITE PERIOD	D			AMRI
VIII A	I JEMDET NASR	D	IV,2	II
VIII B	NASR	C	IV,1	
GAWRA PERIOD		B		IB
	LATE URUK		III,7	
XI	EARLY URUK		III,4	
XII		I		IA
XIII	LATE UBAID		III,1	
UBAID				
XIX	EARLY UBAID		II	
HALAF				
SAMARRA	PROTO UBAID		I	
HASSUNA				
? JARMO				

either within the walls or more often on the slopes outside them. The tombs were used for successive interments over many generations, judging by the varieties of pottery and the number of corpses—300 in tomb A at Jericho—contained in them. The bones are generally found in disorder, but occasionally complete skeletons indicate that the corpse had been originally laid to rest lying contracted on the right side.[1] Macalister[2] described cave 2, II, at Gezer as a 'crematorium', but his account does not provide more convincing evidence for cremation than does Dunand's of the Byblos jar-burials. Even more exactly than in Phœnicia do the collective tombs of Palestine repeat burial practices observed all round the Mediterranean at the dawn of the local metal ages whether in natural caves, rock-cut tombs, or megalithic chambers built above ground. They are certainly more relevant to the latter's origin than the Ghassulian 'dolmens'. In Palestine collective burial in natural caves goes back to mesolithic times, and not even the rock-cut artificial cave can be inspired by the royal burials of Egypt. 'Cup marks' have been noted in some tombs and could be compared with the Natufian basins.

Metal was everywhere known, but seems to have been very scarce. It was perhaps still worked and purveyed by perambulating smiths rather than professionals resident in each township. Flint was still extensively used, but not apparently for axes and adzes. These were presumably made of copper. A stout specimen survives from Beth Shan −XVI. But most of the surviving copper objects—no analysed specimen contained tin—are weapons—daggers or spear-heads. Three types of spear-head were current—with a tapering tang[3]; with the tang bent over to form a hook[4] and with a broad tang folded to form a socket.[5] The last-named is an Early Pharaonic type, the second the oldest dated example of a family, well represented in the Cist Grave period on the Upper Euphrates, at Susa and in Iran.

How far the ceramic industry was industralized is uncertain. In Palestine pots were normally made by hand throughout Early Bronze, but professionals using the wheel may have settled in some townships during E.B.I*b*. Wheel-made vases have been reported

1. Guy, *Megiddo Tombs*, OIP., xxxiii, 1938, 135.
2. *The Excavation of Gezer*, 1912, i, 285.
3. *Mus. J.*, xxiv, pl. iii: Beth Shan −XVI.
4. Loud, *Megiddo II*, pl. 283, 1: Megiddo −XVIII.
5. Guy, *Megiddo Tombs*, 163.

from Megiddo — XVII, Beth Shan — XV, and Jericho — VI,[1] but the diagnosis has been challenged. On the other hand, centrally perforated stone discs some 20 cm. in diameter have been called 'tournettes'.[2]

During Early Bronze we meet besides the grey burnished ware of the Esdraelon culture and the cream-slipped painted ware of Judæa, both proper to E.B.I*a*, pale wares and pale wares covered with a red wash and in E.B.I*b* a fine hard-fired red fabric, termed metallic ware owing to its ringing quality and already encountered in Phœnicia. Decoration might be effected with a comb or by reserving the slip, as in Mesopotamia and Phœnicia, or with the burnishing tool. The latter device produced the lattice burnished ware not found in Palestine before E.B.II but known in Byblos IV and apparently in Hama—K. Though now applied to a pale ware covered with a red wash, the technique is the same as that used on the self-coloured stroke-burnished ware of 'neolithic' Phœnicia and North Syria and must surely be inspired by the same tradition. But at no excavated site has a survival of stroke-burnished ware late enough to inspire lattice-burnishing been observed.

Perhaps the most outstanding form of 'Bronze Age' pottery in Palestine is the ledge-handled jar. Beginning as simple but practical hand-holds in E.B.I*a* with parallels in Gerzean Egypt, the ledges subsequently underwent a development divergent from that which led to Gerzean wavy-handled jars. Spouted jars were also popular; some have the curved spout of the Late Uruk and Gerzean type while an enlarged form of the Ubaid kettle[3] approximates to the Early Helladic askos. The amphoriskos, in Judæa painted in red on a cream slip, occurs from E.B.I*a*.

Apart from a few fayence beads, pottery affords the best evidence for Palestine's foreign trade. Vases in several of the above-mentioned wares and shapes occur as imports in Early Pharaonic tombs at Abydos, Saqqara, Helwan, and Tarkhan. Most of them doubtless reached Egypt by sea from Byblos. But the evidence for Early Pharaonic exports to Palestine is as good, and of the same kind, as that from Byblos. Alabaster bowls of Egyptian manufacture had been offered in the sanctuary at Ai[4] as in the temple of Ba'alat Gebal,

1. Loud, *Megiddo II*, pl. 5; *Mus. J.*, xxiv,   10; *LAAA.*, xix, 1932, 156.
2. Loud, *Megiddo II*, 177; *RB.*, liv, 403. Cf. Mallon, *Teleilat Ghassul*, i, 87, and *LAAA.*, xxiii, 84.
3. Marquet-Krause, *Ay*, pl. lx, 7—no. 587.
4. Marquet-Krause, 19, 29.

while there is an Early Pharaonic slate palette from Jericho — VII.[1]
It is then likely that some of the 'Syrian' vases found in Egypt
had been made and filled with wine or oil in Palestine and
that Egyptian trade with the north did not by-pass the country
altogether.

All the varieties of pottery in question reached Egypt under
Dynasty I. Assuming therefore that not all these imported vases
came from Byblos, they provide *termini ante quos* for the several
sub-periods of Early Bronze. Now lattice-burnished ware is not
attested before E.B.II,[2] combed and metallic wares not till E.B.I*b*.[3]
In fact, all the imports in question belong to E.B.I*b* or E.B.II, rather
than to E.B.I*a*. So E.B.I*b* and the beginning of E.B.II should fall
within the rule of the Ist Dynasty. E.B.I*a* should then be partly
parallel to the Gerzean phase of the predynastic. In fact, the
amphoriskos from Abusir el-Meleq might well be inspired by the
Judæan tradition of E.B.I*a*. The ledge-handled jars of that phase
again are not far removed from the prototype from which Gerzean
wavy-handled jars might have evolved. Spouted vases, too, might
have reached the Nile from the same quarter since they occur from
E.B.I*a* on. However, the earliest published example with a curved
spout comes from Beth Shan — XIV.[4]

Reliable correlations with Mesopotamia are less easily established.
The grey burnished bowls and the associated spouted pots of the
Esdraelon culture are no doubt derived from the Uruk tradition, but
a tradition may be long lived. Two vases from Megiddo, assigned to
the end of E.B.I*a*, had been impressed before firing with cylinder
seals. The style of the designs has been variously interpreted as
Jemdet Nasr and Early Dynastic II.[5] Of course, stylistic comparisons between wooden cylinders, carved to stamp unbaked vases,
and stone cylinders, engraved to seal filled jars, have no more
chronological significance in Palestine than in Phœnicia. Nevertheless the second comparison involving an equation between Early
Dynastic II in Mesopotamia and the First Egyptian Dynasty would
accord perfectly with the estimate of 2900 B.C. as the absolute date

1. *LAAA.*, xxiii, 68.
2. E.g., T. Farah, 4 (*RB.*, liv, 422), Beth Shan — XIV (*Mus. J.*, xxiv, 13).
3. E.g., at T. Farah, 3, and Megiddo — XVIII (*RB.*, lv, 1948, 550).
4. According to Engberg and Shipton, *OIS.*, No. 10, 1934, the type, No. 23A,
occurs already in the earlier 'stages' — VII–V of the Esdraelon culture, equivalent
to E.B.I*a*, at Megiddo.
5. Albright, *Arch. Pal.*, 71; Shipton, *OIS.*, No. 17, 1939, 42.

for the beginning of Early Dynastic II upon which three independent calculations converge.[1]

These long distance correlations are admittedly problematical. The undeniable contacts between Egypt and Palestine do permit some reliable conclusions. The degree of urbanization illustrated by the walled towns of Ai or Jericho —VII was achieved independently of the capital accumulated by the first Egyptian civilization. It was not obviously extended or enriched by drafts on that concentrated social surplus during E.B.I*b* and E.B.II. Again, the rock-cut collective tombs of Palestine were no more inspired by the stairway and rock cut-tombs built for individual pharaohs and nobles of Dynasty I than were the rock-cut family tombs of Byblos II. Metallurgy, too, is not obviously dependent on the Egyptian, still less on the Sumerian of Early Dynastic times.

As for the 'neolithic revolution', the record of food production in Palestine has been carried back from the historically dated horizon of E.B.I*b* to an imposing antiquity and more nearly joined to that of the food-gathering stage than anywhere else. When the ceramic record begins it offers at least hints of connections with the earliest recognizable farmers both in Lower Egypt and Upper Mesopotamia. Even in the sequel one notices a certain parallelism between the chalcolithic of Ghassul and Maadi in which the former should enjoy some priority in as much as the Gerzean, and therefore Maadi, overlap with E.B.I*a* which succeeds the Ghassulian.

The following 'radio carbon' dates have been published by Dr. Libby of Chicago since 1951:

MESOPOTAMIA	NILE VALLEY
Jarmo, Neolithic (p. 104) 4750 B.C.	Fayum Neolithic (p. 35) 4150 B.C.
	el Omari (p. 40) 3300 B.C.
	Khartoum Neolithic (p. 46) 3500 B.C.

all with a margin of error of the order of 500 years.

1. Wright (*BASOR.*, 122, 1951, 52–5) mentions good ceramic evidence for a synchronism between Jericho —VIII and a phase in the Orontes valley (Amuq D), intermediate between those defined by Halafian and local Ubaid pottery. The time relation between Jericho —VIII and the Ghassulian and Esdraelon cultures being still disputed, this involves a further synchronism between Amuq Ubaid and *either* Ghassulian *or* Esdraelon in Palestine, but in any case equates Palestinian E.B. I (?I*a*) with (North) Mesopotamian Uruk, an equation not irreconcilable with our conclusions.

CHAPTER XII

PROOFS OF DIFFUSION

THE table on pp. 232–3 is designed to show the reader one way of comparing rates of cultural progress in the several regions surveyed in the foregoing chapters. Of course, most 'absolute dates' in column 1 are little more than guesses; the correlations of the several sequences are highly speculative; the Mesopotamian sequence could be contracted or extended, leaving the Egyptian column fixed, and the Iranian sequence could be expanded at its expense.

With these reservations the Urban Revolution would have been consummated first in Sumer during the Uruk period; Egyptian, Susian, and Indian civilizations are explicitly later. But, as we have seen, neither are mere reproductions of the Sumerian. Even the script signs are quite distinct. It is indeed conceivable that the Egyptian clerks somehow learned from Sumer the device of investing pictograms with phonetic values. It can hardly be argued that 'Menes' imported Sumerian clerks to train his new civil service, though New Kingdom pharaohs must have done something like that to staff their Foreign Office with cuneiform writers! Both Egypt and India were undoubtedly in contact, direct or indirect, with Sumer before they achieved civilization. But the earliest form of its political counterpart, the State, was different in all regions.

It can indeed be argued that the idea of the State's personification in a divine king was borrowed by Mesopotamia from Egypt. On the other hand, the attractive suggestion that personal gods are all copies of the personified State—of pharaoh—is hardly borne out by the evidence of Mesopotamian art in the Uruk period. At the same time the splendid Jemdet Nasr head of Pl. XXXVI, like the Dancing Girl from Harappa, not only suggests an æsthetic criterion for civilization when compared with the barbaric figures of Pls. IV, XVIII, and XXXVII or even the Lion Hunt palette. It also strongly suggests that a naturalistic rendering of the human form was not

238

inevitably bound up with the portrayal and consequent immortalization of divine kings—'Scorpion', Narmer, Zoser.

Some of the technical inventions on which the four distinct civilizations were based had certainly been diffused. For the table allows us to trace the process from a single starting point. It is, for instance, very probable that both the wheeled vehicle and the potter's wheel were invented in Sumer in Uruk times just before the Revolution. All the vehicular wheels known either from originals or models in the IIIrd millennium from the Indus to the Orontes and from the Persian Gulf to the Oxus were constructed in an identical manner out of three planks. While the Iranian starting point, postulated by McCown, is not absolutely excluded, west of the Tigris the dated examples illustrate a gradual spread from the southeast—to Assyria just before the Gawra period began, to the Khabur by the reign of Sargon, to the Orontes only after his campaigns in the time of Hama —J. Owing to the operation of the sociological factors mentioned in Chapter X, the potter's wheel spread at a rather different rate—to Gawra hardly before the Ninevite phase, to the Orontes by Hama —K, to Byblos III, to Palestine in E.B.1*b*, and even to Egypt by the Pyramid age. Owing to its peculiar physiography Egypt did not need the wheeled cart for transport, relying instead on water. Even so, the idea of the sail was probably imported; the Ubaid model sailing boat from Eridu is certainly appreciably older than the 'foreign' ships painted on Late Gerzean vases or indeed any other extant representation of sails.

Fayence, on the contrary, may very well have been invented in Gerzean Egypt (p. 63) and, on the tabulated chronology, transmitted thence to reach Mesopotamia in Uruk times, the Iranian plateau by Sialk IV, and India before the Harappa period.

Another invention that, though not a technical device and very likely originating in superstitious practices, indirectly contributed to the consummation of the Urban Revolution, can be located with some precision and traced with some confidence. The oldest datable seals are the Halafian 'seal-pendants' of Northern Mesopotamia. Translated into the stamp seal of bead or button form by Ubaid times, the device had reached the Kerkha in the time of Susa I (Early Uruk) and spread thence across southern Persia to Persepolis and beyond. In north-western Persia the stamp appears in Sialk III and Hissar I, perhaps just before the potter's wheel, but (at least in Hissar) divorced from its sealing function. In this mutilated form as the 'seal-amulet' the device reached the Indus.

Meanwhile the stamp seal had been converted into the looped cylinder in Late Uruk times in Sumer. In this form the seal was transmitted to Egypt—directly; for there are no intermediate specimens, dated so early. On the North Mesopotamian steppe normal cylinders of Jemdet Nasr style were in use in the Eye Temple at Brak, but at Gawra cylinders only begin to compete with stamps in the Ninevite period. They reach the Orontes during Hama —K and Judeideh —XII and, converted to a new use for stamping unfired vases, appear on the Mediterranean coast in Byblos IV and in Palestine about the transition from E.B.I*a* to E.B.I*b*.

But the stamp seal had crossed the Euphrates before the cylinder, presumably with Halafian or Ubaid pottery. Though its use for sealing may have been forgotten, it turns up on the Orontes in Hama —L and Judeideh —XIII and was used for stamping vases in Byblos II. Its spread was not arrested by the Taurus nor the Mediterranean. In Central Anatolia stamps, of clay and even copper, and stamp-impressions occur already in the 'Chalcolithic' of Alishar.[1] Then beyond the Aegean clay stamps—and one in stone—are associated with painted pottery and sling bullets in the Neolithic A of Thessaly and again, but always in clay, in the Gumelnitsa tells of Thrace, the Körös culture of the Banat, and the Danubian II or Lengyel culture of Moravia.[2] Even the familiar filled cross design is faithfully reproduced in Anatolia, in Thessaly, and even on the Maros in Hungary. Could a more convincing proof of diffusion from Hither Asia to our continent be demanded? Early Minoan button seals, too, are descended from the same stock, but are thought to have reached Crete by a more circuitous route via Egypt.[3]

The diffusion of metallurgy, however, remains more nearly a postulate. By the beginning of the IIIrd millennium we are confronted with distinct assemblages of fully differentiated local types in Egypt, Mesopotamia, and the Indus valley. The distinctive 'Sumerian' types can be traced back through Susa B, Sialk III, 4, and Gawra —VIII at least to Late Uruk times. Inferentially divergent specialization had begun even in the Ubaid phase with the creation, or translation into metal, of the shaft-hole axe.

By the second half of the IVth millennium metallurgy must have reached a high technical level, judging by the use of silver and lead in Susa C, Jemdet Nasr Mesopotamia, Byblos II and Gerzean Egypt.

1. van der Osten, *The Alishar Hüyük*, *OIP.*, xxviii, 82.
2. Childe, *Dawn*, 60, 95, 103, 126; *AJA.*, xliii, 16.
3. Matz, *Die frühkretischen Siegel*, 1928, 29.

Even tin bronze had been discovered, if only rarely used, before 3000 B.C. in view of the published analyses of objects from Gawra —VIII and T. Ghassul. But before that date, owing to the accidents of excavation, the known distribution of metal finds is so irregular that its pattern provides no reliable pointer to a single focus. The types themselves are at first so simple that they might have been devised independently in several regions.

The first relatively specialized type that could be used as an argument for diffusion is the knot-headed pin. But it is a long lived device and is first found, almost simultaneously, in regions so far apart as Gerzean Egypt and Sialk IV! Only a little later the scalloped or crescentic axe is represented in Early Pharaonic Egypt and on the Middle Euphrates in Early Dynastic I. But it, too, enjoyed a long popularity, surviving in Phœnicia and North Syria till 2000 B.C. and reaching Susa in the latter part of the IIIrd millennium.

In that millennium the most distinctive Sumerian types enjoyed only a very limited distribution. But a group of derivative types, first found together as an assemblage in Phœnicia and North Syria during the Cist Grave period (? after 2250 B.C.) were explicitly diffused. Spear-heads, derived from the Early Dynastic Sumerian series, but provided with a hooked tang,[1] reappear in Cyprus, Cilicia, Central Anatolia, Troy, and the Cyclades, but also in Hissar III in Iran. Specimens from Tarsus and the Royal Tombs of Alaca[2] reproduce even detailed peculiarities, like the slits in the blade seen in the weapon from Til-Barsib shown in Pl. XXXIX, 1. Of course, the hooked tang is traceable much earlier in Palestine and lasts well into the IInd millennium. Equally, 'Sumerian' spear-heads, without the hook, crossed the Caucasus and were deposited in a chieftain's tomb at Novosvobodnaya, in the Kuban basin.[3]

Similarly, derivatives of the Sumerian shaft-tube axe, approximating to the Cist Grave form of Pl. XXXIX, 1, in the crescentic nick at the end of the shaft-tube, reached Lemnos in the Early Aegean period[4] and were subsequently elaborated in Hungary during the local Middle Bronze Age. Again, wire neck-rings with recoiled ends penetrated to Central Anatolia, and at least one example is known

1. Discussed and illustrated by Schaeffer, *Strat. comp.*, 38, figs. 80, 168, 172, 174, 239, 245; and *Mission en Chypre*, Paris, 1936, 42 ff.
2. Schaeffer, *Strat. comp.*, figs. 82, 4; 172, 4; 176, 23.
3. Childe, *Dawn*, fig. 75.
4. *Arch. Anz.*, 1937 (*Jahrbuch d. Instituts.*, lii), 170, fig. 22.

from Central Europe in a grave of the late neolithic Baden culture.[1] But all three types—wiry neck-rings, hook-tanged spear-heads, and elaborated axes—though not associated, had been known east of the Tigris apparently before they appeared together in the cist graves of the Upper Euphrates.

After 2000 B.C. these wiry neck-rings were reproduced by casting in Phœnicia and thence introduced into Europe by the 'Torque-Bearers' together with a whole series of older Sumerian types of pins and earrings[2] and the Phœnician eyelet celt that became the Italian flanged celt with notched butt in Europe. These were the types manufactured and distributed by the first local metal industry in Central Europe and thus illustrate the diffusion of metallurgy across the Alps.

The foregoing types are surely specialized enough to demonstrate diffusion, but it is hardly the diffusion of metallurgy itself, at least not to Anatolia nor the Aegean. Though the chronology of Minoan Crete and the Troad may need quite drastic deflation,[3] the earliest metal-work from Crete, Lesbos, and Alishar cannot possibly be brought down to the reign of Sargon. The Early Minoan daggers are not derived from any known Oriental type. On the contrary, the evidence from the Aegean and Anatolia taken together with that from northern Persia lends support to Frankfort's[4] hypothesis of a primary cradle of metallurgy in Transcaucasia. At the same time intercourse of the Aegean islanders with Egypt and even Mesopotamia may be deduced from Cycladic marble reported from Protodynastic graves in Egypt and perhaps from the block vases from the same context and from Early Dynastic Sumer. Metallurgy and other discoveries could be diffused in the Aegean from Egypt or Phœnicia without passing over the Anatolian plateau.

But the use of metal required economic organization as well as technical knowledge; the diffusion of metallurgy should mean the diffusion of both knowledge and organization. The Urban Revolution itself evoked the latter. The wealth accumulated in the sacred or royal granaries of Mesopotamia and Egypt made it worth while for a whole class of the population to engage in the production and distribution of metal and other raw materials. It guaranteed a market

1. Childe, *Dawn*, 113.
2. Schaeffer, *Ugaritica*, ii, Paris, 1950, 56–115.
3. E.g., Matz, *Historia*, i (Baden Baden, 1950), 185–194; Milojčic, *BSA.*, xliv, 1949, 258–306.
4. *Ant. J.*, viii, 233.

for the product. But in practice the market, or at least the chief consumer, was the State. Now in Egypt the pharaonic State provided not only the capital (food, gear, baggage-animals) for the extraction and distribution of copper but also the personnel employed. Copper and turquoise were won from Sinai[1] by periodical expeditions dispatched by the pharaohs and protected by the royal army from interference by local beduin tribes. Some Sumerian dynasts, too, have recorded expeditions that they sent out to get metal, building stone, or timber, and these may have been like the pharaohs'. Such, of course, did nothing to enrich the barbarians whose territories they traversed.

But the early Sumerian temples can hardly have obtained their supplies in this way. In Early Dynastic times written documents show that they relied upon the services of the *damkur* or professional merchant. Even the relations between Early Pharaonic Egypt and Palestine or Phœnicia seem to have been of a more reciprocal, commercial character. Whether or no commercial expeditions were equipped by the State, they must conciliate the communities to be visited. The Egyptian vases offered in the temples of Byblos and Ai, in the first case in the name of the pharaoh as the personification of the State, show how permission to trade was obtained by Egyptians. Perhaps the metal ewer of Late Uruk shape, borne by Narmer's squire, is the result of similar approaches by Mesopotamian merchants to the Egyptian State. In any case, like the stone vases, it shows how types of vessel, familiar only from cheap pottery copies, were actually diffused over distances too great for the transport of fragile vases.

Regular traffic established on some such basis between the urban markets and the mines or quarries or forests provided machinery for the distribution of the raw materials in intervening regions, too poor alone to support such regular trade. So grave finds show metal in regular use for tools and weapons in the Syrian villages along the frequented steppe route from Lower Mesopotamia to the Amanus and Taurus, while it was available only rarely and used almost exclusively for weapons in the contemporary villages of Palestine since Egyptian–Syrian trade was then mainly maritime.

At the same time, regular traffic with urban centres should promote an approximation to civilized organization in the producing and intermediate regions. The representative of the local community, whether a deity or a chief, would find himself in control of surplus

1. Petrie, *Researches in Sinai*, London, 1906.

243

wealth no longer derived from the freewill offerings or customary gifts of the community's members. Thus, he gained a certain economic independence. Even when the raw materials were obtained by military force, resistance to the armed aggression whether of pharaonic mining expeditions or the imperalist campaigns of Sargon and his successors to the 'Cedar Forest' and 'the Silver Mountain', would consolidate the authority of war chiefs. The royal tomb of Til-Barsib, if correctly dated just after the campaigns of the Agade dynasts, aptly documents the point. Moreover, such warlike ventures would bring home to barbarians the value of metal. For tools, flint is almost as good as copper, but flint daggers are much more liable to snap with fatal results in hand-to-hand fighting! Stone Age barbarians would be as helpless against civilized troops with copper weapons and helmets as were the Aztecs against the Spaniards.

Still, if the want for metal were thus converted into an urgent need, some sporadic use, and therefore some kind of want, were fairly widespread even before the Urban Revolution started. To account for the distribution of the one and the diffusion of the other we can only appeal to the picture of a continuum of mobile populations drawn in Chapter II. The wanderings of marine shells in Badarian and Halafian times prove that materials were being transported by human agency, and so that ideas could be diffused, over vast distances very soon after the Neolithic Revolution. The growth of social surpluses, made possible by the new economy, provided the material condition for the intensification and extension of that traffic. But its mechanism still remains a matter of speculation. *A fortiori*, it would seem unprofitable to-day to ask how or whence the Neolithic Revolution itself was diffused. We shall, however, make one observation. The frontier between two early neolithic cultural provinces, characterized respectively by self-coloured pottery and bows and by pale pottery and slings, coincides with the divide between Mediterranean and Arabian Sea drainage in North Syria. But Schiemann has recently suggested just that area as the primary focus of wheat-growing. Immediately to the south began a third early neolithic province, which might on one view have extended into Lower Egypt. But the view favoured by most Egyptologists, making Merimde later than the Tasian, requires an independent centre of wheat growing in Africa.

BIBLIOGRAPHY

BOOKS CITED IN MORE THAN ONE CHAPTER

ALBRIGHT, W. F. *The Archæology of Palestine*, London, 1949.

BAUMGÄRTEL, E. *The Cultures of Prehistoric Egypt*, Oxford, 1947. (*CPE.*)

BRUNTON, G. *Qau and Badari*, i, London, 1927.

—— *Mostagedda*, London, 1937.

—— *Matmar*, London, 1948.

—— and CATON-THOMPSON. *The Badarian Civilization*, London (British School of Archæology in Egypt), 1928.

CAPART. *Primitive Art in Egypt*, London, 1905.

CATON-THOMPSON, G. *The Desert Fayum*, London, 1935.

CHILDE, V. G. *The Dawn of European Civilization*, London, 1950.

CONTENAU, G. *Manuel d'Archéologie orientale*, Paris, 1924–9.

DELOUGAZ and LLOYD, *Pre-Sargonid Temples of the Diyala Region*, *OIP.*, lviii, 1942.

DUNAND, M. *Fouilles de Byblos*, Paris, 1939.

—— *Byblia Grammata*, Beyrouth, 1945. (*BG.*)

EMERY, W. B. *Hor-Aha* (Excavations at Saqqara), Cairo, 1939.

—— *Great Tombs of the First Dynasty*, Cairo, 1949.

EVANS, A. *The Palace of Minos at Knossos*, London, 1921–28.

ELIOT, H. W. *Excavations in Mesopotamia and Western Iran*, Cambridge, Mass. (Harvard University), 1950. (*EMWI.*)

FRANKFORT, H. *Cylinder Seals*, London, 1939.

—— 'Archæology and the Sumerian Problem,' *OIS.*, 4, 1932. (*ASP.*)

—— *Studies in the Early Pottery of the Near East*, London (R. Anthrop. Institute, Occasional Papers, 6 and 8), 1925–27.

Gawra i, see Speiser.

Gawra ii, see Tobler.

GHIRSHMAN, R. *Fouilles de Sialk*, Paris, 1938–9.

HALL and WOOLLEY. *Ur Excavations*, i: *al'Ubaid*, London, 1927.

Harappa, see Vats.

MACKAY, E. *Further Excavations at Mohenjo-daro*, New Delhi, 1938 (*Mohenjo-daro*, ii).

—— *Chanhu-daro Excavations*, 1935–6, New Haven, 1943.

McCOWN, D. *The Comparative Stratigraphy of Early Iran*, *OIS.*, 23, 1942. (*CSEI.*)

BIBLIOGRAPHY

MacIver, R. *El Amrah and Abydos*, London (Egypt Exploration Fund), 1902.

Marshall, J., and others. *Mohenjo-daro and the Indus Civilization*, London, 1932. (*Mohenjo-daro*, i.)

Mohenjo-daro, see Mackay, and Marshall.

Mond and Myers. *The Cemeteries of Armant*, London (Egypt Exploration Society), 1937.

Perkins, A. *The Comparative Archæology of Early Mesopotamia*, OIS., 25, 1950. (*CAEM.*)

Petrie, W. M. F. *Royal Tombs*, i, London (Egypt Exploration Fund), 1900.

—— *Royal Tombs*, ii, London (Egypt Exploration Fund), 1902.

—— *Diospolis Parva*, London (Egypt Exploration Fund), 1902.

—— *The Labyrinth and Gerzeh*, London (British School of Archæology in Egypt), 1911.

—— *Tarkhan*, i, London (British School of Archæology in Egypt), 1912.

—— *Tarkhan*, ii, London (British School of Archæology in Egypt), 1913.

—— *Tools and Weapons*, London (British School of Archæology in Egypt), 1916.

—— *Prehistoric Egypt*, London (British School of Archæology in Egypt), 1917.

Piggott, S. *Prehistoric India*, London, 1950. (*PI.*)

Reisner, G. *The Development of the Egyptian Tomb down to the Accession of Cheops*, Cambridge, Mass. (Harvard), 1936.

Schaeffer, C. A. E. *Stratigraphie Comparée et Chronologie de l'Asie Occidentale*, Oxford, 1948.

Scharff, A. *Die Altertümer der Vor- und Frühzeit Ägyptens*, Staatliche Museen zu Berlin (*Mitteilungen aus der ägyptischen Sammlung*, 4–5), i, 1931; ii, 1929.

—— *Grundzüge der ägyptischen Vorgeschichte* (*Morgenland*, xii), Leipzig, 1927.

Speiser, E. A. *Excavations at Tepe Gawra*, i (Publications of the American School of Oriental Research), 1935 (*Gawra i*).

Tobler. *Excavations at Tepe Gawra*, ii, Philadelphia, 1950 (*Gawra ii*).

Vats, M. S. *Excavations at Harappa*, New Delhi (Archæological Survey of India, 1940).

Watelin, *Kish*, iv, Paris, 1934.

Winckler, H. *The Rockdrawings of Southern Upper Egypt*, London (Egypt Exploration Society), i, 1938; ii, 1939.

Woolley, L. *Ur Excavations*, ii, *The Royal Cemetery*, London, 1934.

ABBREVIATIONS

ADFU-W.   *Ausgrabungen der Deutschen Forschungsgemeinschaft in Uruk-Warka,* Berlin.

AfO.   *Archiv für Orientforschung,* Vienna.

AJA.   *American Journal of Archæology,*

Anatolian Studies   *Anatolian Studies,* London (British Institute of Archæology at Ankara).

Ancient India   *Ancient India,* New Delhi (Archæological Survey of India).

Annales du Service des Antiquités de l'Egypte, Cairo.

Antiquity   *Antiquity,* Southampton.

Ant. J.   *Antiquaries' Journal,* London (Society of Antiquaries).

ÄZ.   *Zeitschrift für ägyptische Sprache usw.,* Berlin.

BASOR.   *Bulletin of the American School of Oriental Research.*

CAH.   *Cambridge Ancient History* (First Edition).

Chron. d'Egypte   *Chronique d'Egypte,* Brussels (Musées du Cinquantennaire).

IPH., Mem.   Archives de l'Institute de Paléontologie humaine, *Memoires,* Paris.

Iraq   *Iraq,* London (British School of Archæology in Iraq).

JEA.   *Journal of Egyptian Archæology,* London (Egypt Exploration Society).

JNES.   *Journal of Near Eastern Studies,* Chicago.

JRAI.   *Journal of the Royal Anthropological Institute,* London.

JRAS.   *Journal of the Royal Asiatic Society,* London.

LAAA.   *Annals of Archæology and Anthropology,* Liverpool.

L'Anthr.   *L'Anthropologie,* Paris.

MAGW.   *Mitteilingen der anthropologischen Gesellschaft in Wien.*

Man   *Man,* London (Royal Anthropological Institute).

MASI.   *Memoirs* of the Archæological Survey of India, New Delhi.

MDOG.   *Mitteilungen der deutschen Orient-Gesellschaft,* Berlin.

Mus. J.   *Museum Journal,* Philadelphia (University of Pennsylvania).

MDP.   *Memoires de la Délegation en Perse* (subsequently *de la Mission Archéologique en Iran*), Paris (Ministry of Public Instruction).

OIC.   University of Chicago, Oriental Institute, *Communications.*

OIP.   University of Chicago, Oriental Institute, *Publications.*

OIS.   University of Chicago, Oriental Institute, *Studies in Ancient Oriental Civilization.*

OIAS.   University of Chicago, Oriental Institute, *Assyriological Studies.*

OLZ.   *Orientalische Literatur-Zeitung,* Berlin.

PPS.   *Proceedings of the Prehistoric Society,* Cambridge, Cambs.

RASI.   *Annual Reports* of the Archæological Survey of India, New Delhi.

ABBREVIATIONS

RB.	*Revue Biblique.*
Rec. Const.	*Recueil des notices et Memoires* de la Société archéologique de Constantine.
Rev. Ass.	*Revue d'Assyriologie*, Paris.
Sumer	*Sumer*, Baghdad (Antiquities Department, Iraq).
Syria	*Syria*, Paris.
UVB.	*Vorlaufige Berichte über die von der Notgemeinschaft der deutschen Wissenschaft in Uruk unternommenen Ausgrabungen:* published in the *Abhandlungen der preuss. Akademie der Wissenschaften, phil.-hist. Kl*, Berlin (iii and iv in Jg, 1932; v, 1933, vi–vii, 1935; viii, 1936; ix, 1938; x, 1939; xi, 1940).

INDEX

A-anni-padda, 10, 13, 171
Abusir el-Meleq, 65, 72, 73, 94, 236
Abydos, 82–8, 95, 98, 151, 152, 155, 163, 235
Adametz, L., 47
adzes, stone, 93, 105, 107, 108, 110, 116, 141, 191, 193, 209, 229; copper, 90; *see also* axes, transverse; axe-adzes; celts
Agrab, Tell, 170
Aha, 83, 85, 154, 156
Ai, 100, 230–239, 243
alloys, 129, 157, 177; *see also* bronze, tin
almonds, 231
al'Ubaid, *see* Ubaid
amazonite, 36, 47, 117, 177
amphoriskoi, 90, 230, 235–6
Amri, 173, 186–7, 203
amulets, 68, 71, 97, 130, 111; axe, 39, 229; fly, 71, 183, 196
Anau, 177, 193, 195, 196, 202
anthropology, physical, 29, 34, 40, 42, 46, 50, 75, 99, 155, 175, 220
apes, 96
areas of temples, towns, and villages, 64, 73, 134, 156, 168, 174, 199, 211, 229, 231
arches (true), 151, 168
Arkell, A., 46
Armant, 42, 58, 65
armies, 169
arrow-heads, tanged, 20, 29, 41, 74; transverse, 56, 68, 72, 79, 93, 129; hollow-based, 33, 36, 37, 40, 42, 56; leaf shaped, 42, 129, 137, 195, 215, 220, 225, 227; copper, 160, 178
arrow-butts, 145, 160
arsenic, 177
art styles, 60, 81, 100, 134, 138, 155,

164, 167, 170, 173, 181–2, 200, 203, 219, 238; *see also* rock-pictures, seals, mosaics, sculpture
Aryas, 185, 188
asses, 17, 31, 54, 65, 88, 106, 176, 197, 231
Assur, 208
Aterian, 20, 46, 48
axes, flint, 33, 36, 41, 55, 62, 220, 225; stone, 36, 38, 40, 47, 107, 116, 209; copper, flat, 63, 74, 90, 92, 116, 137, 177, 199, 200, 202, 230, 234; copper, salloped, 92, 149, 159; 241; copper, eyelet, 216, 222, 242; copper, shaft-hole, 116, 135, 137, 145, 159, 187, 200, 202, 206, 240, 241; copper, transverse (adzes), 141, 159, 241
see also battle-axes, celts, tranchets, amulets, double-axes
axe-adzes, 178, 187
Aurignacian, 10

Badari, 2, 8, 9, 33, 42, 52, 58, 224
Bakun, 198, 201
barley, 25, 29, 32, 33, 35, 37, 40, 42, 110, 176, 221
barrows, 229
basins, rock-cut 29; *see also* cup-marks, quern
baskets, 36, 37
basketry models for pottery, 34, 58, 138, 161, 191, 198
bathrooms, 178, 184
Baumgärtel, E., 46, 76
beads, segmented, 45, 182, 212; winged, 30, 111; etched carnelian, 170, 183, 197; glazed stone, 45, 43, 59; *see also* amulets, fayence, lapis lazuli

PLATE I

Shell Inlay from Royal Tomb at Ur

PLATE II

a. Mouflon Ram

b. Urial Ram
Zoological Gardens, London

PLATE III

a. Neolithic basket from Fayum
(*Photo: G. Caton-Thompson*)

b. Rippled Badarian vases
British Museum

PLATE IV

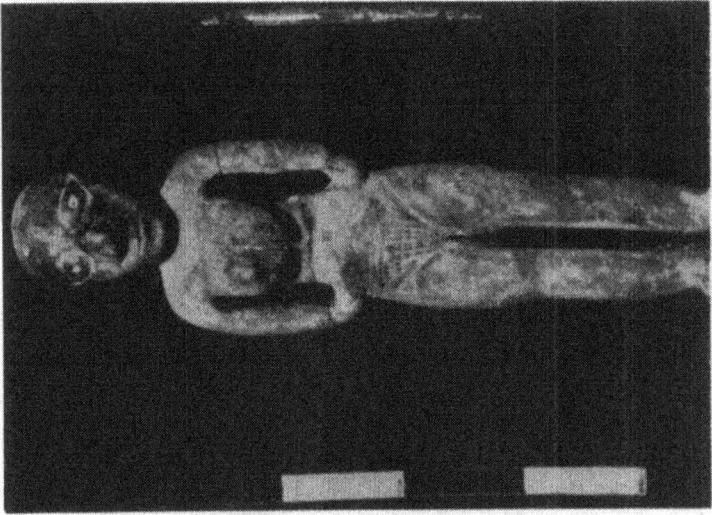

a. Badarian Figurine

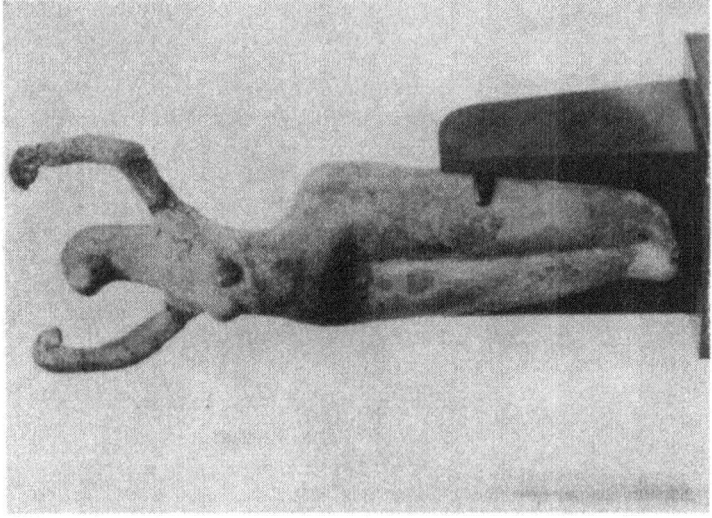

b. Amratian Figurine

British Museum

PLATE V

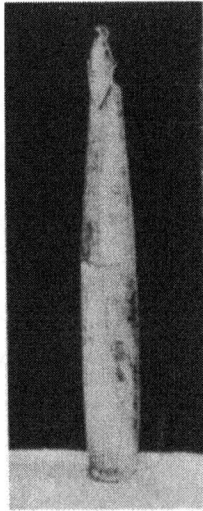

a. Tusk Figurine

b. Black-topped vases
Royal Scottish Museum

PLATE VI

a. Basalt and alabaster vases
Royal Scottish Museum

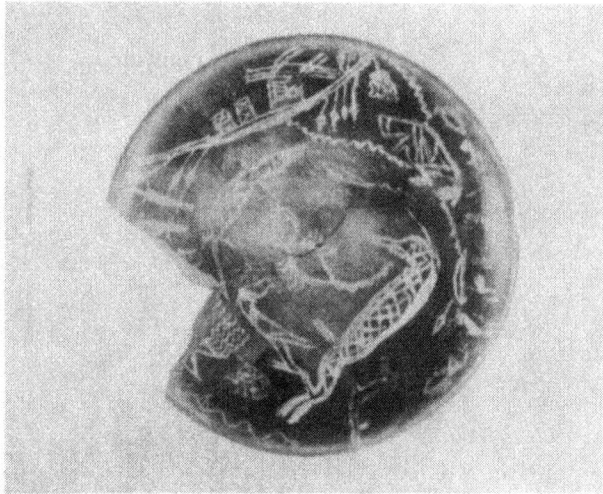

b. Interior of White Cross-lined bowl showing boat
Egyptian Museum, Cairo

Plate VII

b

Tomb groups from Diospolis Parva, Egypt Exploration
Society, illustrating (a) figurines wearing penis sheath
(b) pointed mace, alabaster vase, disc-shaped mace, steato-
pygous figurine, disc-shaped mace, stone vase, rhomboid
slate palette

PLATE VIII

a

b

Tomb groups from Diospolis Parva, Egypt Exploration
Society, illustrating (*a*) top row, slate pendants and theriomorphic palette, below, clay models, tags, rubber, sickle-
flint, and fish-tailed blade; (*b*) top, figurines, combs and
theriomorphic palette; middle, bracelets; bottom,
amulets, tags and combs

PLATE IX

a. Stone vases and copies in Decorated pottery;
Royal Scottish Museum

b. Gerzean Wavy-handled jar and its descendants

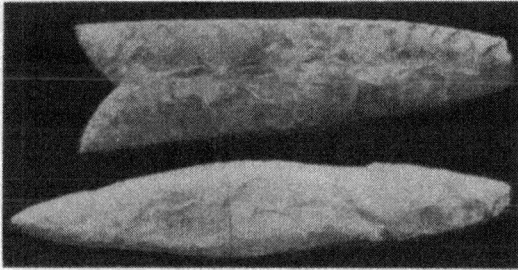

c. Swallow-tailed blade and dagger of flint;
Egypt Exploration Society

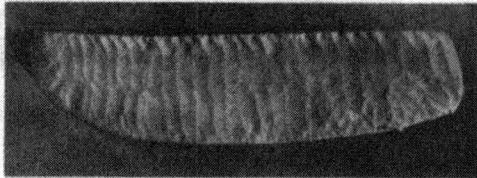

d. Flint knife showing serial flaking

PLATE X

a. Amratian model cattle
Egypt Exploration Society

b

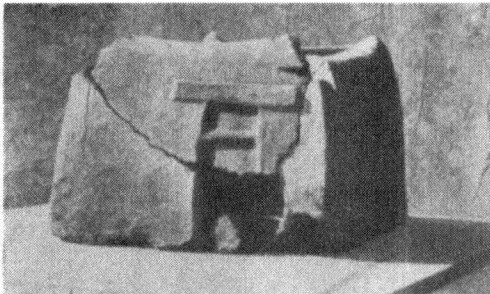

c

b-c. Gerzean model of house

PLATE XI

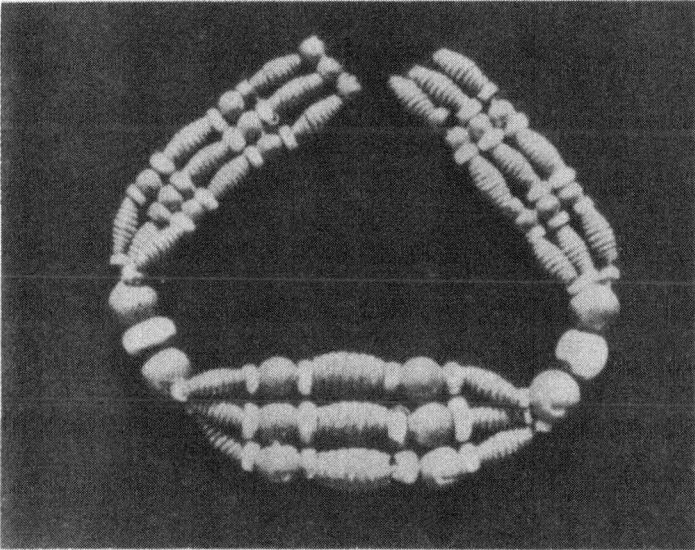

Bracelets of gold, amethyst and lapis lazuli from tomb of
King Zer; ¾
Egypt Exploration Society

The Lion Hunt palette
British Museum

PLATE XII

PLATE XIII

The Lion Hunt stele from Erech
Iraq Museum, Baghdad

PLATE XIV

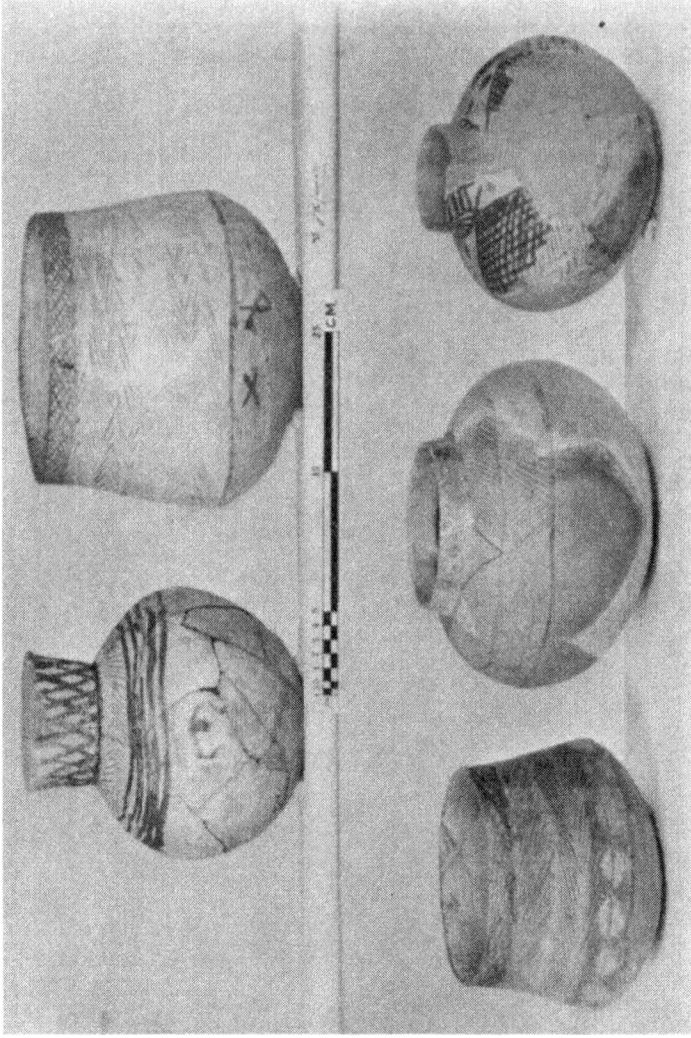

Hassuna Painted and Incised vases
Iraq Museum, Baghdad

PLATE XV

a

b

Stone-lined stairway tomb of First Dynasty, Ezbet el-Wâlda
(Helwan) (robbers' entry bottom left, in (*b*))

PLATE XVI

a. Polychrome Halafian dish; after Mallowan; ¼

b. Painted beaker from Samarra; ¼
British Museum

PLATE XVII

Vases from Tell Halaf
Tell Halaf Museum, Berlin

PLATE XVIII

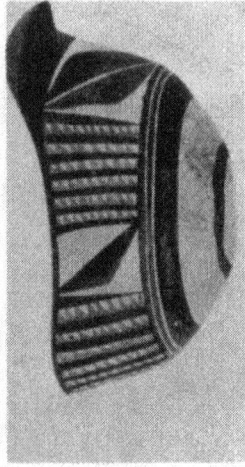

a. Ubaid " Sauce-boat "

b. Samarran Beaker

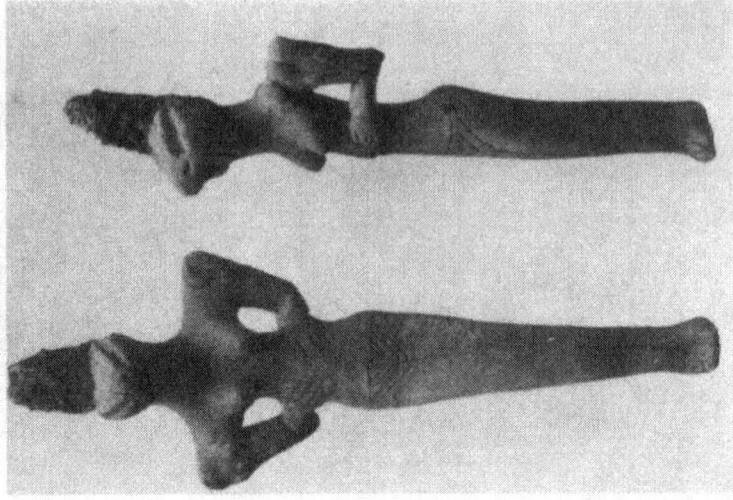

c. Ubaid Figurines

British Museum

PLATE XIX

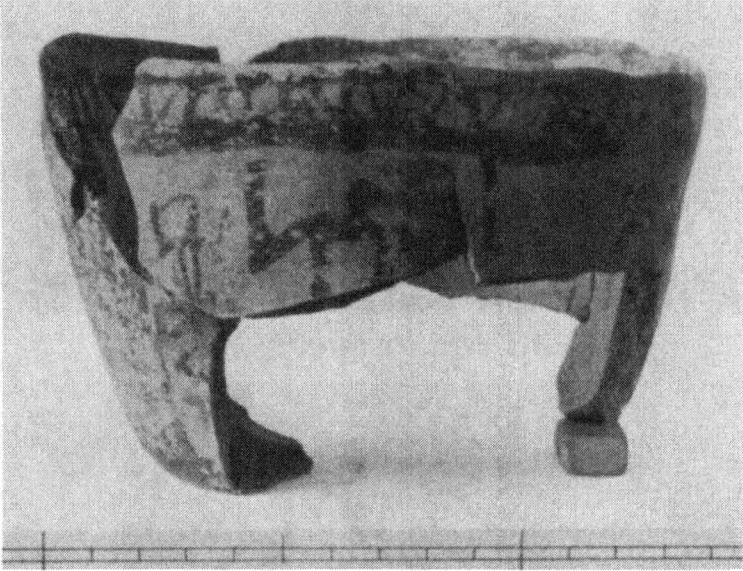

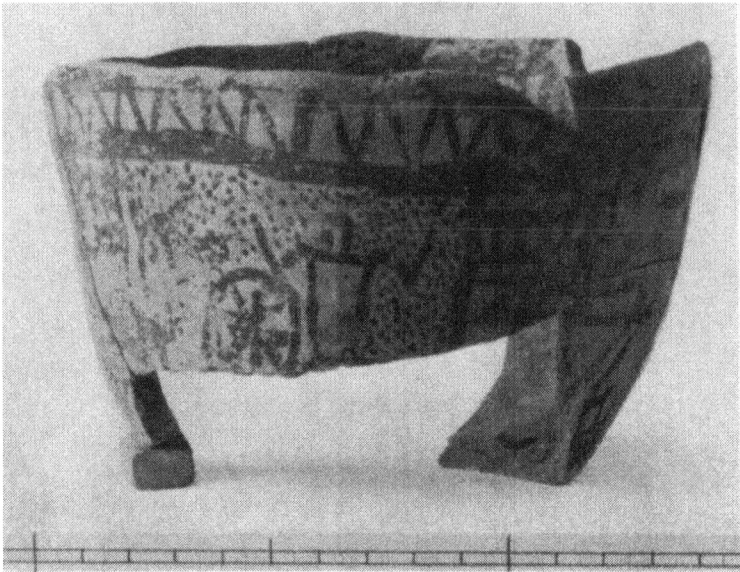

Halafian vase with alleged representation of a " chariot "

PLATE XX

a. Stone boar of Jemdet Nasr period, Ur

b. Carved stone vase, Erech; ⅔
British Museum

c. Uruk seal from Erech; ⅔
Iraq Museum

PLATE XXI

Spouted vase from Jemdet Nasr; ¼

Polychrome vases from Jemdet Nasr
Ashmolean Museum, Oxford

Bowls from Susa I
Musée du Louvre, Paris

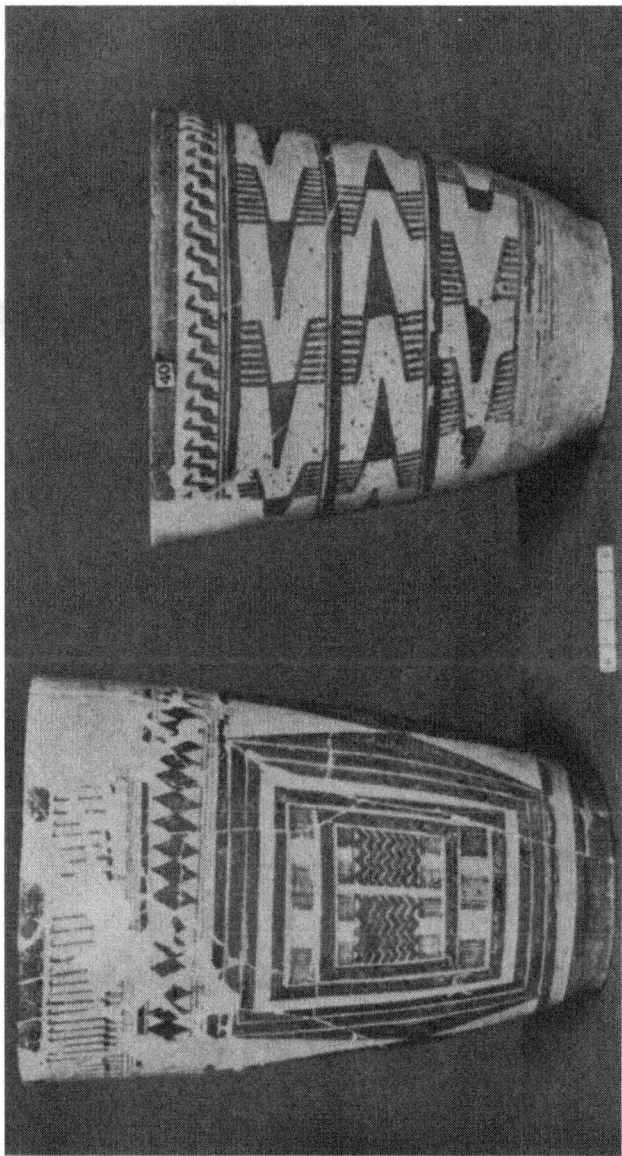

Plate XXIII

Tumblers from Susa I
Musée du Louvre, Paris

PLATE XXIV

a. Bas-relief showing chariot, Ur

b. Silver Boat from Royal Tomb, Ur
British Museum

PLATE XXV

a. Rein-ring with mascot from Queen Shub-ad's tomb, Ur

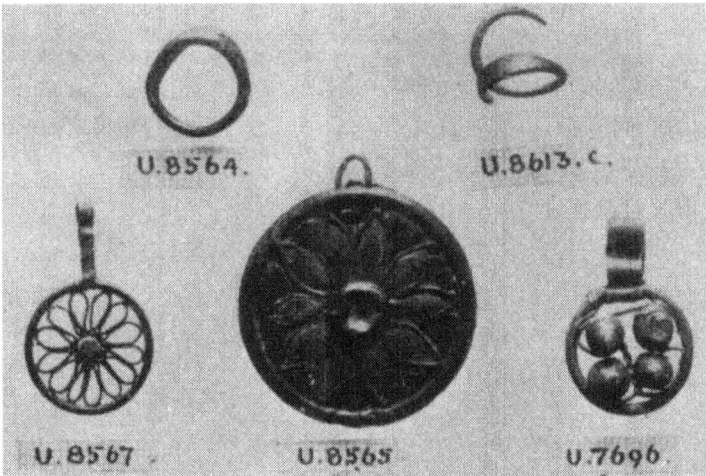

b. Ear-rings and pendants from Royal Cemetery, Ur
British Museum

PLATE XXVI

a.　Gold dagger with lapis
hilt and its sheath, Ur

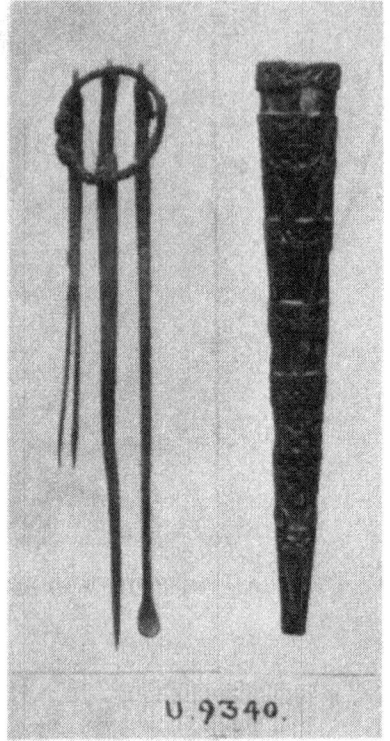

U.9340.

b.　Gold toilet set and its case, Ur
British Museum

PLATE XXVII

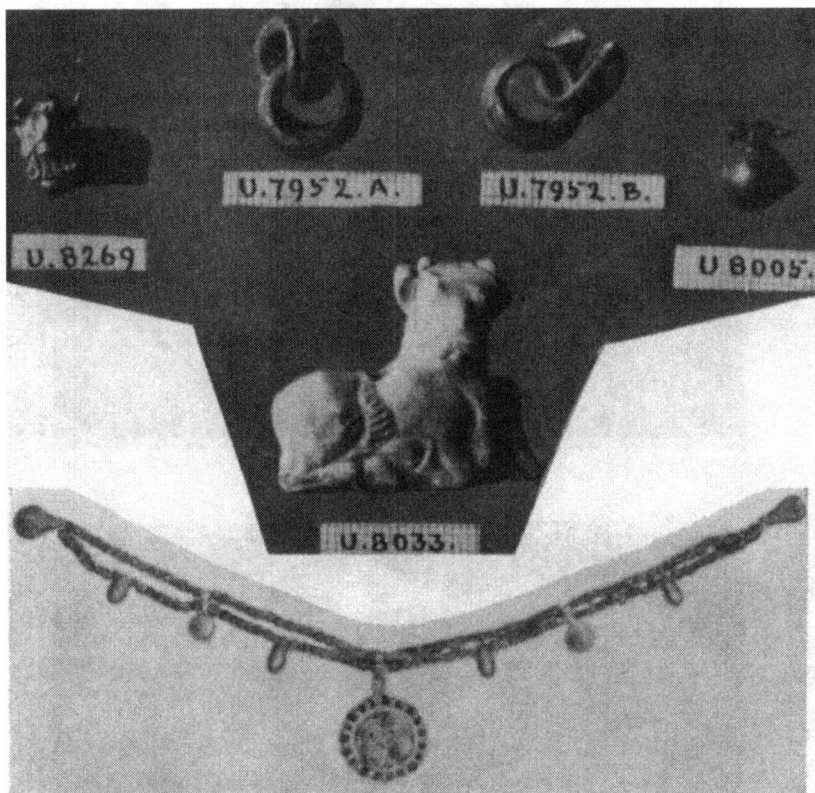

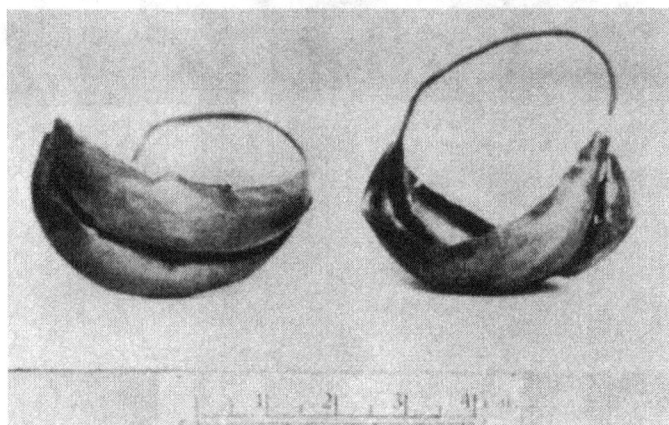

Jewelry from Royal Cemetery, Ur
British Museum

PLATE XXVIII

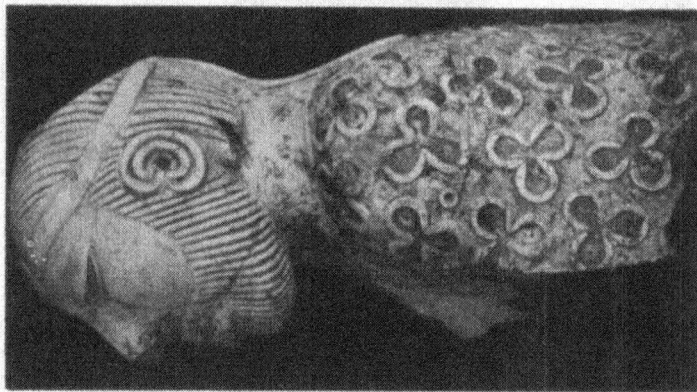

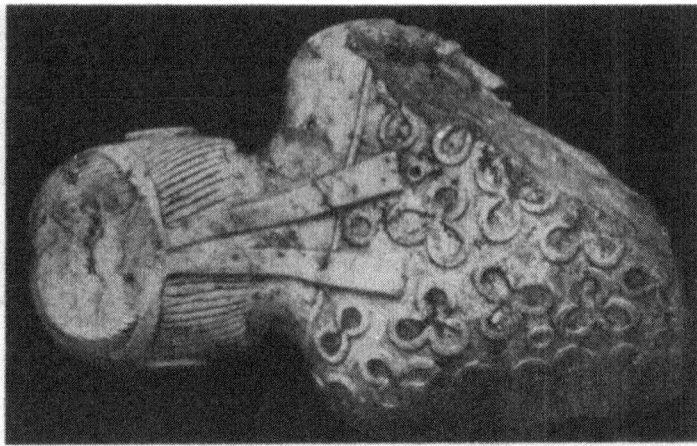

Stone statuette from Mohenjo-daro
Archaeological Survey of India

PLATE XXIX

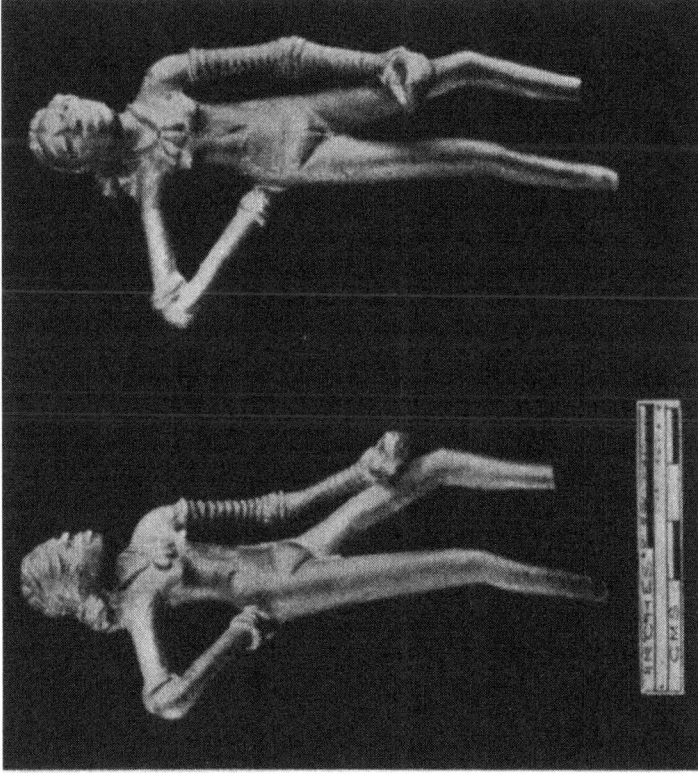

a. Copper statuette of Dancing Girl, Harappa; Central Asian
Museum, Delhi

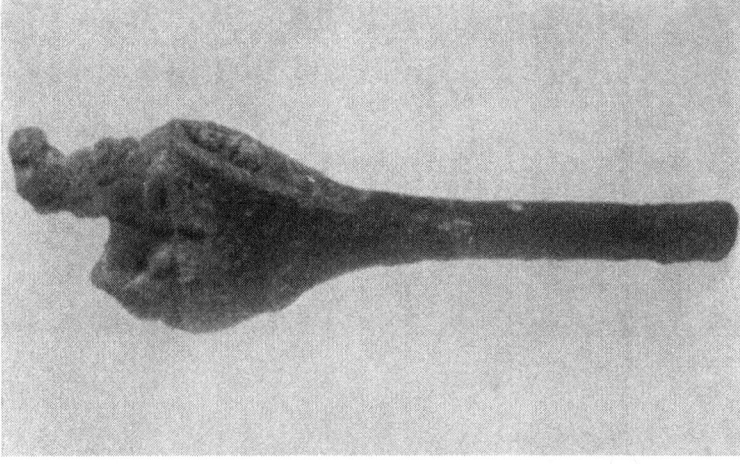

b. Copper wand surmounted by a
camel, Khurab; $\frac{1}{1}$
Peabody Museum, Harvard

PLATE XXX

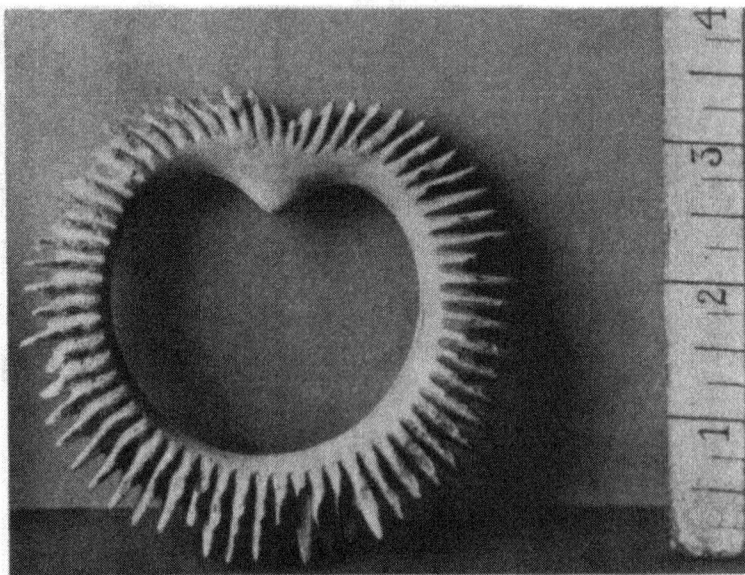

Seals and amulet from Mohenjo-daro, $\frac{1}{1}$; and fayence
bracelet from Harappa

PLATE XXXI

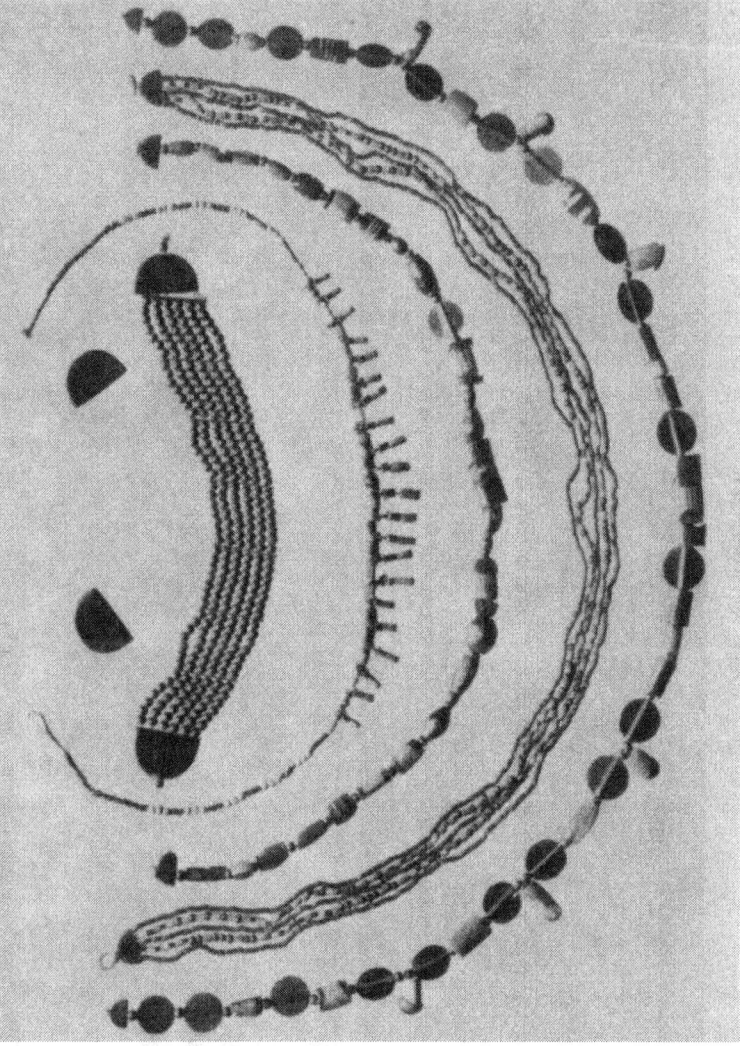

Jewelry from Mohenjo-daro

PLATE XXXII

Painted vase from Mohenjo-daro

PLATE XXXIII

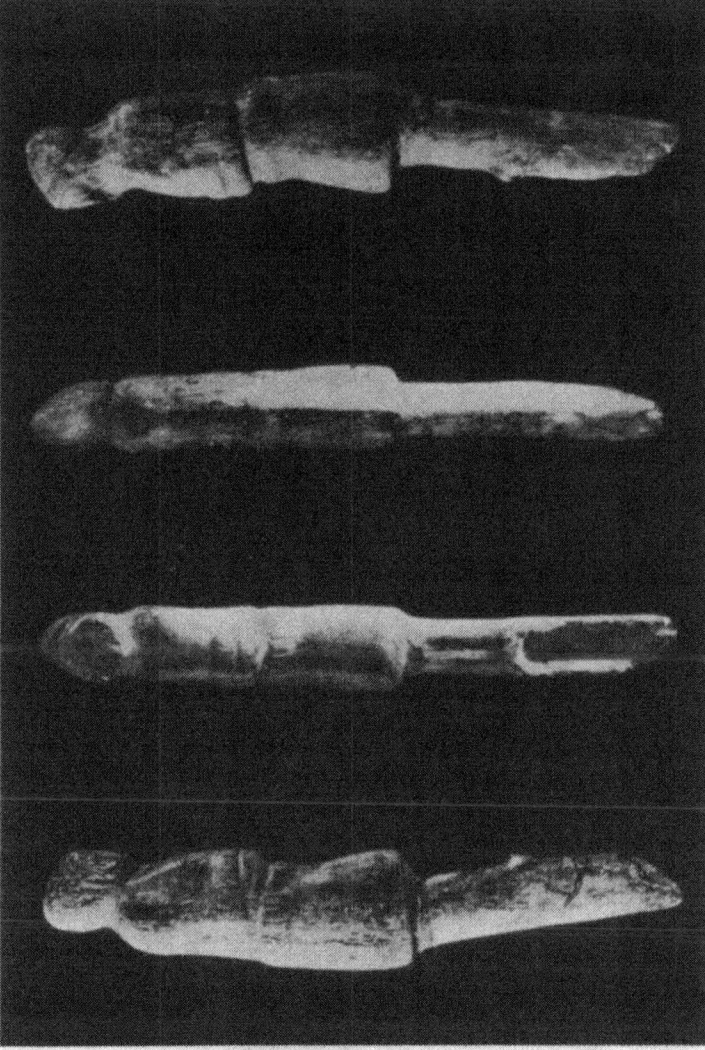

Carved sickle-handle of bone, Sialk I; $\frac{2}{3}$

PLATE XXXIV

Painted pottery from Sialk II

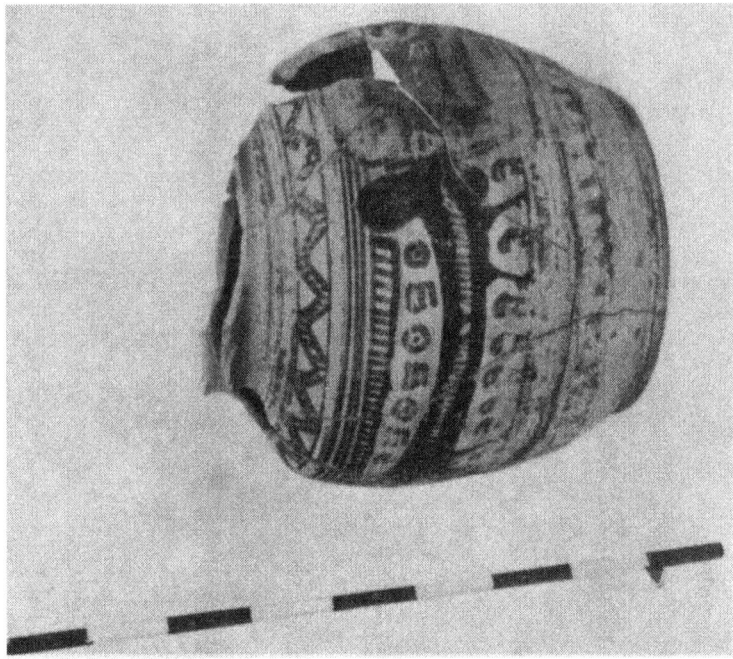

PLATE XXXV

a. Pot from Mehi, painted in Kulli style

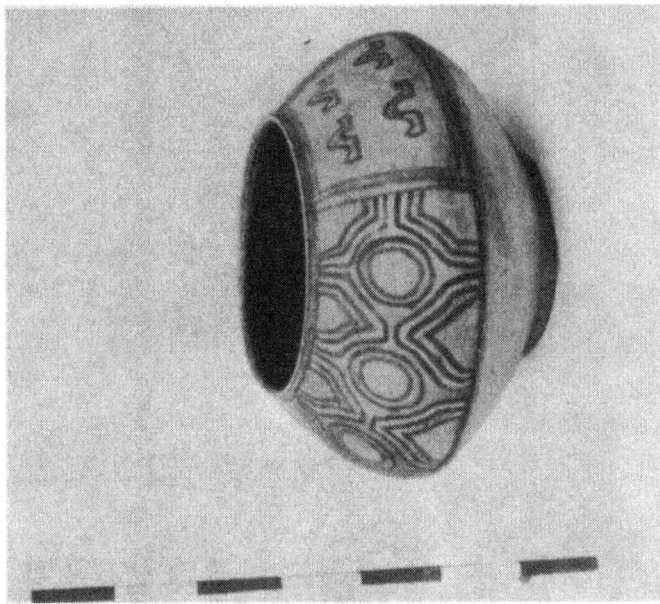

b. Polychrome vase from Nal

Central Asian Museum, Delhi

PLATE XXXVI

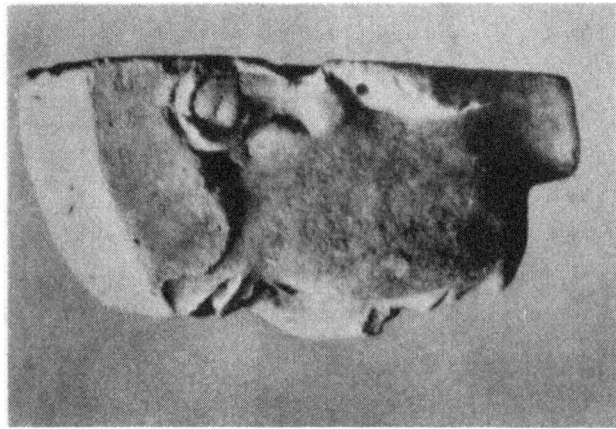

Alabaster head from Erech; $\frac{2}{5}$
Iraq Museum

PLATE XXXVII

Alabaster head from the Eye Temple at Brak; $\frac{2}{5}$
Iraq Museum

PLATE XXXVIII

Dish, $\frac{1}{3}$, and squat pot, $\frac{2}{5}$, from Shahi-tump cemetery;
Central Asian Museum, Delhi

PLATE XXXIX

Copper axe, daggers and spearheads from Til-Barsib; eyelet celt
from Byblos IV, $\frac{1}{3}$; daggers from tombs of Byblos II, $\frac{1}{4}$

For Product Safety Concerns and Information please contact our EU
representative GPSR@taylorandfrancis.com
Taylor & Francis Verlag GmbH, Kaufingerstraße 24, 80331 München, Germany

9 781138 817241